The AudioPro Home Recording Course

a comprehensive

multimedia

recording text

by Bill Gibson

MIXBOOKS

236 Georgia Street • Suite 100 • Vallejo • CA 94950

Library of Congress card number: 96-078454

Cover art direction and design: Tami Needham
Cover photograph: Michael Mendelson
Design consultant: Michael Zipkin

Book design and layout: Bill Gibson

Computer graphics: Bill Gibson

Production staff: Mike Lawson, publisher; Lisa Duran, editor; Georgia George, production director; Tom Marzella, production assistant

Instrumental Performances: Bill Gibson, except "Acoustic Drums and Percussion" chapter (Wade Reeves on drum set)

Recording engineer: Bill Gibson

236 Georgia Street, Suite 100
Vallejo, CA 94590
(707) 554-1935

Also From MixBooks:
The AudioPro Home Recording Course, Volumes I, II, and III
Modular Digital Multitracks: The Power User's Guide
The Art of Mixing
Professional Microphone Techniques
Sound for Picture 2nd Ed.
The Mixing Engineers Handbook
Live Sound Reinforcement

Also From EMBooks:
Making the Ultimate Demo 2nd Ed.
Anatomy of a Home Studio
Making Music With Your Computer 2nd Ed.

MixBooks is an imprint of artistpro.com, LLC

Printed in Auburn Hills, MI

ISBN 0-918371-10-4

Contents

List of Audio Examples   vii   Preface   1

Chapter One   2

The Mixer

The Mixer Layout   2

Split vs. In-line   2

Professional Amplifiers   3
Proper Wire 7

Studio Monitors   7
Near-Field Reference Monitors 7
Far-Field Monitors 8

Connectors   8
RCA Connectors 9
Quarter-Inch Phone Connectors 9
XLR Connectors 10
Plugging In 11

Electrical Power   11
Powering Up 13
Powering Down 13
Grounding 13
Ground Hum 13

Connecting to the Mixer   14
Input Stage/Impedance 17
Direct Box 18
Passive vs. Active DIs 18
Phantom Power 19
Line Level 19
+4dBm vs. -10dBV 20

Getting Sound Into the Board   20
The Preamp 20
Attenuator 22
Meters 23
Phase 23
Input Level Comparison 26

More Signal Path   27
Channel Insert .27

Managing the Signal Path   29
Input Faders 29
The Effects Bus 32
Pre and Post 32
Using the Aux Bus 33
The Headphone Bus 34
Track Assignment 34
Three Practical Applications
for the Combining Bus 35
Three Practical Applications for Splitting a
Signal Using a Y 36
Pan 37
Gain Structure .38
Ping-ponging .39
Which Tracks Should I Bounce Together? 39
Solo 41
Mutes 41

The Equalizer   42
Hertz 43
Definition of Frequency Ranges 47
Bandwidth 48
Personal 4-track Multitrack 48
Sweepable EQ .49
Parametric EQ .50
Graphic EQ 51

Other Types of EQ   51
Notch Filter 51
Highpass Filter .52
Lowpass Filter .52

The Monitor Section   53
Control Room Monitor Selector 54
Stereo to Mono 55
Stereo Master .56
Talkback/Communications 56
Test Tones 56
Reference Tones 57

Patch Bays   58

Session Procedures   58
Basic Procedure 58

Conclusion   60

Chapter Two   62

Signal Processing

Intro to Signal Processors   **62**
Slang/Terminology 62

Signal Processor Basics   **62**

Dynamic Processors   **67**
The VCA 69
Compressor/Limiter 69
Threshold 73
Attack Time 74
Release Time 76
Ratio 76
Summary 76
Gain Reduction 76
Proper Use of the Compressor/Limiter 77
Gate/Expander 80
Gates vs. Expanders 82

More About Equalizers   **84**

Effects Processors   **85**
Delay Effects 85
Slapback Delay 85
Doubling 89
Modulation 89
Phase Shifter 90
Flanger 90
Chorus 90
Phase Reversal and Regeneration 91
Stereo Effects 92

Reverberation Effects   **92**
Hall Reverb 93
Chamber Reverb 95
Plate Reverb 95
Room Reverb 95
Reverse Reverb 95
Gated Reverb 98
Predelay 98
Diffusion 98
Decay Time 98
Density 99

Conclusion   **99**

Chapter Three   100

Microphones

Microphones: Our Primary Tools   **100**

Condenser Microphones   **101**
Operating Principle of the Condenser Mic 101
Phantom Power 102

Moving-coil Mics   **104**
Operating Principle of the Moving-coil Mic 104

Ribbon Mics   **106**
Operating Principle of the Ribbon Mic 108

Pickup/Polar Patterns   **109**
Cardioid 109
Omnidirectional 110
Bidirectional 110

Frequency Response Curve   **111**

Conclusion   **111**

Chapter Four   112

Guitars and Guitar Sounds

Recording Guitars   **112**

Direct Electric   **112**
Advantages of Running Direct 113
Levels 116
Transients 116
Tuning/Instrument Selection .117
Pickup Types 118
Basic Types of Electric Guitars 118
Compressor/Limiter/Gate/Expander 120
Delay 121
Should I Print Reverb or Delay to Tape? 122
Electronic Doubling 122
Multi-effects 124
Chorus/Flanger/Phase Shifter 124
Reverb 124
Panning 125
Equalizing the Guitar 126

Amplified Electric   **127**
Mic Techniques 128
The Most Common Approach to
Miking an Amp 128
Combining the Miked and Direct Signals 134

Acoustic Guitars   **134**
Mic Techniques 136
Tuning/Instrument Selection 139
Picks 139
Dynamic Processing and the Acoustic Guitar 139
Equalizing the Acoustic Guitar 142
Reverb 143
Double Tracking the Acoustic Guitar 143
Distortion 144

**Synthesized and Sampled Guitar
Sounds**   **144**

Conclusion   **145**

Kick Drum   **166**
Equalizing the Kick Drum 167
Effects on the Kick 169
Recording Levels for Kick Drum 169

Snare Drum   **169**
Mic Choice for Snare Drum 172
Reverberation on the Snare Drum 173
Equalizing the Snare Drum 174
Recording Levels for Snare Drum 174

Toms   **174**
Equalizing the Toms .174
Reverberation on the Toms 174

Overhead Microphones   **178**

Isolating the Drum Tracks   **181**

Miscellaneous Percussion   **182**

Application of Techniques   **184**

Click Track   **184**

Conclusion   **185**

Credits   **185**

Chapter Five   146

Acoustic Drums and Percussion

The Percussion Family   **146**

Theories of Drum Miking   **147**

**Recording a Drum Set With One
Microphone**   **149**
Be Mobile! 152

Recording a Kit With Two Mics   **153**

Recording a Kit With Three Mics   **156**

Recording a Kit With Four Mics   **159**

Close-mike Technique   **159**

Drum Conditioning   **161**

Muffling the Drum   **162**

Drum Sticks   **165**

Chapter Six   188

Synchronization/Drum Machines

Introduction to Drum Machines   **188**

Patching in the Drum Machine   **189**

Sub-mixing   **193**

Time Code and Sync Pulse   **193**
Sync Pulse 193
SMPTE/Time Code 194
MIDI Time Code 195
Using Time Code 196

Drum Machine Recording Levels   **197**

Programming   199
Real-Time Programming   199

Separating and Organizing Tracks   200
24 Tracks 201
16 Tracks 202
8 Tracks 203
4 Tracks 204

Kick Drum   205
Tuning the Kick 206
Equalizing the Kick 206
Recording Levels for the Kick Drum 207
Panning the Kick 210

Snare Drum   211
Recording Levels for the Snare Drum 212
Tuning the Snare 213
Gating the Snare 213
Compressing the Snare Sound 213
Reverberation on the Snare 216
Panning the Snare 221

Toms   221
Recording Levels for Toms 221
Tuning Drum Machine Toms 222
Equalizing the Toms 222
Reverberation on Toms 223
Panning the Toms 223

Cymbals   224
Reverb on Cymbals 225

Percussion   226

More Stuff   229

Conclusion   230

Glossary   232

Index   239

Acknowlegments   245

Audio Examples

CD-1

Chapter 1 The Mixer

Track 1
Introduction

Track 2
Audio Example 1-1 60-Cycle Hum...13

Track 3
Audio Example 1-2 Mix 1...14
Audio Example 1-3 Mix 2...14
Audio Example 1-4 Mix 3...14

Track 4
Audio Example 1-5 Direct Boxes...19
Audio Example 1-6 Direct Boxes...19
Audio Example 1-7 The Overdriven Input...22

Track 5
Audio Example 1-8 Attenuator Adjustment...22

Track 6
Audio Example 1-9 Phase Reversal...25
Audio Example 1-10 Phase Reversal...25
Audio Example 1-11 Phase Reversal...25

Track 7
Audio Example 1-12 Proper Input Levels...27
Audio Example 1-13 Low Input Levels Resulting in a Noisy Mix...27
Audio Example 1-14 High Input Levels Causing Distortion...27

Track 8
Audio Example 1-15 Dry Guitar...33
Audio Example 1-16 Dry Guitar...34
Audio Example 1-17 Reverb Only...34
Audio Example 1-18 Blending Wet and Dry...34

Track 9
Audio Example 1-19 Direct Guitar...37
Audio Example 1-20 The Miked Amp...37
Audio Example 1-21 Combining Direct and Miked Signals...37

Track 10
Audio Example 1-22 Synth Sound A...38
Audio Example 1-23 Synth Sounds B and C...38
Audio Example 1-24 Synth Combination...38

Track 11
Audio Example 1-25 Bouncing Multiple Instruments to One
  Tape Track...39

Track 12
Audio Example 1-26 Soloing...41

Track 13
Audio Example 1-27 60Hz...43
Audio Example 1-28 120Hz...43
Audio Example 1-29 240Hz...43

Audio Example 1-30 500Hz...43
Audio Example 1-31 1kHz...44
Audio Example 1-32 2kHz...45
Audio Example 1-33 4kHz...45
Audio Example 1-34 8kHz...45
Audio Example 1-35 16kHz...45

Track 14
Audio Example 1-36 Bass (Flat)...46
Audio Example 1-37 Bass (Cut 250Hz)...46

Track 15
Audio Example 1-38 Guitar (Flat)...46
Audio Example 1-39 Guitar (Boost 250Hz)...46

Track 16
Audio Example 1-40 Guitar and Bass Together...46

Track 17
Audio Example 1-41 Flat...47
Audio Example 1-42 Highs (Above 3.5kHz)...47
Audio Example 1-43 Mids (250Hz to 3.5kHz)...47
Audio Example 1-44 Lows (Below 250Hz)...47

Track 18
Audio Example 1-45 Flat (Reference)...47
Audio Example 1-46 Brilliance...47
Audio Example 1-47 Presence...47
Audio Example 1-48 Upper Midrange...47
Audio Example 1-49 Lower Midrange...47
Audio Example 1-50 Bass...47
Audio Example 1-51 Sub-bass...47

Track 19
Audio Example 1-52 Simple Stereo Mix...56
Audio Example 1-53 Stereo Mix in Mono...56

Chapter 2 Signal Processing

Track 20
Audio Example 2-1 Hall Reverb...65
Audio Example 2-2 Plate Reverb...65
Audio Example 2-3 Gated Reverb...65

Track 21
Audio Example 2-4 Slapback...65

Track 22
Audio Example 2-5 Echo...65

Track 23
Audio Example 2-6 Doubling...65

Track 24
Audio Example 2-7 Chorus...65

Track 25
Audio Example 2-8 Flanging...65

Track 26
Audio Example 2-9 Phase Shifting...65

Track 27
Audio Example 2-10 Vocal Without Compression...65
Audio Example 2-11 Vocal With Compression...65

Track 28
Audio Example 2-12 Parametric EQ...66

Track 29
Audio Example 2-13 S's and T's...74
Audio Example 2-14 S's and T's...76

Track 30
Audio Example 2-15 No Compression...80
Audio Example 2-16 3dB Gain Reduction...80
Audio Example 2-17 6dB Gain Reduction...80
Audio Example 2-18 9dB Gain Reduction...80
Audio Example 2-19 Pumping and Breathing...80

Track 31
Audio Example 2-20 Guitar: No Gate...83
Audio Example 2-21 Guitar: Gated...83

Track 32
Audio Example 2-22 Hi-hat: No Expander...84
Audio Example 2-23 Hi-hat: Expander...84

Track 33
Audio Example 2-24 Sweeping 50 to 500Hz...84
Audio Example 2-25 Sweeping 100Hz to 5kHz...85
Audio Example 2-26 Sweeping 2.5 to 15kHz...85
Audio Example 2-27 Sweeping a Narrow Bandwidth...85

Track 34
Audio Example 2-28 250ms Slapback...87
Audio Example 2-29 50ms Slapback...87

Track 35
Audio Example 2-30 Repeating Delays...87
Audio Example 2-31 11ms Vocal Delay...89

Track 36
Audio Example 2-32 The LFO...89
Audio Example 2-33 Extreme Speed and Depth...90

Track 37
Audio Example 2-34 Phase Shifter...90
Audio Example 2-35 Flanger...90
Audio Example 2-36 Chorus...91
Audio Example 2-37 Inverting Phase...92
Audio Example 2-38 Stereo Chorus...92

Track 38
Audio Example 2-39 Simulated Reverb...93
Audio Example 2-40 Reverberation...93

Track 39
Audio Example 2-41 Hall Reverb...95
Audio Example 2-42 Chamber Reverb...95
Audio Example 2-43 Plate Reverb...95
Audio Example 2-44 Room Reverb...95
Audio Example 2-45 Reverse Reverb...95
Audio Example 2-46 Gated Reverb...98

Track 40
Audio Example 2-47 Predelay...98

Track 41
Audio Example 2-48 Diffusion...98

Track 42
Audio Example 2-49 Decay Time...99

Chapter 4 Guitars and Guitar Sounds

Track 43
Audio Example 4-1 Single Coil...119

Track 44
Audio Example 4-2 Double Coil...119

Track 45
Audio Example 4-3 Hollow-Body Electric Jazz Guitar...119

Track 46
Audio Example 4-4 No Compression...120
Audio Example 4-5 With Compression...120

Track 47
Audio Example 4-6 Buzzy Distortion...121
Audio Example 4-7 Simulated Tube Distortion...121
Audio Example 4-8 Simulated Rock Stack...121

Track 48
Audio Example 4-9 The 250ms Delay...121
Audio Example 4-10 The 62.5ms Delay...121

Track 49
Audio Example 4-11 The 23ms Double...123
Audio Example 4-12 The Live Double...123

Track 50
Audio Example 4-13 Chorus...124

Track 51
Audio Example 4-14 Phase Shifter...124

Track 52
Audio Example 4-15 Multiple Effects...124

Track 53
Audio Example 4-16 Hall Reverb...124

Track 54
Audio Example 4-17 Adjusting Predelay...125

Track 55
Audio Example 4-18 Conflicting Guitars...126
Audio Example 4-19 Equalized for Mono...126

Track 56
Audio Example 4-20 Boost and Cut 100Hz...126
Audio Example 4-21 Boost and Cut 200Hz...126
Audio Example 4-22 Boost and Cut 300Hz...126
Audio Example 4-23 Boost and Cut 550Hz...126
Audio Example 4-24 Boost and Cut 4kHz...126
Audio Example 4-25 Boost and Cut 10kHz...127

Track 57
Audio Example 4-26 Clean Small Solid-state Amp...128
Audio Example 4-27 Clean Large Tube Amp...128

Track 58
Audio Example 4-28 Distorted Small Solid-state Amp...128
Audio Example 4-29 Distorted Large Tube Amp...128

Track 59
Audio Example 4-30 Mic at the Center of the Speaker...129
Audio Example 4-31 Mic at the Outer Edge of the Speaker...130

Track 60
Audio Example 4-32 Condenser Mic Seven Feet From the Amp...130

Track 61
Audio Example 4-33 Close-miking the Amp...130

Track 62
Audio Example 4-34 Combining the Close and Distant Mics...130

Track 63
Audio Example 4-35 Miking the Amp in the Shower...131

Track 64
Audio Example 4-36 Multiple-Room Miking...134

Track 65
Audio Example 4-37 Combining Miked and Direct Signals...134

Track 66
Audio Example 4-38 Acoustic Guitar Direct In...134
Audio Example 4-39 Miking the Acoustic Guitar...135

Track 67
Audio Example 4-40 The Steel String Acoustic Guitar...136

Track 68
Audio Example 4-41 The Nylon String Classical Guitar...136

Track 69
Audio Example 4-42 The Sound Hole...137
Audio Example 4-43 Behind the Bridge...137
Audio Example 4-44 Over the Neck...138
Audio Example 4-45 Over the Neck, Near the Sound Hole...138

Track 70
Audio Example 4-46 Three Feet Away...138
Audio Example 4-47 Smaller Room...138
Audio Example 4-48 The Bathroom...138

Track 71
Audio Example 4-49 Thin Pick...139
Audio Example 4-50 Thick Pick...139

Track 72
Audio Example 4-51 No Compression...140
Audio Example 4-52 Compressed...140

Track 73
Audio Example 4-53 Cut 150Hz...142
Audio Example 4-54 Boost 12kHz...142
Audio Example 4-55 Cut 300Hz...142
Audio Example 4-56 Boost 4kHz...142
Audio Example 4-57 Boost and Cut 2kHz...142

Track 74
Audio Example 4-58 Chamber Reverb...143

Track 75
Audio Example 4-59 Flange With Delay...143

Track 76
Audio Example 4-60 Acoustic Guitar...143
Audio Example 4-61 Adding the Double Track...143

CD-2

Chapter 5 Acoustic Drums and Percussion

Track 1
Audio Example 5-1 Mic in Front...151

Track 2
Audio Example 5-2 Mic Over Drummer's Head...151

Track 3
Audio Example 5-3 Overhead...152

Track 4
Audio Example 5-4 Eight Feet Away...152

Track 5
Audio Example 5-5 Plate on the Set...152

Track 6
Audio Example 5-6 One Mic Over Kit, One in the Kick...155

Track 7
Audio Example 5-7 Stereo X-Y...155

Track 8
Audio Example 5-8 Head Baffle...156

Track 9
Audio Example 5-9 Three Microphones...158

Track 10
Audio Example 5-10 X-Y Overhead, One in the Kick...158

Track 11
Audio Example 5-11 Snare, Kick and X-Y...159

Track 12
Audio Example 5-12 Snare, Kick, Toms and X-Y...160

Track 13
Audio Example 5-13 A Tom Out of Tune...161
Audio Example 5-14 A Tom in Tune...161

Track 14
Audio Example 5-15 Kick Attack...167

Track 15
Audio Example 5-16 Kick Tone...167

Track 16
Audio Example 5-17 Kick Three Inches Away...167

Track 17
Audio Example 5-18 Kick 12 Inches Outside...167

Track 18
Audio Example 5-19 Cut 300Hz...168
Audio Example 5-20 Cut 300Hz, Boost 80Hz and 4kHz...168

Track 19
Audio Example 5-21 Lots of Kicks...169

Track 20
Audio Example 5-22 Snare Tuned Low...170
Audio Example 5-23 Snare Tuned High...170
Audio Example 5-24 Tight Top and Bottom...171
Audio Example 5-25 Snare Without Dampening...172
Audio Example 5-26 Snare With Weather Stripping...172

Track 21
Audio Example 5-27 Snare From One Foot...173
Audio Example 5-28 Snare From Two Inches...173

Track 22
Audio Example 5-29 Snare Reverb With 2.5 Second Decay Time...173

Track 23
Audio Example 5-30 Snare With Gated Reverb...174

Track 24
Audio Example 5-31 Roll Off 100Hz, Boost 250Hz and 5kHz...174

Track 25
Audio Example 5-32 Lots of Snares...174

Track 26
Audio Example 5-33 Tom at 0VU...176
Audio Example 5-34 Tom at +5VU...176

Track 27
Audio Example 5-35 Tom at 0VU...176

Track 28
Audio Example 5-36 Roll Off 100Hz, Cut 300Hz, Boost 5kHz...177

Track 29
Audio Example 5-37 Lots of Toms...178

Track 30
Audio Example 5-38 X-Y Panned Hard...178

Track 31
Audio Example 5-39 Panning the Hi-hat...180

Track 32
Audio Example 5-40 Hi-hat Miked at the Outer Edge...180
Audio Example 5-41 Hi-hat Miked at the Bell...181

Track 33
Audio Example 5-42 Adjusting the Gate...181

Track 34
Audio Example 5-43 Reverb on the Gated Snare...181

Track 35
Audio Example 5-44 Bypassing the Gate...181

Track 36
Audio Example 5-45 Soloing Percussion...184

Chapter 6 Synchronization/Drum Machines

Track 37
Audio Example 6-1 Mono Drums...189

Track 38
Audio Example 6-2 Outputs Separated...190

Track 39
Audio Example 6-3 Outputs Low...197
Audio Example 6-4 Outputs Maximum...197

Track 40
Audio Example 6-5 Quantized Pattern...200
Audio Example 6-6 Human Feel...200

Track 41
Audio Example 6-7 Kick Drums...206

Track 42
Audio Example 6-8 Simple Kick...206
Audio Example 6-9 Tuning the Kick...206

Track 43
Audio Example 6-10 Cut Mids...206

Track 44
Audio Example 6-11 Enhance Lows...207

Track 45
Audio Example 6-12 Before and After...207

Track 46
Audio Example 6-13 Noisy Kick...207
Audio Example 6-14 Gate the Kick...208

Track 47
Audio Example 6-15 Kick Reverb...209

Track 48
Audio Example 6-16 Short Reverb...209

Track 49
Audio Example 6-17 Gated Reverb...209
Audio Example 6-18 Plate Reverb...210

Track 50
Audio Example 6-19 Snare Drums...211

Track 51
Audio Example 6-20 Simple Snare...211
Audio Example 6-21 8kHz...212
Audio Example 6-22 4kHz...212
Audio Example 6-23 2kHz...212
Audio Example 6-24 250Hz...212
Audio Example 6-25 100Hz...212

Track 52
Audio Example 6-26 Gate the Snare...213

Track 53
Audio Example 6-27 No Compression...216
Audio Example 6-28 Compressed Snare...216

Track 54
Audio Example 6-29 Normal Snare...216
Audio Example 6-30 Compressed Snare...216
Audio Example 6-31 Gate the Compressed Snare...216

Track 55
Audio Example 6-32 Ambience...220

Track 56
Audio Example 6-33 Add Large Reverb...220

Track 57
Audio Example 6-34 Two Reverbs...220

Track 58
Audio Example 6-35 Three Reverbs...220

Track 59
Audio Example 6-36 Toms...221

Track 60
Audio Example 6-37 Tuned Tom...222

Track 61
Audio Example 6-38 100 to 500Hz...222

Track 62
Audio Example 6-39 7 to 9kHz...223
Audio Example 6-40 3 to 5kHz...223

Track 63
Audio Example 6-41 Clean Drums...223

Track 64
Audio Example 6-42 7 to 12kHz...224

Track 65
Audio Example 6-43 3 to 5kHz...224

Track 66
Audio Example 6-44 1.5 to 2.5kHz...224

Track 67
Audio Example 6-45 200 to 600Hz...224

Track 68
Audio Example 6-46 Cut Below 80Hz...225

Track 69
Audio Example 6-47 Reverb on Hi-hat...225

Track 70
Audio Example 6-48 Crash With Plate...225

Track 71
Audio Example 6-49 Real Cymbals With Sequence...225

Track 72
Audio Example 6-50 Tambourine...226
Audio Example 6-51 Oversaturated Tambourine...226
Audio Example 6-52 Result of Oversaturation...226
Audio Example 6-53 Properly Recorded Tambourine...227

Track 73
Audio Example 6-54 Balanced Percussion...229

Track 74
Audio Example 6-55 Distracting Triangle...229

Track 75
Audio Example 6-56 Reverb Panned Away...229
Audio Example 6-57 Reverb Panned Away...229

Track 76
Audio Example 6-58 Small-Room Reverb...229

Track 77
Audio Example 6-59 Add Acoustic Ambience...230

Preface

The AudioPro Home Recording Course teaches you specific concepts and techniques that will improve the overall quality of your audio recordings so that they approach the same audio quality that you hear on the radio and on CDs and cassettes. To do this, the first two chapters together cover enough concepts and terms so that we're all talking the same language. The remaining chapters focus on specific recording techniques as they relate to different types of instruments, kinds of sounds and practical recording situations.

This is a complete course. The explanations are designed to progressively build your recording skills throughout the course. I might introduce a topic with a very minimum of information, then later in the course I'll expand the explanation and support the concepts further with audio and text examples. Read all printed material and listen carefully to the audio examples provided on the accompanying compact discs. (You'll find the audio examples listed by CD and track number as they appear in the chapter.) The information in each complements the other, and together they offer a complete course. Each part of this course is important.

I've designed *The AudioPro Home Recording Course* for the person who is already doing some recording or at least has a small setup on which to practice. To make this a hands-on experience, I'll give you specific assignments to do in each chapter (with visual aids provided by the accompanying illustrations) with your own setup.

If I use a term that is unfamiliar to you, please refer to the Glossary for its definition. At first, we'll keep things as simple as possible to avoid brain burnout. As you progress through this course, you'll build your knowledge and technical abilities step by step.

This material will really help you get sounds that are competitive. Persevere! Keep fine-tuning your craft. If you're serious about audio as a career or if you're doing music just for the fun of it, this course is for you. The techniques described herein are going to help you make better use of your recording time. Your music will only benefit from your deeper understanding of the studio as a musical tool.

The primary tools of the musical trade, for both the professional and the amateur, are available everywhere, right off the shelf. Technology is more affordable now than ever before. With a mixer, some keyboards or guitars, a microphone and a sequencer, almost anyone can create a solid musical work that can be complete on its own or polished off in a professional recording studio. With some motivation, imagination and education, you can (in your own hometown) make your music a financially, emotionally and artistically profitable venture.

We're going to approach recording from a musical perspective. You'll study recording examples that fit real musical situations, and you'll learn solutions to common problems that will help you enhance your music. In doing so, you'll establish a base of common knowledge.

Chapter 1 The Mixer

The Mixer Layout

We begin with the mixing board. Our approach throughout this course is that the mixing board is one of the engineer's musical instruments. Always let the music lead the way through technology. Let your ears and your heart tell you what the musical sounds should be, then use the tools of the trade to get those artistically inspired sounds.

In this first section, we'll cover the following concepts: mixer configurations, amplifiers, speaker connections and studio monitors. This information will help you identify your mixer configuration and ensure that your speakers are connected properly to your amplifier. Once this is completed, you'll have a point of reference for new knowledge, and you can be sure that what you are hearing can be trusted.

First we'll look at how a typical mixer is laid out. Then we'll study the location of each control. Later in this chapter, I'll explain each control in detail so you'll know what each feature is and how it works. Please look at Illustration 1-1 as we go through this. The terms mixer, console, board, mixing desk, desk and audio production console are used interchangeably.

Mixers have a number of channels, each typically having the same controls. These controls can include an attenuator (also called a *pad*); a phase switch; a preamp control; auxiliary sends; equalization; a pan control; track assignments; solo, mute and PFL buttons and the input fader. In understanding how one channel works, you can understand how they all work.

To the right of the channels, there is often a monitor section. In the monitor section, there is usually a master volume control for adjusting listening levels, a monitor selector (where we choose what we listen to), master aux send levels, a test tone oscillator, a stereo master fader, a stereo/mono button, a headphone jack and on some mixers, we also see the output level controls for the track assignment bus.

Split vs. In-line

If your mixer has faders to the right of the channel input faders and if these faders adjust the level of the final output to the multitrack, then your mixer is called a *split mixer* or *console*.

Some mixers have the level controls to the multitrack (typically knobs instead of faders) near the top of each channel. These are called *in-line consoles*. Look at Illustration 1-2 to help visualize the difference between a split and an in-line console. Illustration 1-1 is a split console. The module in Illustration 1-2 is an example of an in-line module.

Split and in-line mixers each have their

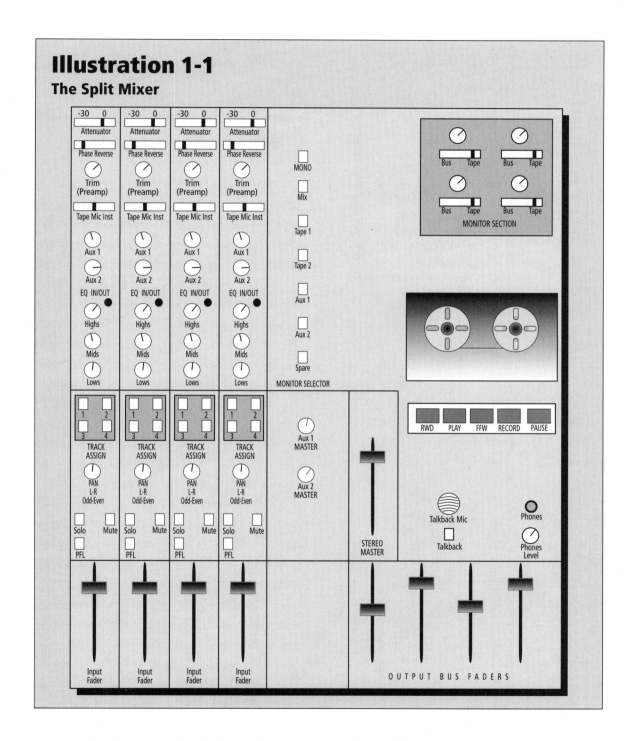

Illustration 1-1
The Split Mixer

own set of advantages, but both can be very effective and flexible while sonically supporting your musical ideas. I've worked a lot on both types and have adjusted quite easily because I understand how each configuration operates. My goal is to explain the basics in simple enough terms that you'll be able to integrate all concepts seamlessly into any recording situation.

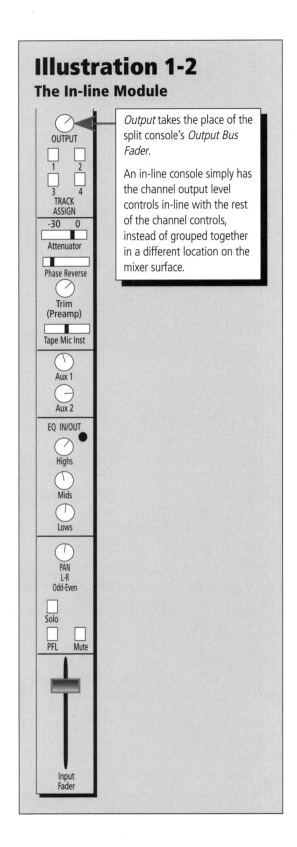

Illustration 1-2
The In-line Module

Output takes the place of the split console's *Output Bus Fader.*

An in-line console simply has the channel output level controls in-line with the rest of the channel controls, instead of grouped together in a different location on the mixer surface.

OUTPUT

1   2
3   4
TRACK ASSIGN

-30   0
Attenuator

Phase Reverse

Trim (Preamp)

Tape Mic Inst

Aux 1

Aux 2

EQ IN/OUT

Highs

Mids

Lows

PAN L-R Odd-Even

Solo

PFL   Mute

Input Fader

Take a look at your mixer to see which kind of controls you have. Identify whether you have a split or in-line mixer.

Professional Amplifiers

Connecting the mixer to your power amp is an important step. Use quality line cables (like the type you use for a guitar or keyboard) to connect the output of the mixer to the input of the power amp. Many wires are specially designed for minimal signal loss. This means a better signal-to-noise ratio. Quality wires and connectors also last longer and create fewer problems.

When I use the term quality in referring to equipment, I don't necessarily mean the most expensive. For home use, it's rarely justifiable to purchase the top of the line. By quality I do mean a product that's produced by an established and reliable manufacturer. If you buy from a trusted name, you should at least be able to count on product support and quality control.

Using a quality power amp is very important. Distortion is a primary cause of ear fatigue, and an amplifier that produces less distortion over longer periods of time causes less fatigue and damage to your ears.

If you have a professional power amp with a rating of at least 100 watts RMS and if you use a good quality reference monitor designed for studio use, you'll be able to work on your music longer with less ear fatigue. When I use the term *professional* in regard to amplifiers, I mean an industrial strength unit, designed for constant use in a pro setting. Compared to a consumer home amplifier, amps designed for pro use generally have better specifications, therefore helping to reduce ear fatigue. They use high

Illustration 1-3
Mixer Configurations

Mixers are designed in various configurations. These configurations can be labeled 4X2, 8X4X2, 16X8X2, and so on. The *X's* between the numbers stand for the word "by," so 4X2 is "4 by 2". There are many different possibilities, but the system is easy to understand.

The first number indicates the number of channel inputs that are available. If your mixer has 8 inputs, then your first number would be 8.

The remaining numbers refer to the different subgroups that these inputs can be combined to. For example, if your mixer has 8 inputs that can be mixed to a stereo output, your configuration would be 8X2.

If your mixer has 20 inputs that can be assigned to 8 tape tracks that can be mixed down to a stereo master output and can also be combined into a mono output that's separate, then your configuration would be 20X8X2X1.

If you have a personal multitrack 4-track with 6 channel inputs that can be assigned to any of the 4 tracks that can then be mixed down to stereo, your configuration would be 6X4X2.

Look at your mixer, determine your configuration and write it down. Start with the number of mic inputs, subgroups, then main outs (like stereo and/or mono).

Assignment: RMS

Find out what the RMS power rating is on your amplifier. Even if you have a home entertainment system, this rating will be in the owner's manual.

If you go shopping for a new amp, I suggest buying a professional quality amplifier rated between 100 and 200 watts RMS from a well known manufacturer.

It isn't necessary to get the most expensive or the most powerful (although that *is* pretty fun). More power is good if you can afford it, because it assures you of less distortion from the amp itself, but be careful if your speakers aren't capable of handling as much power as your amp can deliver. Speakers will often indicate, right on the back by the terminals, the maximum amount of power they can handle safely.

quality components, therefore lasting longer and working harder for longer periods of time. Reputable manufacturers offer the best service and support. Fast, quality service is invaluable when you're making money with your equipment.

Using a small system designed for home entertainment can get you by for a while, but as you become more serious and are spending more and more time recording, investing in a good amp and speakers is necessary. See Illustration 1-3 for the assignment on RMS.

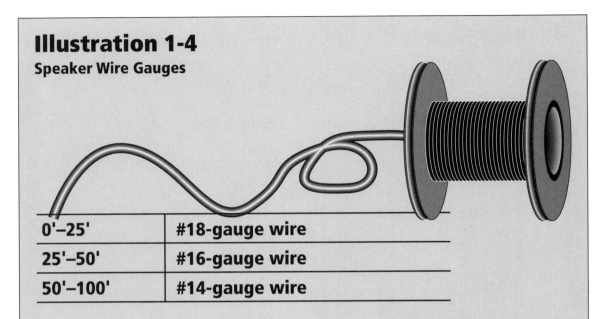

Illustration 1-4
Speaker Wire Gauges

0'–25'	#18-gauge wire
25'–50'	#16-gauge wire
50'–100'	#14-gauge wire

Always use heavy-duty wire designed specifically for use with speakers. The chart above indicates suggested wire gauges for varying lengths.

The smaller the wire number, the thicker the wire. Thicker wire has less resistance to signal. To have minimal degradation of signal in longer runs, we use thicker wire.

Wire can be very expensive, especially if you buy the top of the line. For home studio use, it's rarely justifiable or necessary to buy "the best." Buying a good, heavy-duty wire of the appropriate gauge in the middle price range is usually safe.

Be sure to use designated speaker wire for speakers—not a regular guitar cable (line cable). Both wires in a speaker cable must be identical. A guitar cable has one single center conductor with a braided shield acting as the other wire. Using a guitar cable as a speaker cable is an inefficient way to carry the amplified audio signal to the speakers and can be taxing on the power amplifier sending the signal.

Speaker wire often looks like the power cord on a standard lamp in your house. In fact, a heavy-duty 18-gauge lamp wire can work well as speaker cable in a pinch.

Whenever you're monitoring in stereo, be absolutely certain that the red post on the back of the power amp is connected to the red post on the back of both speakers and that black goes to black! If these are connected backwards on one of the two monitors, the speakers are said to be *out-of-phase*. When this happens, a sound wave that is sent simultaneously to both speakers (panned center) moves one speaker cone out while it moves the other speaker cone in. Speakers connected out-of-phase work against each other instead of with each other. What you hear from them is inaccurate and unpredictable, especially in the lower frequencies.

Proper Wire

Use the proper wire to connect your speakers to your power amp. **Speaker wire is not the same as a guitar cable**. Use designated speaker wire. Guitar cable is designed to carry signals like those from a keyboard to a mixer, not power from an amplifier to speakers. Also, choosing wire that's too thick or too thin for your situation can cause a problem with the efficiency of your amp and speakers.

Ask a salesperson which wire gauge and type is best for your situation. Let them know how long a run it is from your power amp to your speakers, what kind of connectors your amp has, plus the brand of your amp and its power rating. If the salesperson gives you a glazed look when you recite all of these specifications, this indicates that they don't understand your situation. I suggest you get a second opinion.

As a rule of thumb, a good quality 18-gauge speaker wire works well in most cases. Refer to Illustration 1-4 for suggested wire gauge numbers for a specific wire length.

Studio Monitors

Selecting speakers is the key to producing good sounds that reliably transfer from your system to a friend's system or your car stereo. One of the most annoying and frustrating audio recording problems is a mix that sounds great on your system but sounds terrible everywhere else.

Part of the solution to this is experience with analytical listening on your system to music that you know sounds good everywhere. Possibly, an even bigger part of the solution to this problem lies in the use of *near-field reference monitors*. Industry standards are continually changing and the market for near-field reference monitors has become very competitive. There are great new products available from all major speaker manufacturers, and most are very reasonably priced (typically between $300 and $1000 per pair).

Several manufacturers are producing high priced near-field reference monitors—some with built-in, factory-calibrated amplifiers. Often these speaker pairs cost several thousands of dollars and are very accurate and quite fun to listen to, but they aren't necessary for most home studio applications.

Near-Field Reference Monitors

A near-field reference monitor is designed to be listened to with your head at one point of an equilateral triangle (approximately three feet, or one meter, on each side) and the speakers at the other two points. The speakers should be facing directly at your ears and are ideally about 10 degrees above the horizontal plane that's even with your ears (Illustration 1-5). With this kind of a system, the room that you're monitoring in has a minimal effect on how you hear the mix. These monitors should sound pretty much the same in your studio at home as they do in any studio in the world.

If the room is minimally affecting what you hear, then the mix that you create will be more accurate and will sound good on more systems. Changing to a near field reference monitor gives you immediate gratification through more reliable mixes, plus it lets you start gaining experience based on a predictable and accurate listening environment.

Not just any small speaker works as a near-field reference monitor. In fact, speakers that aren't designed specifically for this application

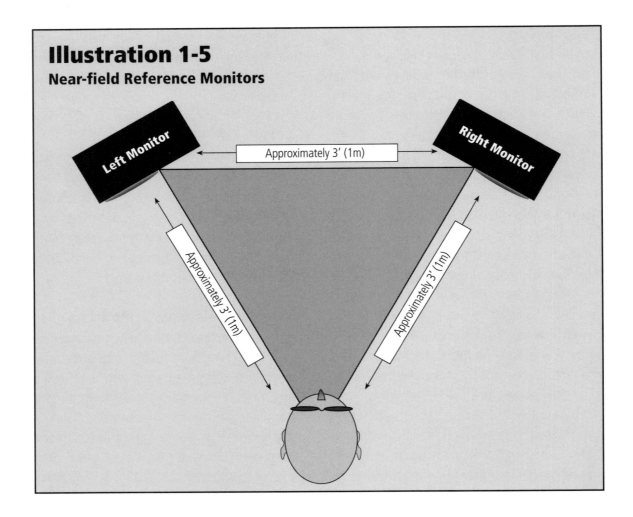

Illustration 1-5
Near-field Reference Monitors

Left Monitor

Right Monitor

Approximately 3' (1m)

Approximately 3' (1m)

Approximately 3' (1m)

produce poor results and unreliable mixes when positioned as near-field reference monitors.

Far-field Monitors

Far-field monitors are designed to be farther away from the mixing engineer, and their sound is greatly affected by the acoustics of the room they're in. Larger rooms have more air to move, so they require larger monitors to move that air. These monitors can be very expensive.

In order to get great results from far-field monitors, they must be used in a studio that has been acoustically designed for a smooth and even balance of frequencies within the room.

Since this can involve actual construction and often plenty of expense and since near-field reference monitors can produce excellent results, the obvious choice for most home setups is a pair of near field reference monitors.

Connectors

We encounter several types of connectors when hooking audio equipment together. In this section, we cover RCA connectors, 1/4-inch connectors, XLR connectors, adapters, plugging in, powering up/down, grounding and hums.

RCA Connectors

RCA phono connectors are the type found on most home stereo equipment and are physically smaller in size than the plug that goes into a guitar or keyboard (Illustration 1-6). RCA phono connectors are very common in home-recording equipment and are among the least expensive connectors.

Quarter-inch Phone Connectors

Quarter-inch phone connectors are the type found on regular cables for guitars or keyboards. These connectors are commonly used on musical instruments and in home and professional recording studios.

Notice that a guitar cable has one tip and one sleeve on the connector (Illustration 1-7). In a guitar cable, the wire connected to the tip

Illustration 1-6
RCA Phono Plug and Jack

carries the actual musical signal. The wire carrying the signal is called the *hot wire* or *hot lead.* The sleeve is connected to the braided shield that's around the hot wire. The purpose of the shield is to diffuse outside interference, like electrostatic interference and extraneous radio signals.

The other type of 1/4-inch phone connector is the type found on stereo headphones. This plug has one tip, one small ring (next to the tip)

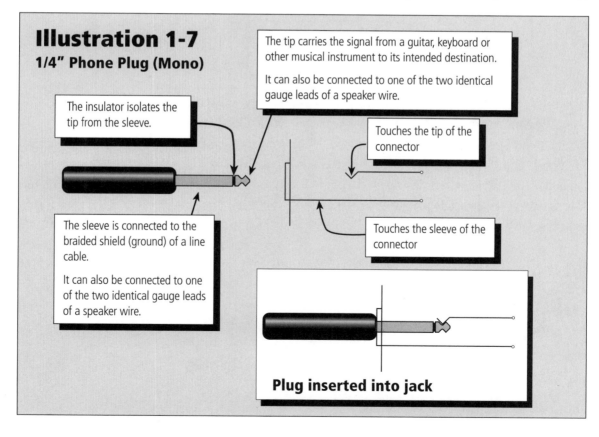

Illustration 1-7
1/4" Phone Plug (Mono)

The tip carries the signal from a guitar, keyboard or other musical instrument to its intended destination.

It can also be connected to one of the two identical gauge leads of a speaker wire.

The insulator isolates the tip from the sleeve.

Touches the tip of the connector

The sleeve is connected to the braided shield (ground) of a line cable.

It can also be connected to one of the two identical gauge leads of a speaker wire.

Touches the sleeve of the connector

Plug inserted into jack

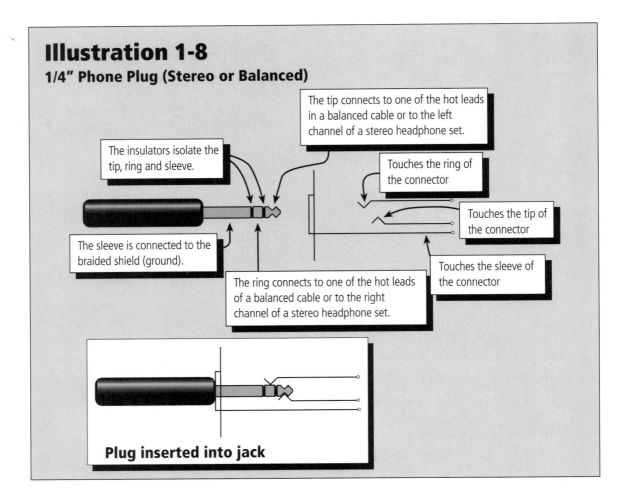

Illustration 1-8
1/4" Phone Plug (Stereo or Balanced)

The tip connects to one of the hot leads in a balanced cable or to the left channel of a stereo headphone set.

The insulators isolate the tip, ring and sleeve.

Touches the ring of the connector

Touches the tip of the connector

The sleeve is connected to the braided shield (ground).

Touches the sleeve of the connector

The ring connects to one of the hot leads of a balanced cable or to the right channel of a stereo headphone set.

Plug inserted into jack

and a sleeve (Illustration 1-8). In headphones, the tip and ring are for the left and right musical signal, and the sleeve is connected to the braided shield that surrounds the two hot wires. This connector can be used for other devices that require a three-point connection.

XLR Connectors

XLR connectors are the type found on most microphones and the mic inputs of most mixers (Illustration 1-9). Two of the three pins on this connector carry the signal, and the third is connected to the shield. The reason for the two hot leads has to do with reducing noise in a bal-

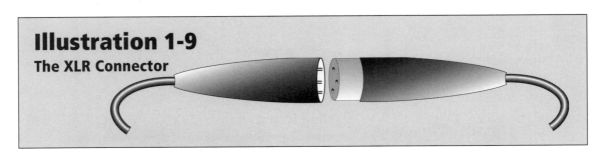

Illustration 1-9
The XLR Connector

Illustration 1-10
Adapters

The center post on the RCA phono plug corresponds to the tip on the RCA-to-1/4" phone plug adapter.

The tip and the ring on the 1/4" tip-ring-sleeve phone plug correspond to pins 2 and 3 on the 1/4" phone plug-to-XLR adapter. The sleeve corresponds to pin 1. The pin numbers of the XLR connector are imprinted on the connector end itself. They're located next to the base of the pins on the male XLR connector and next to the holes on the female XLR connector.

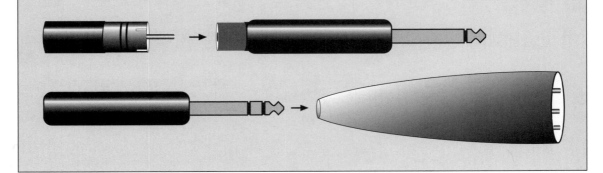

anced low-impedance mic cable. The details involved here are covered later in this course.

It's not uncommon to find cables with an XLR on one end and a 1/4-inch phone plug on the other or cables that have been intentionally wired in a nonstandard way. These are usually for specific applications and can be useful in certain situations. Check wiring details in your equipment manuals to see if these will work for you.

There are other types of connectors, but RCA phono, 1/4-inch phone and XLR are the most common. It's okay to use adapters to go from one type of connector to another, but always be sure to use connectors and adapters with the same number of points. For example, if a plug has a tip, ring and sleeve, it must be plugged into a jack that accepts all three points (Illustration 1-10).

Plugging In

The output of your mixer might have multiple outputs for connection to different amplifier inputs. The stereo line output is the correct output from the mixer to be plugged into the power amplifier. This might also be labeled Main Output, Mains, Mix Out, Control Room Monitor Output, Out to Amp, or Stereo Out. **If your mixer has XLR outputs available and if your power amp has XLR inputs, patch these points together as your first choice.** This output typically provides the most clean and noise-free signal.

Electrical Power

When plugging into the power outlet, use power strips that have protection against power surges and spikes. These can be picked up for a reasonable price at most electrical supply stores.

Spikes and surges are fluctuations in your electrical current that rise well above the 120-volt current that runs most of your equipment. Surges generally last longer than spikes, but both usually occur so quickly that you don't even notice them. Since power surges and spikes can seriously damage delicate electronic circuits, protection is necessary for any microprocessor-controlled equipment (computers, synthesizers, mixers, processors, sequencers, printers, etc.).

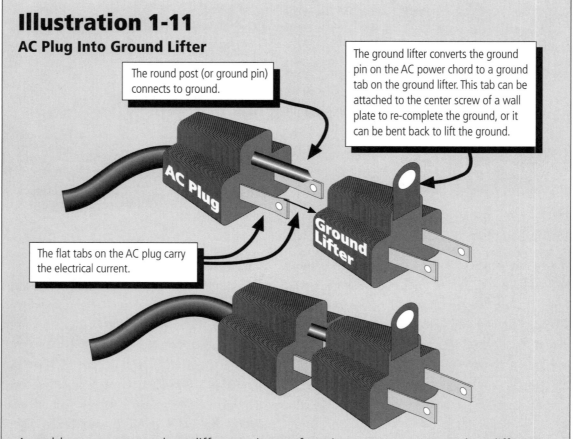

Illustration 1-11
AC Plug Into Ground Lifter

The round post (or ground pin) connects to ground.

The ground lifter converts the ground pin on the AC power chord to a ground tab on the ground lifter. This tab can be attached to the center screw of a wall plate to re-complete the ground, or it can be bent back to lift the ground.

The flat tabs on the AC plug carry the electrical current.

A problem can occur when different pieces of equipment are connected to different outlets. An inconsistency in ground and in-house wiring can produce a low hum in your audio signal. When this happens, you can use a ground lifter on the piece of equipment causing the hum. The ground lifter is the adapter that accepts all three prongs from a standard AC cable but turns the ground pin into a tab. This tab can be screwed to the wall plate mounting screw if the ground needs to be completed at the outlet, or if you need the ground disconnected at that point, simply bend the ground tab back and leave it disconnected.

Possible danger! Refer to Illustration 1-13 and consult a qualified electrician about your unique setup.

Powering up

- Turn on the mixer and outboard gear (like delays, reverbs and compressors) *before* the power amps.
- Always turn power amps on *last* to protect speakers from pops and blasts as the rest of the electronic gear comes on.

Powering down

- Turn power amps off *first* to protect speakers, then turn the mixer and outboard gear off.

Grounding

Grounding is a very important consideration in any recording setup! **The purpose of grounding is safety.** If there's an electrical short, or a problem in a circuit, the electricity may search out a path other than the one intended. Electricity is always attracted to something connected to the ground we walk on (the earth). The reason for the third pin, called the ground pin, on your AC power cable is to give an electrical problem like this somewhere to go (Illustration 1-11).

The ground pin in your electrical wiring is ideally connected, through the third pin on your power cord, to a grounding rod, which is a metal rod that's stuck at least six feet into the earth. Another possible source of ground is a metal pipe like the water supply pipe to your hot-water heater. This can be an excellent ground, but be sure the metal pipe at the heater is not connected to plastic pipe before it gets to ground.

If you happen to touch equipment that isn't properly grounded and if you are standing on the ground, you become just the path to the ground that the electricity is looking for. This could, at the very least, be painful or, at worst, even fatal. Properly grounding a piece of equipment gives potentially damaging electrical problems a path, other than you, to ground.

Ground Hum

Aside from causing physical pain, grounding problems can induce an irritating hum into your audio signal. If you have ever had this kind of noise show up mysteriously and at the worst times in your recordings, you know what true frustration is.

Audio Example 1-1 60-Cycle Hum
CD-1: Track 2

Sixty-cycle hum is the result of a grounding problem where the 60-cycle electrical current from the wall outlet is inducing a 60-cycle-per-second tone into your musical signal.

To make matters worse, this 60-cycle tone isn't just a pure and simple 60 Hertz sine wave. A sine wave is the simplest wave form and, in fact, is the only wave form that has a completely smooth crest and trough as it completes its cycle (Illustration 1-12). We could easily eliminate a 60-cycle sine wave with a filter. Sixty-cycle hum has a distinct and distracting wave form, which also includes various harmonics that extend into the upper frequencies.

It's very important to have your setup properly grounded in order to eliminate 60-cycle hum and for your own physical safety while operating your equipment. For some practical solutions to some grounding problems, see Illustration 1-13.

Illustration 1-12
The Sine Wave

There are 360° in the complete cycle of a sine wave. This is the simplest wave form, having a smooth crest and trough plus complete symmetry between positive and negative air pressure.

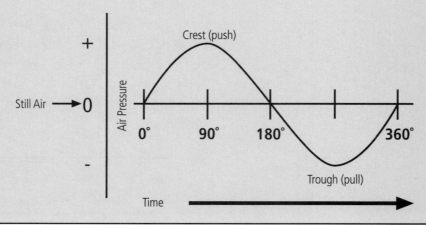

Connecting to the Mixer

Audio Examples 1-2, 1-3 and 1-4 are mixed in three different ways—same music and board but different mixes. Notice the dramatic differences in the effect and feeling of these mixes. Even though they all contain the same instrumentation and orchestration, the mixer combined the available textures differently in each example.

Audio Examples 1-2, 1-3 and 1-4
Mixes 1, 2 and 3
CD-1: Track 3

The mixer is where your songs are molded and shaped into commercially and artistically palatable commodities. If this is all news to you, there's a long and winding road ahead. We'll take things a step at a time, but for now you need to know what the controls on the mixer do. No two mixers are set up in exactly the same way, but the concepts involved with most mixers are essentially the same.

In this section, we'll cover those concepts and terms that relate to the signal going to and coming out of the mixing board. These concepts include:
- High and low impedance
- Direct boxes and why they're needed
- Phantom power
- Line levels

A mixer is used to combine, or mix, different sound sources. These sound sources might be:
- On their way to the multitrack
- On their way to effects from instruments or microphones
- On their way from the multitrack to the monitor speakers, effects or mixdown machine

We can control a number of variables at a

Illustration 1-13
Grounding Buzzes and Hums

Let's look at some practical solutions to the persistent hums and buzzes that vex so many recording setups. Once your studio is on the right path electrically, your frustration level should drop significantly.

Hire a Pro

The best approach to a persistent grounding problem is to hire a qualified electrician to rewire your studio so that all available electrical outlets have the ground terminals running to the exact same perfect ground. The ideal situation is to have a completely separate electrical feed run into your studio by the power company. These circuits should be filtered and relayed. When designed properly, if there is a loss of power, circuits will come back on in an order determined by the relay network. It's also a great idea to have any computer-based gear on a power backup system. These backup systems have battery power that will continue the flow of current to your equipment if there's a power loss or failure. You only need to be saved once by one of these systems to be a firm believer in their use.

This solution is obviously impractical for most home users. You might spend as much money to get a truly professional electrical system as many home recordists spend on their recording equipment altogether. Please keep in mind, though, that you might benefit greatly by a simple consultation with an experienced studio wiring technician.

Lifting the Ground

Lifting the ground is accomplished when the third prong on an AC power cable does not plug into the power outlet.

The ground can be lifted on any piece of gear that has a three-prong wall plug by plugging that wall plug into a small adapter that accepts all three prongs from the power chord at the in end but only has two prongs coming out of the out end. See Illustration 1-11. If the power cord has only two prongs, the ground has already been lifted.

Lifting the ground doesn't necessarily mean nothing is grounded; it simply means that a particular piece of equipment isn't grounded twice to conflicting grounds. Many home studios have the ground lifted on all pieces of gear except one. In such a case, all gear that's part of the network grounds to that one piece, even though their individual power cord grounds aren't connected.

If all grounds are lifted, it's advisable to connect all of the individual chassis grounds together with zip cord, lamp wire or #10 insulated wire. Most pieces of equipment have ground terminals on their back panels. If there is no ground terminal, connect

continued...

Illustration 1-13
...continued

the ground wire to any screw that goes into the metal chassis. It's easiest if you connect all of these wires to one terminal strip, mounted close to your gear, then connect the terminal strip to a true ground. A true ground can be difficult to find, but try the hot water supply pipe to your hot water tank, the center screw on one of your wall AC outlet face plates or have an electrician install and verify a true ground source.

Disconnect Shields

Another way to eliminate hum is to disconnect the shield at one end of your line cable (patch cable, instrument cable, guitar cord, etc.), usually at the end closest to your mixer. This can break the ground loop and solve the problem. To disconnect the shield on a cable, you must open the connector and either cut or unsolder the braided shield from the lug it's connected to. It can be convenient to keep a couple of cables like this around. Mark them clearly and indicate the end with the disconnected shield.

Danger, Danger

Anyone who has ever played in a real live garage band knows that there's always danger when electrical equipment, musicians and cement floors coexist in the same room. The cement floor is connected directly to the ground, and you can become a very attractive option for electricity in search of ground if you're standing on the cement. Remember, the human body can conduct the flow of 20 to 30 amps of 110-volt alternating current (AC). Since this can be, at the very least, very painful or, at worst, even lethal, be cautious.

In Summary

Proper grounding can be the single most important factor in keeping your system quiet and buzz free. A poorly designed system can have many hums and other unwanted sounds and noises. Paying attention to detail here and hiring some professional help will make your home studio far more functional and tons more fun.

Keep in mind that you've just seen some practical solutions to common problems, but real electrical wiring and system design should be handled by a professional electrician. Studio grounding is a specialized application, so look for an electrician with expertise in this field. Hiring the right electrician with the right bag of tricks for the studio is a very worthwhile investment.

number of points in the pathway from the sound source to the recorder and back. This pathway is called the *signal path*. Each point holds its own possibility for degrading or enhancing the audio integrity of your music.

Input Stage/Impedance

Let's begin at the input stage, where the mics and instruments plug into the mixer. Mic inputs come in two types: high-impedance and low-impedance. There's no real difference in sound quality between these two as long as each is used within its limitations (Illustration 1-14).

The main concern when considering impedance is that high-impedance outputs go into high-impedance inputs and low-impedance outputs go into low-impedance inputs.

Impedance is, by definition, the resistance to the flow of current measured in a unit called an ohm. Imagine two pipes: one large and one small. More water can go through the large pipe with less resistance than the same amount of water through the small pipe. I think we would all agree that a city water reservoir would be easier to drain through a six-foot diameter pipe than through a straw. The large pipe represents low-impedance (low resistance). The small pipe represents high-impedance (high resistance).

Now, we can put a numerical tag on impedance. *High impedance* has high resistance, in the range of 10,000 to 20,000 ohms (a small pipe). *Low impedance* has low resistance, in the range of 150-1000 ohms (a large pipe).

A high-impedance instrument plugged into a low-impedance input is expecting to see lots of resistance to its signal flow. If the signal doesn't meet that resistance, it'll overdrive and distort the input almost immediately, no matter how low you keep the input level.

Illustration 1-14
Hi Z vs. Lo Z
Balanced Low Impedance

Balanced low-impedance inputs, abbreviated lo Z, use a three pin connector—typically XLR (Illustration 1-9). The advantage to balanced low-impedance mics and mic inputs is that cables can be very long (up to about 1000 feet) with no signal loss and minimal noise and interference. This type of design uses a clever scheme that cancels any noise, radio signal or electrostatic interference that joins the signal between the mic and the mixer input. This is the system of choice for a serious setup.

Unbalanced High Impedance

High-impedance inputs, abbreviated hi Z, generally accept a regular guitar cable with 1/4" phone plugs (Illustration 1-7). High-impedance systems are limited since cables can be no longer than 20-30 ft. without noticeable electrostatic noise, radio interference and other types of noises. Most guitars and keyboards have high-impedance outputs. They must be plugged into high-impedance inputs. The line input on a mixer will usually work well with high-impedance instrument outputs.

A low-impedance mic plugged into a high-impedance input meets too much resistance to its signal flow. Therefore, no matter how high you turn the input level up, there's insufficient level to obtain a proper amount of VU reading. The water from the large pipe can't all squeeze into the small pipe fast enough.

So, what is the solution if you have a high-impedance guitar that you want to plug into a low-impedance mixer or a low-impedance mic that you want to plug into a high-impedance guitar amp?

Direct Box

It's possible, acceptable and standard procedure to use a direct box to match a high-impedance output to a low-impedance input or vice versa. A direct box is also called a line-matching transformer, impedance-matching transformer, impedance transformer or DI (direct injection). Its sole purpose is to change the impedance of the instrument or device plugged into its input.

Impedance transformers work equally well in both directions—low to high or high to low. Using the same transformer, you can plug a high-impedance instrument into the high-impedance input and then patch the low-impedance output into a low-impedance input, or, if necessary, you can plug low-impedance into the low-impedance end and come out of the transformer high-impedance.

Passive vs. Active DIs

There are two main types of direct boxes: passive and active. Passive direct boxes are the least expensive and generally do a fine job of matching one impedance in to another impedance out. Active direct boxes are usually more expensive and contain amplifying circuitry that requires power from a battery or other external power supply. These amplifying circuits are used to enhance bass and treble. An active direct box typically gives your signal more punch and clarity in the high frequencies *and* low frequencies.

Illustration 1-15
The Direct Box

The hi Z input is a Y. One side of the Y sends the signal to the transformer; the other side of the Y sends the signal to the Out to Amp jack. This makes it possible for instruments to plug into the direct box then into the amplifier from the Out to Amp jack.

If you hear a loud ground hum after plugging into the direct box, it will usually go away if you flip the Ground Lift switch.

Most DIs have a Pad to help keep strong signals from overdriving the console inputs.

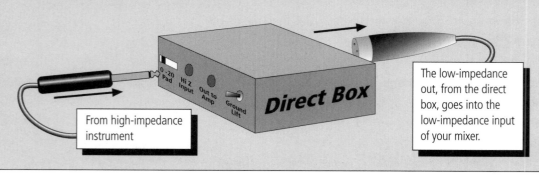

From high-impedance instrument

Direct Box

The low-impedance out, from the direct box, goes into the low-impedance input of your mixer.

Audio Example 1-5 is a bass through a passive direct box.

Audio Example 1-6 is the same bass through an active direct box.

Audio Examples 1-5 and 1-6 Direct Boxes
CD-1: Track 4

The difference between these two examples can be subtle, but it's often the nuances that make the difference between okay and brilliant! A 10 percent improvement of each track really impacts the final product, especially when recording 8, 16, 24 or more tracks. Optimize every step of your recording process! It makes a noticeable difference.

Direct boxes typically have a ground lift switch (Illustration 1-15). Try flipping this switch if you can hear a noticeable 60-cycle ground hum along with the instrument sound. There is usually one position that eliminates hum.

Phantom Power

Condenser microphones and active direct boxes need power to operate. If they don't receive it, they won't work. This power can come from a battery in the unit or from the phantom power supply located within the mixer.

Phantom power (a very low amperage 48-volt DC current) is available at any mic input that has a phantom power switch. Since amperage is the actual punch behind the voltage and since phantom power has a very low amperage, there's little danger that this power will cause you any physical harm, even though the power travels to the mic or direct box through the same mic cable that the musical signal travels to the mixer.

Phantom power requirements can vary from mic to mic so check your mic specifications to insure that the mic is getting the power it needs. Voltage requirements are typically between 12 and 52 volts. Most mics that require low voltages have a regulatory circuit to reduce higher voltages so that normal 48-volt phantom power can be used without damaging the mic. Microphones that require higher voltages won't usually sound all that great until they get the power they require. These mics often come with their own power supply.

Your mixer might not have phantom power built in. Most microphone manufacturers offer external phantom power supplies for one or more mics. Simply plug the phantom power supply into an AC outlet, then plug the cable from the mic or direct box into the phantom power supply. Finally, patch from the XLR output of the phantom power supply into the mixer mic input.

Phantom power is preferred over battery power because it is constant and reliable, whereas batteries can wear down, lose power and cause the mic or direct box to operate below its optimum specification (even though it might still be working).

If the mic or direct box doesn't need phantom power, it's good practice to turn the power off on those channels, though it isn't absolutely essential. Many consoles have phantom power on/off switches. Some mixers have phantom power that stays on all of the time. This is okay but if there's an on/off switch, turn it on when you need it and off when you don't.

Line Level

Line in and *line out* are common terms typically associated with tape recorder inputs and outputs and mixer inputs and outputs. The signal that comes from a microphone has a strength that's called *mic level,* and a mixer needs to have that signal amplified to what is called *line level.* The amplifier that brings the mic level up to line level is called the *mic preamp.* We'll study mic preamps later in this chapter.

Instrument inputs on mixers are line level. An input that is line level enters the board after the microphone preamp and is, therefore, not affected by its adjustment.

Some mixers have attenuators on the line inputs and the mic inputs to compensate for different instrument and tape recorder output levels. As we optimize each instrument or voice recording, we must optimize the gain structure at each point of the signal path. When all the levels are correct for each mic preamp, line attenuator, fader, EQ, bus fader, etc., we can record the cleanest, most accurate signal. When one link of this chain is weak, the overall sonic integrity crashes and burns.

Mixers that have only one 1/4-inch phone input on each channel typically have a Mic/Line switch. Select the appropriate position for your situation. In *mic* position the input goes through the preamp. In *line* position (possibly called *instrument* position) the preamp is not included.

+4dBm vs. -10dBV

You might have heard the terms *plus four* or *minus 10* (+4 or -10) used when referring to a mixer, tape recorder or signal processor.

This is another consideration for compatibility between pieces of equipment, aside from the low impedance/high impedance dilemma. Different equipment can have different relative line level strength. This is tagged in dB and the two options are +4dBm or -10dBV.

When we use the term *dB* it's useful to keep in mind that it is a term that expresses a ratio between two powers and can be tagged to many different types of power that we encounter in recording.

With our option of +4dBm, dB is being tagged to milliwatts; and with -10dBV, dB is being tagged to volts. Without going into the math of it all, let's simply remember that +4 equipment only works well with other +4 equipment, and -10 equipment only works well with other -10 equipment.

Some units let you switch between +4 and -10, so all you do is select the level that matches your system. There are also boxes made that let you go in at one level and out at the other. Refer to Illustration 1-16 for more details about +4 and -10.

Getting Sound Into the Board

At first glance, mixers can be very intimidating to new users. Don't forget, for the most part each channel has exactly the same controls. So, if we can use and understand one channel, we've already won most of the battle. In this section, we begin to see what each control can do. As you grasp these concepts thoroughly, the mixer becomes a creative tool rather than a formidable adversary.

The Preamp

One of the first things your signal from the mic sees as it enters the mixer is the mic preamp (sometimes called the input preamp or simply the preamp). The preamp is actually a small amplifier circuit, and its controls are generally at the top of each channel. The *preamp level* con-

Illustration 1-16
More Details About +4 vs. -10

Most +4 gear is balanced low-impedance. This is the type that's used in a true blue professional recording studio and uses either an XLR connector or some other type of three-pin connector, like a stereo headphone type of plug (tip-ring-sleeve). Gear can also be of the unbalanced variety and still operate at +4. This equipment will use RCA or 1/4" phone connectors.

We most often think of -10 gear as being unbalanced. This type of gear is considered semipro. Most home recording equipment operates at -10dBV. Gear that uses RCA phono type plugs or regular mono guitar plugs is usually -10dBV.

Some pieces of equipment will have a switch somewhere that will let you select whether they operate at +4 or -10. A +4 output is too strong for a -10 input, and a -10 output is too weak for a +4 input.

When used properly and with shorter cable runs, there should not be a noticeable difference in sound quality from a unit operating at -10 as opposed to +4, even though +4 is the professional standard.

+4dBm balanced equipment works especially well when longer cable runs are necessary, like in a large recording studio, or when radio interference and electrostatic noises are a particular problem.

If you are considering signal processors (reverbs, compressors, gates, etc.), mixers or tape recorders, you must always maintain compatibility between +4 and -10 equipment.

Units are available which allow +4 and -10 gear to work perfectly together. Plug in one end at +4, and the signal comes out the other end at -10, or vice versa.

trols how much a source is amplified and is sometimes labeled as the Mic Gain Trim, Mic Preamp, Input Preamp, Trim, Preamp or Gain.

A signal that's been patched into a microphone input has entered the mixer before the preamp. The preamp needs to receive a signal that is at mic level. Mic level (typically 30-60dB below line level) is what we call the strength of the signal that comes out of the mic as it hears your music. A *mic level* signal must be amplified to a signal strength that the mixer wants. Mixers work at line level so a mic level signal needs to be amplified by the preamp to line level before it gets to the rest of the signal path.

Best results are usually achieved when the preamp doesn't need to be turned all the way up. A preamp circuit usually recirculates the signal back through itself to amplify. This process can add noise, then amplify *that* noise, then amplify *that* noise, etc. So, use as little preamplification as possible to achieve sufficient line level.

Many boards have an LED (light-emitting diode, or red light) next to the preamp control. This is a peak level indicator and is used to indicate peak signal strength that either is or is getting close to overdriving the input. The proper way to adjust the preamp control is to turn it up until the peak LED is blinking occasionally, then decrease the preamp level slightly. It's usually okay if the peak LED blinks a few times during a recording.

Attenuator

It's a fact that sometimes the signal that comes from a microphone or instrument into the board is too strong for the preamp stage of your mixer. This can happen when miking a very loud instrument, like a drum or electric guitar amp, or when accepting the DI of a guitar or bass with particularly powerful pickups. Some microphones can also produce a stronger signal than others. If the signal is too strong going into the preamp, then there will be unacceptable distortion. When this happens at the input, there's no fixing it later.

This situation requires the use of an attenuator, also called a pad. This is almost always found at the top of each channel by the preamp level control. An *attenuator* restricts the flow of signal into the preamp by a measured amount or, in some cases, by a variable amount. Listen to Audio Example 1-7 to hear the sound of an overdriven input. This example would sound clean and clear if only the attenuator switch were set correctly!

Audio Example 1-7 The Overdriven Input
CD-1: Track 5

Most attenuators include 10, 20 or 30dB pads, which are labeled -10dB, -20dB, or -30dB.

If there's noticeable distortion from a sound source, even if the preamp is turned down, use the pad. Start with the least amount of pad available first. If distortion disappears, all is well. If there's still distortion, try more attenuation.

Once the distortion is gone, use the preamp level control to attain sufficient input level. Listen to Audio Example 1-8 to hear the dramatic difference this adjustment can make in the clarity of an audio signal.

Audio Example 1-8 Attenuator Adjustment
CD-1: Track 5

Again, if the input stage of your mixer has a red peak LED by the input level control, it's desirable to turn the input up until the peak LED blinks occasionally, then back the level off slightly. This way we know we have the signal coming into the mixer as hot as possible without distortion. This is good.

Ideally, we'll always record electronic instruments with their output at maximum going into the board. This procedure results in the best possible signal-to-noise (S/N) ratio and provides a more surefire way to get the instrument back to its original level for a punch-in or retake.

If you don't have an attenuator and if you are recording from an instrument like bass, keyboard or guitar through a direct box, you can turn the output of the instrument down slightly to keep from overdriving the input preamp. Be sure to mark or notate the position of the instrument's controls (especially volume) so you can duplicate levels for a future punch-in or retake.

Meters

We must use meters to tell how much signal is getting to the console, tape recorders, outboard gear, etc. There are a few different types of meters, and they don't all work in the same way.

VU meters are the most common type of meter. VU stands for volume unit. This meter reads average signal levels, not peak levels or fast attacks. A VU meter has a needle that moves across a scale from about -20VU up to about +5VU. The act of moving the needle's physical mass across the VU scale keeps this meter from being able to follow fast attacks.

Peak meters or *peak LEDs* can accurately meter fast attacks from percussive instruments. Nearly instantaneous, sharp attacks, like those from any metal or hard wood instrument that is struck by a hard stick or mallet, are called *transients*. Peak meters contain a series of small lights that turn on immediately in response to a predetermined voltage. Since there's no movement of a physical mass (like the VU meter's needle), peak meters are ideal for accurately indicating transients. Refer to Illustration 1-17 for more detail about these types of meters.

Phase

Phase is a very important and often misunderstood factor in recording. Imagine the complete cycle of a sound wave as being like a wave in water. This wave has a crest, which pushes on your eardrum, and a trough, which pulls on your eardrum (Illustration 18).

If two signals are electronically *out of phase* their waveforms can be mirror images of each other. When this happens, there can be cancelation of all or part of your sound. As the crest of waveform A pushes on your eardrum, the trough of waveform B pulls on your eardrum with the same amount of energy. This results in either no movement of the eardrum (no perceived sound) or reduced movement of the eardrum (altered, inaccurate sound).

If two waveforms are *in phase*, they crest and trough together. This results in a doubling of the amount of energy from that waveform, or twice the amount of air being moved.

When multiple microphones are used in the same room, sounds can reach the different mics at different times and probably at different points in the cycle of the wave. They combine at the mic out of phase. That's why it's always best to use as few mics as possible on an instrument or group of instruments in the same. Fewer mics means fewer phase problems.

This theory also pertains to the way speakers operate. If two speakers are in phase and they both receive the identical waveform, both speaker cones move in and out at the same time. If two speakers are out of phase and if they both receive the identical waveform, one speaker cone moves in while the other speaker cone moves out. They don't work together. They fight each other, and the combined sound they produce is not reliable.

This problem doesn't show up as much in a stereo mix, but anytime your mix is played in mono or anytime you are combining multiple microphones to a single tape track, this can be the worst problem of all. To hear the effect of combining a sound with itself in and out of phase, listen to the guitar in Audio Examples 1-9, 1-10 and 1-11. Audio Example 1-9 is the original track playing into one channel of the mixer. In Audio Example 1-10, the signal is split and run into another channel of the mixer. Notice the volume increase as the two channels are combined. Audio Example 1-11 shows the

Illustration 1-17

Transients

A transient attack is the percussive attack present in all percussion instruments when one hard surface is struck with a hard stick, mallet or beater (cymbals, tambourine, cowbell, claves, guiro, shakers, maracas, etc.). Transient attacks are also a consideration when recording acoustic guitar (especially steel string played with a pick) or acoustic piano.

VU Meters

A VU meter is the most common type of meter. VU stands for volume unit. This meter is capable of reading average signal levels, not peak levels or fast attacks. A VU meter has a needle that physically moves across a scale from about -20VU up to about +5VU.

Instruments with a very fast, percussive attack have levels that can't be read accurately by a standard VU meter, which responds too slowly to register the attack.

Peak Meters

A peak meter uses LEDs (or other types of lights) instead of the physically moving needle of a standard VU meter.

Peak meters are capable of metering transients, but different types of peak meters have different speeds and meter transients with varying degrees of accuracy.

Peak meters are necessary for recording digitally, since our primary goal, using a digital recorder, is to not record above a certain level with any signal. When recording digitally, always try to obtain the highest meter reading without going past 0. If digital recordings are made with levels too low, the full resolution of the digital recording process isn't realized. Low level digital recordings can sound grainy and harsh.

Adjusting Record Levels for Transients

When recording instruments that contain transients and metering with a standard VU meter, adjust levels so that the loudest part of the track registers between -9VU and -7VU. This approach results in much more accurate and clean percussive type tracks. The transient is usually at least 9VU hotter than the average level, so when the standard VU Meter reads -9VU the tape is probably seeing 0VU. If you meter 0VU on a transient, the tape might see +9VU!

Peak LEDs are fast enough in their response to accurately meter transients. A peak LED is normally just one red light that comes on when the signal is about to oversaturate the tape or overdrive a circuit.

continued...

Illustration 1-17

...continued

It's usually okay for the peak LED that lives in one corner of a VU meter to blink occasionally, but if it's on continuously, find the instrument, instruments or frequencies that are making it come on and back the levels off.

When a peak LED comes on, it means that, even though the VU is registering well within acceptable limits, the actual level that's reaching tape is getting pretty hot.

In a mix, if the average or VU level is conservative but the peak LEDs are always on, there's probably a percussion instrument in your mix that's too loud, and even if it doesn't sound too loud on your system, it'll probably sound too loud on other systems.

Metering with peak meters, although potentially more accurate, can lead to recording with very conservative levels which can result in recordings that contain more noise in relation to the signal.

Standard VU meters, with a little education and experience, are still the preferred method of metering for most analog recording situations.

---

sound difference as the phase is reversed on the second track. The tracks combined are obviously thin and reduced in level. Imagine if that happened to the guitar track in a mix as it was played on mono AM radio.

Audio Examples 1-9, 1-10 and 1-11
Phase Reversal
CD-1: Track 6

The nature of combining sounds dictates that there is always phase interaction. We wouldn't want to hinder that because good phase interaction gives our music depth and richness. However, we *do* want to be particularly aware of phase interactions that can have an adverse effect on the quality of our music.

If your mixer has a phase switch on each channel, it's probably at the top of the channel by the preamp and attenuator controls. Its purpose is to help compensate for phase interaction problems. For practical use, listen to your mixes in mono. If you notice that too many instruments get softer, disappear or just seem to sound funny in mono, then there's probably a phase problem between some of the tracks. Change the phase of some of the tracks that might be combining in a problematic way until the mix sounds full and smooth in mono.

Short delay times, chorus and phasing effects can also cause these kinds of problems in mono, so you might also need to change some delay times to help even things out. There will be more about this when we cover mixdown. Once you've located and solved the phase problems, your mix will sound just as good in stereo, and you'll be ready for television or AM radio.

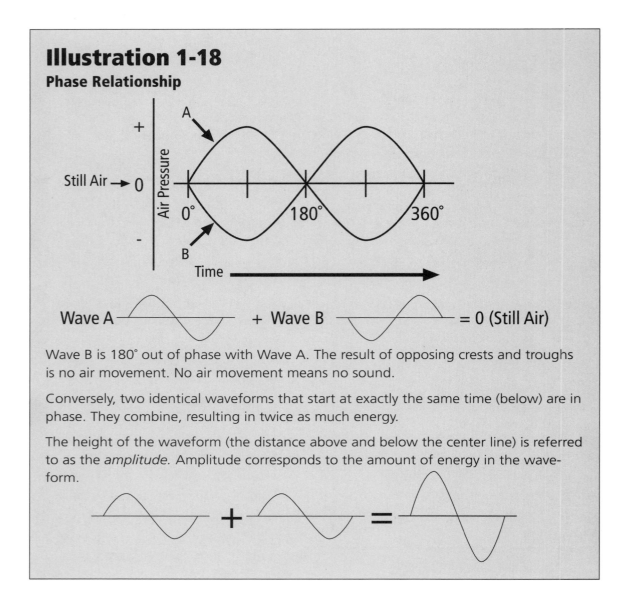

Illustration 1-18
Phase Relationship

Wave A + Wave B = 0 (Still Air)

Wave B is 180° out of phase with Wave A. The result of opposing crests and troughs is no air movement. No air movement means no sound.

Conversely, two identical waveforms that start at exactly the same time (below) are in phase. They combine, resulting in twice as much energy.

The height of the waveform (the distance above and below the center line) is referred to as the *amplitude.* Amplitude corresponds to the amount of energy in the waveform.

It's a good idea to be checking for phase problems when recording tracks to the multitrack. Some mixers that have phase reversal switches have them operable only on the mic inputs and not on the tape inputs. Therefore, they're unavailable during mixdown.

Input Level Comparison

These initial variables (preamp, attenuator, meters and phase) are very important points for us to deal with. Any good engineer has a solid grasp of these crucial parts of the signal path. These are the basics; you'll continually return to them for clean, quality, professional recordings.

As reinforcement of the importance of

proper adjustment of the input stage of your mixer, listen to Audio Examples 1-12, 1-13 and 1-14. If your signal isn't clean and accurate at the input stage, it won't be clean and accurate anywhere.

Audio Example 1-12 Proper Input Levels
CD-1: Track 7

Audio Example 1-13
Low Input Levels Resulting in a Noisy Mix
CD-1: Track 7

Audio Example 1-14
High Input Levels Causing Distortion
CD-1: Track 7

We must have proper levels coming into the mixer before we can even begin to set levels to tape. Any distortion here is magnified at each point. Any noise that exists here is magnified at each point. Listen to the effects of improper level adjustment at the input. Audio Examples 1-12, 1-13 and 1-14 use the same song, the same mixer and the same tracks with different input levels.

More Signal Path

Remember, *signal path* is simply the route that a signal takes from point A to point B. For speed and efficiency in any recording situation, it's essential that you're completely familiar with the signal paths involved in your setup.

Any good maintenance engineer knows that the only surefire way to find a problem in a system is to follow the signal path deliberately from its point of origin (point A, for example, the microphone) to its destination (point B, the speakers).

There are several possible problem spots between point A and point B. A thorough knowledge and understanding of your signal path lets you deal with any of these problems as quickly as possible. See Illustration 1-19 for an assignment on signal path.

Channel Insert

Most modern mixers have what is called a *channel insert* (Illustration 1-20). This is the point where a piece of outboard signal processing can be plugged into the signal path on each individual channel. If your mixer has inserts, they're probably directly above or below the microphone inputs.

A channel insert lets you access only one channel at a time and is used to include a signal processor in the signal path of that specific channel. The processor you insert becomes a permanent part of the signal path from that point on. An insert is especially useful when using a compressor, gate or other dynamic processor.

A channel insert utilizes a send to send the signal (usually as it comes out of the preamp) to the signal processor. The signal processor output is then patched into the return of the channel insert. This completes the signal path, and the signal typically continues on its way through the EQ circuit and on through the rest of its path. To understand the different types of inserts, refer to Illustrations 1-21A through 1-21D.

A channel insert and an effects bus are similar in that they deal with signal processing. An insert affects one channel only. Inserts are

Illustration 1-19
Assignment: Signal Path

Many owner's manuals give a schematic diagram of exactly what the signal path is in a mixer. You may not be totally into reading diagrams, but there's a lot to be learned by simply following the arrows and words. The basis of electronics is logic. Most complex electronic tasks can be broken down into small and simple tasks. That's exactly how the recording world is. What seems like an impossible task at first isn't so bad when you realize it consists of several simple tasks performed in the right order.

An example of a typical signal path might be: The microphone goes into the microphone input, which goes to the attenuator, which goes into the preamp, which goes into the equalizer, which goes to the track assignment, which goes to the tape recorder, which comes back to the mixer at the monitor section, which goes to the master volume fader, which goes to the main stereo output of the mixer, which goes to the power amp in, which goes to the speakers, which go to your ears, which go to your brain, which makes you laugh or cry.

Try making a simple map of your signal path, using boxes with the appropriate words and arrows pointing from box to box.

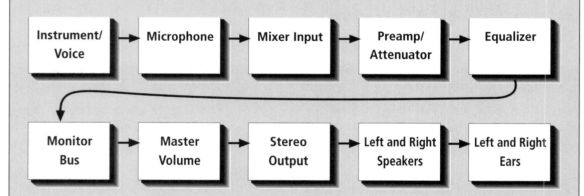

A thorough understanding of your signal path is the answer to most trying circumstances you'll come across. Build a diagram like this for the most common recording situations you encounter, including:

- Recording tracks
- Mixing down
- Sending from aux buses to effects
- Setting up the headphone bus

ideal for patching dynamics processors into a signal path. An effects bus (like aux 1 or aux 2) lets you send a mix from the bus to an effect, leaving the master mix on the input faders without effects. The output of the effect is then plugged into the effects returns or open channels on the mixer. This is good for reverbs and multi-effects processors.

Managing the Signal Path

This section covers input faders, gain structure, buses, track assignments, pan, solo and mute.

Input faders

Once everything is set properly at the preamp, use the input faders to set the recording level to tape (Illustration 22). During recording, these faders adjust the recording level to tape. On any recording mixer, there's a different control that determines listening volume. During mixdown these faders often control the volume of each track in the mix, but in tracking, their sole purpose is recording level adjustment to the multitrack.

When recording most instruments, adjust the recording level so that VU meters read 0VU to +2VU at the peaks (strongest parts of the track). For percussive instruments that have transient attacks, also called *transient peaks,* the VU meter should read around -9VU to -7VU at the

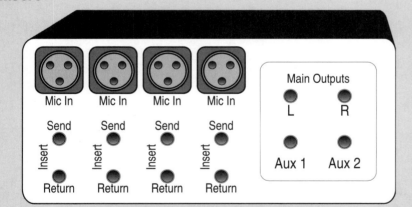

Illustration 1-20
Channel Insert

Many mixers have a channel insert. This is the point where an outboard signal processor can be plugged into the signal path. If your mixer has inputs, they're probably directly above or below the mic inputs.

A channel insert will have a send that sends the signal, usually as it comes out of the preamp, to the processor. The output of the signal processor is then patched into the return of the channel insert. This completes the signal path. The signal then continues on its way through the EQ circuit and on through the rest of its path.

Illustration 1-21

Three Common Types of Channel Inserts

1. A Simple Send and Return With Separate 1/4" jacks

Inside the mixer, the send is normally connected to the return when no plugs are in the jacks. With this sort of setup, the send and return are said to be *normalled,* because they are normally connected together. That connection can be interrupted by inserting a plug into one or both of the jacks.

1-21A Normalled Jacks

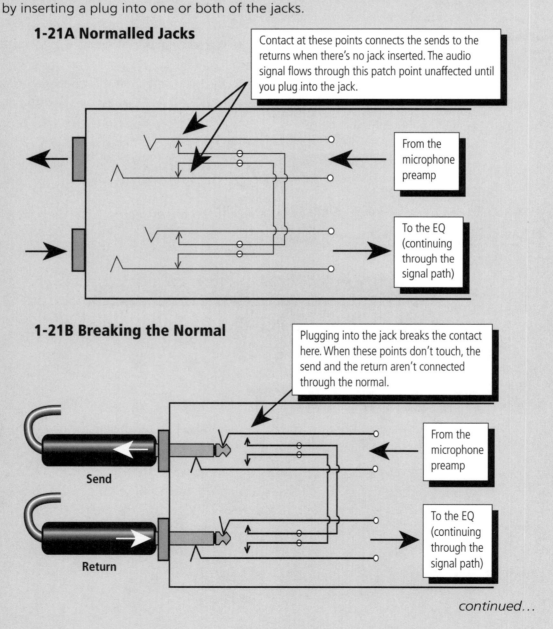

Contact at these points connects the sends to the returns when there's no jack inserted. The audio signal flows through this patch point unaffected until you plug into the jack.

From the microphone preamp

To the EQ (continuing through the signal path)

1-21B Breaking the Normal

Plugging into the jack breaks the contact here. When these points don't touch, the send and the return aren't connected through the normal.

Send

Return

From the microphone preamp

To the EQ (continuing through the signal path)

continued...

Illustration 1-21

...continued

2. Jumpered Sends and Returns

This method also uses separate send and return jacks (usually RCA phono), but instead of being normalled internally, the send is connected to the return using a simple jumper plug. The send and return are only connected when the jumper is plugged into both RCA jacks at once. If this jumper is removed, you won't hear the signal. When outboard processing is needed, simply remove the jumper, patch the send to the input of the processor and then patch the processor output to the return.

1-21C The Jumper

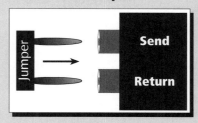

3. The Single Insert Jack

Another common type of insert uses a single insert jack. To utilize this type of insert, you must use a special Y cable, like the one in 1-21D (male tip-ring-sleeve stereo 1/4" phone plug to two female tip-sleeve mono 1/4" phone jacks).

Plug the male stereo phone plug into the insert. Next, use a line cable to connect one of the female mono connectors to the processor input, and patch the output of the processor into the other female mono connector. You might need to experiment to determine which of the mono connectors is the send and which is the return. Once everything is working, label the Y cable so it will be easy to use next time you need it.

1-21D Single Insert Jack

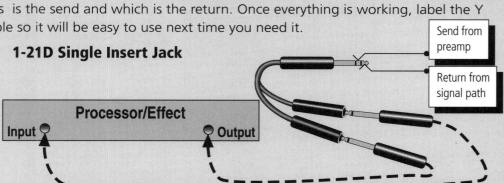

peaks. We'll cover more about this later.

The Effects Bus

When we discuss the input faders as a group, we're talking about a bus. The term bus is confusing to many, but the basic concept of a bus is simple—and very important to understand. A *bus* usually refers to a row of faders or knobs.

If you think about a city bus, you know that it has a point of origin (one bus depot) and a destination (another depot), and you know that it picks up passengers and delivers them to their destination. That's exactly what a bus on a mixer does. For example, in mixdown the *faders* bus has a point of origin (the tape tracks) and a destination (the mixdown recorder). Its passengers are the different tracks from the multitrack.

Most mixers also have auxiliary buses, or effects buses (Illustration 1-23). *Aux buses* (also called cue sends, effects sends or monitor sends) operate in the same way as the faders bus. An aux bus (another complete set of knobs or faders) might have its point of origin at the multitrack or the mic/line inputs. It picks up its own set of the available passengers (tracks) and takes them to their own destination (usually an effects unit or the headphones).

When a bus is used with an effect, like a reverb, delay or multi-effects processor, the individual controls on the bus are called *effects sends* because they're sending different instruments or tracks to the effects unit on this bus. The entire bus is also called a *send*.

Return is a term that goes with send . The send sends the instrument to the reverb or effect. The *return* accepts the output of the reverb or effect as it returns to the mix.

Pre and Post

Aux buses often include a switch that chooses whether each individual point in the bus hears the signal *before* it gets to the EQ and fader (indicated by the word *pre*) or *after* the EQ and fader (indicated by the word *post*).

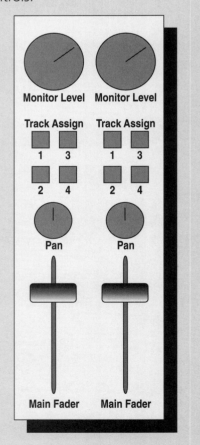

Illustration 1-22
Input Faders

Monitor Level controls receive signals from the multitrack output. When recording tracks to the multitrack, adjust the record levels with the Main Fader and adjust the listening volumes with the Monitor Level controls.

Pre lets you set up a mix that's totally separate from the input faders and EQ. This is good for headphone sends. Once the headphone mix is good for the musicians, it's best to leave it set. You don't want changes you make for your listening purposes to change the musicians' mix in the phones.

Post is good for effects sends. A bus used for reverb sends works best when the send to the reverb decreases as the instrument or voice fader is turned down. Post sends are perfect for this application since the send is after the fader. As the fader is decreased, so is the send to the reverb, maintaining a constant balance between the dry and affected sounds. If a pre send is used for reverb, the channel fader can be off, but the send to the reverb is still on. When your channel fader is down, the reverb return can still be heard, loud and clear.

Using the Aux Bus

Imagine there's guitar on track 4, and it's turned up in the mix. We hear the guitar clean and dry. *Dry* means the sound is heard without effect. The guitar in Audio Example 1-15 is dry.

Audio Example 1-15 Dry Guitar
CD-1: Track 8

If the output of aux bus 1 is patched into a reverb, and the aux 1 send is turned up at channel 4, we should see a reading at the input meter of the reverb when the tape is rolling and the track is playing. This indicates that we have a successful send to the reverb.

The reverb can't be heard until we patch the output of the reverb into either an available, unused channel of the mixer or into a dedicated

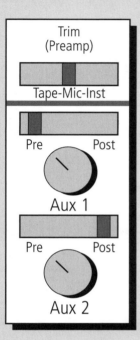

Illustration 1-23
Aux Buses With Pre and Post

On Aux 1, the Pre-Post switch is set to Pre. This lets the Aux 1 bus hear the signal *before* it gets to the EQ and fader.

On Aux 2, the Pre-Post switch is set to Post. This lets the Aux 2 bus hear the signal *after* it has gone through the EQ and fader circuitry.

effects return. If your mixer has specific effects returns, it's often helpful to think of these returns as simply one or more extra channels on your mixer.

Once the effects outputs are patched into the returns, raise the return levels on the mixer to hear the reverb coming into the mix. Find the adjustment on your reverb that says wet/dry. The signal coming from the reverb should be 100 percent wet. That means it's putting out only reverberated sound and none of the dry sound. Maintain separate control of the dry track. Get the reverberated sound only from the completely wet returns. With separate wet and dry control, you can blend the sounds during mixdown to produce just the right sonic blend. Listen to Audio Examples 1-16, 1-17 and 1-18 to hear the dry and wet sounds being blended in the mix.

Audio Example 1-16 Dry Guitar
CD-1: Track 8

Audio Example 1-17 Reverb Only
CD-1: Track 8

Audio Example 1-18 Blending Wet and Dry
CD-1: Track 8

The Headphone Bus

If your mixer has a headphone bus, or if you're using an auxiliary bus to send a signal to the headphones, patch the output of that bus into a headphone amplifier. You'll hear the mix you've sent to the headphone amp (from the headphone bus) when you plug headphones into the outputs of the headphone amp. The individual auxiliary buses on a mixer are hardly ever powered to run headphones or speakers.

If there's an output on your mixer or personal 4-track recorder labeled Headphones, it's probably powered, and you won't need a headphone amp. If you're patching this output into an amp, the powered send will overdrive the input. The resulting sound will be distorted and

unsatisfactory. If the headphone output is minimally powered, you might be able to patch it into a separate headphone amp, but you must be careful to keep the headphone output level low.

The headphone output often listens to the main faders. In some cases, there's a selector to let you listen to different buses.

Track Assignment

The track assignment section, also called the bus assign section, is used to send whatever is received at the input of the mixer (mic, instrument or tape) to any one or a combination of output buses. These bus outputs are normally connected to the inputs of the multitrack.

A board designed to be used with a 4-track recorder gives you the option of sending your signal to any one or more of the four main outputs of the mixer that are connected to the multitrack recorder inputs.

Track assignments can also combine two or more outputs to one input. See Illustration 1-24 for an example of how the track assignments help you route mic input 1 and instrument input 2 to tape recorder track 3.

Avoid patching the outputs of two or more instruments (or other devices) together through a Y cable into one input. This typically overdrives and distorts the input (Illustration 1-25). Anytime you sum (combine) multiple outputs to one input, use a circuit like the track assignment circuit on your mixer. This is designed specifically to maintain proper impedance and signal strength for its destination input. This type of circuit is also called a combining bus, combining matrix, summing bus, summing matrix, switching matrix, track assignment bus or track assignment matrix.

Three Practical Applications for the Combining Bus

1. When miking a drum set with multiple mics (kick, snare, toms, overheads): If the mics are being combined and then recorded on one track of the multitrack, you must use a combining bus to achieve satisfactory results

2. When direct ins from a bass and a keyboard are being printed to one track on the multitrack: If the instrument outputs are being combined then recorded onto one track of the multitrack, you must use a combining bus to achieve satisfactory results

3. When two or more tracks of the multitrack are being run back through the mixer and bouncing, or ping-ponging, to one of the other available tracks: If the tracks are being combined and then recorded onto one track of the multitrack, you must use a combining bus to achieve satisfactory results

Illustration 1-24
Assign Mic 1 and Instrument 2 to Track 3

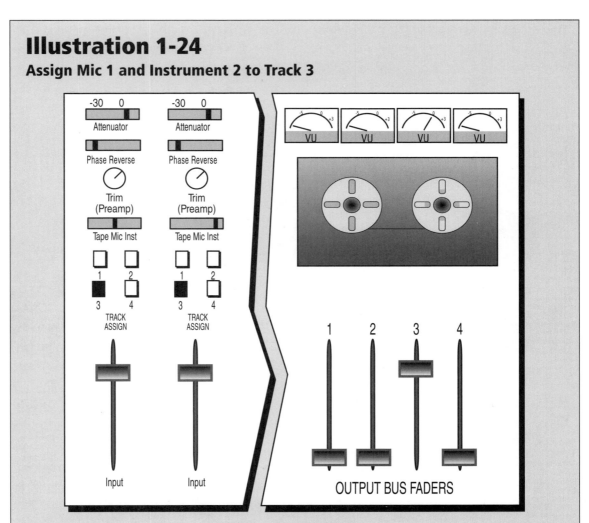

Press the 3 button on the track assigns to combine the mic and instrument for recording onto track 3. Notice the position of each switch on this mixer.

It *is* acceptable to split one output from an instrument or other equipment with a simple Y cable (Illustration 1-26). No electronic circuitry is necessary. Most outputs can be split up to about five times with no adverse effect on the signal.

Three Practical Applications for Splitting a Signal Using a Y

1. When sending a guitar to the direct input of a mixer and simultaneously to an amplifier: You can use a Y cable out of the guitar or the guitar effects setup
2. When sending a microphone signal to a live system and simultaneously to a recording sys-tem: A Y cable is also called a splitter; a split-ter box usually has a snake that plugs into the recording board and outputs (or another snake) that plug into the live mixing board
3. When plugging the final output of a mixer into two or more mixdown recorders: If you're using a patch bay, all connections can be made with short, high quality patch cords for optimum signal transfer

Audio Examples 1-19, 1-20 and 1-21 dem-onstrate the sound of splitting the guitar signal with a Y cord straight out of the guitarist's ef-fects. One side of the Y goes directly to the mixer through a direct box. The other side is sent to an amplifier. The amp is miked and the micro-

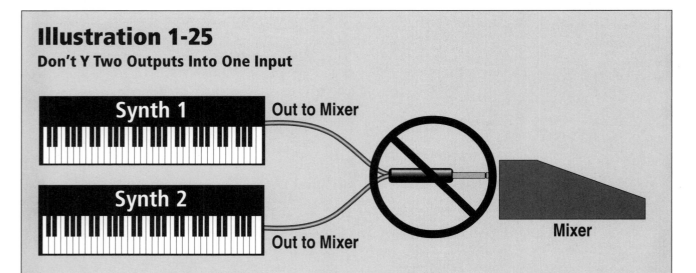

Illustration 1-25
Don't Y Two Outputs Into One Input

Synth 1 — Out to Mixer

Synth 2 — Out to Mixer

Mixer

It is *not* good to Y two or more instruments into one input, because they will overdrive the mixer input. The resulting sound will probably be distorted. You might get by with this if you have two weak sound sources and an input with plenty of headroom, but as a rule, this is unacceptable.

To successfully record two or more sources to one track or to one channel of a mixer, you must use a combining bus, such as the track assign bus on your mixer. If you're out of channels on your mixer, consider buying a small inexpensive mixer to augment your system. Plug multiple sound sources (like your MIDI sound modules) into your small mixer, then patch the output of that mixer into your main mixer.

phone is plugged into the mixer. This setup works well with a guitar, synth, drum machine or any other electronically generated sound source (Illustration 1-27).

Audio Example 1-19 demonstrates the direct guitar sound.

Audio Example 1-19 Direct Guitar
CD-1: Track 9

Illustration 1-26
Splitting One Output to Multiple Inputs

Synth

To Input

Mixer

To Input

Amplifier

Outputs can be split several times with little or no adverse effect on the signal. In this case, the synth is split with a Y cord and sent simultaneously to the mixer and amplifier.

Listen to the miked amplifier in Audio Example 1-20.

Audio Example 1-20 The Miked Amp
CD-1: Track 9

We can combine the direct and miked guitar to one tape track with the track assignment bus. Listen to Audio Example 1-21 as the guitar sounds combine in different levels to create a new and interesting texture.

Audio Example 1-21
Combining Direct and Miked Signals
CD-1: Track 9

Pan

The *pan control*, sometimes called the *pan pot* (for panoramic potentiometer), is used to move a track in the stereo panorama. Sounds are positioned at any point in the left to right spectrum (between the left and right speakers). Some pan controls are either all the way left or all the way right with no position in between, but panning is usually infinitely sweepable from full left to full right or anywhere in between. Often the pan control is used for selecting odd or even track assignment on the multitrack bus assignments. Odd is left and even is right.

You can use the pan control along with the track assignment bus to combine multiple instruments, like several keyboards, to a stereo pair of tape tracks. This can give you a very big sound while letting you get the most out of your equipment pool by conserving tracks and freeing up sound modules.

Listen to Audio Examples 1-22, 1-23 and 1-24. Three sounds are combined and panned

Illustration 1-27
The Y Inside the DI

Synth

Direct Box

Input

Mixer

Mic In	Mic In	Mic In	Mic In	Main Outputs
Send	Send	Send	Send	L R
Insert	Insert	Insert	Insert	Aux 1 Aux 2
Return	Return	Return	Return	

Most direct boxes have a Y built in. Input and Out to Amp are connected together to form an internal Y. The input also goes to the transformer on its way to the mixer. The Y lets you take the signal being fed into the Input of the DI and patch it out of the Out to Amp jack into any hi Z amplifier.

around to create a unique sound that can't be gotten out of any single synth. A mixer lets you create a sound that's different from any other. Combining textures like this is called *layering* or sometimes *doubling*.

Audio Example 1-22 is synth sound A.

Audio Example 1-22 Synth Sound A
CD-1: Track 10

Listen to Audio Example 1-23 to hear synth sounds B and C combine with synth sound A.

Audio Example 1-23 Synth Sounds B and C
CD-1: Track 10

In Audio Example 1-24, synth sounds A, B, and C combine at different levels to become one unique and interesting sound.

Audio Example 1-24 Synth Combination
CD-1: Track 10

Gain Structure

It's necessary to consider gain structure as we control different levels at different points in the signal path. *Gain structure* refers to the relative levels of the signal as it moves from the input to the EQ and out the fader to the track assignment bus and onto the multitrack.

We've already discussed the proper method for adjusting the input preamp level, and we've heard some examples of music recorded with the input stage too cold and too hot. These examples give an obvious demonstration of the importance of proper level adjustment at this primary stage. Each stage with user-controlled levels carries its own importance to the integrity of your signal. Ideally, you'll be able to adjust each stage to be as hot as possible, with minimal distortion.

Some mixers have a suggested setting for input faders and track assignment bus faders. These suggested settings (referred to as *unity points*) are usually indicated by a grayed area near the top of the fader's throw or numerically by a zero indication. Try placing the input and track assignment bus faders to their ideal settings. Then adjust the input preamp for proper recording level. This is a safe approach and works well much of the time.

Experiment with different approaches to find what works best with your setup. No approach works every time, so remember to trust your ears. If your sound is clean and punchy but the settings don't seem to be by the book, you're better off than if you have textbook settings on your mixer with substandard sound.

Confidence in your control of the gain structure can take time and experience, so start practicing. See what happens when you try a new approach. See Illustration 1-28 for an assignment on gain structure.

Ping-ponging

Let's take a closer look at track assignments as they're used for bouncing tracks (or ping-ponging). Bouncing tracks means one or more tracks on the multitrack are being rerecorded onto an open track of the same multitrack.

Since the input of a mixer can be switched to listen to mic, line or tape, you select the input of two or three channels to listen to the tape. Once you've done this, for example, on tracks 1, 2 and 3, you can assign these channels to track 4 at the track assignment bus.

Put track 4 into Record Ready and use the faders of 1, 2 and 3 to set up the proper mix. Next, bounce those three tracks onto one by simply pressing play and record. Now start laying new parts down on 1, 2 and 3 as you listen to track 4 (Illustration 1-29).

Beware of bouncing to adjacent tracks. You run the risk of internal feedback of the tape machine anytime you bounce from a track to either track directly next to it. A lot depends on the alignment of your tape machine heads and the adjustment of your playback and record electronics. Digital multitrack formats like the ADAT and 8mm systems have no problem bouncing to adjacent tracks.

Which Tracks Should I Bounce Together?

If you have the option of choosing which tracks to bounce together, the best rule of thumb is to bounce an instrument with primarily low frequencies (like a bass) with an instrument that has primarily high frequencies (such as a tambourine). This lets you adjust their relative levels by adjusting EQ. Turning down the highs turns down the tambourine; turning down the lows turns down the bass. Listen to Audio Example 1-25 to hear a demonstration of this theory.

Audio Example 1-25
Bouncing Multiple Instruments to One Tape Track
CD-1: Track 11

Illustration 1-28
Gain Structure

We've already discussed the proper method for adjusting the input preamp level, and we've heard some examples of music recorded with the input stage too low and too high. These examples give an obvious demonstration of the importance of proper level adjustment at this primary stage. It's equally important that you maintain a sufficient level to keep your signal strong and clean at each available point of level adjustment.

Some mixers have a suggested setting for input faders and track assignment bus faders. These suggested settings are usually denoted by a grayed area near the top of the fader's throw. Some faders indicate this suggested operating range by using a numeric scale that starts at the bottom of the fader throw with negative numbers increasing to 0 and then increasing to positive numbers up to the top of the fader throw. The 0 setting on these faders is the suggested operating setting. Zero is usually an about an inch from the top of the fader throw.

If you adjust the input level properly, if the input fader is somewhere close to the ideal setting, and if the track assign bus/record level fader is also close to the ideal, all should be well. If one or more of these settings is abnormally high or low, you might have a problem with your gain structure.

Experiment with different approaches to find what works best with your setup. Remember to trust your ears. If your sound is clean and punchy but the settings don't seem to be by the book, that's better than having a textbook setting on your mixer and a substandard sound.

The Primary Dangers

If the input level is abnormally high (even if the signal isn't noticeably distorted), the input fader and/or track bus fader might be abnormally low. Faders work more smoothly and are easier to control in the upper part of the fader throw. When the fader is abnormally low, it's much more difficult to fade an instrument down or to fine-tune the record levels or monitor levels.

If the preamp level is destructively high, the signal will overdrive the mixer and the integrity of the entire signal path will be jeopardized. The preamp adjustment is very important. An improper setting here will result in surefire failure.

If the preamp level is abnormally low, the input fader and/or the track bus fader might be abnormally high. When this happens, the inherent noise that resides in your mixer is turned up further than it needs to be. Therefore, we end up with more noise in relation to signal (an undesirable signal-to-noise ratio). This is bad.

continued…

Illustration 1-28
...continued

Assignment: Gain Structure

Practice changing the gain structure with your equipment. Plug an instrument into your mixer, assign it to a tape track, play a part and adjust the input fader to achieve a 0VU reading on your recorder.

Now, change the gain structure by raising or lowering the preamp level, the input fader level and the track assignment bus fader level. When you make one change, adjust the other controls up or down so that you maintain a reading of 0VU.

Keep a list of the differences in sound quality and the types of settings that produced these sounds, good or bad. This should help you in properly adjusting your own gain structure.

Solo

A Solo button turns everything off except the soloed track. This lets you hear one track or instrument by itself, as if it were a solo. Listen as I press the Solo button on different tracks in Audio Example 1-26. You can also combine solos to hear a group of tracks together.

Audio Example 1-26 Soloing
CD-1: Track 12

This feature is very useful in evaluating a track for cleanliness of signal and quality of sound. It's often impossible to tell what's really going on with a track when listening to it in the context of the rest of the arrangement.

Another type of solo is the *PFL* which stands for Pre-Fader-Listen. The PFL button solos a channel immediately before the fader. This can give an accurate picture of how a particular channel is sounding just as it's going into your mix or just before it gets to the multitrack.

There are often several solo points along the signal path. These different solo buttons are very handy for isolating a problem. Sometimes there's an input solo to let you verify the signal integrity as it enters the mixer. If the sound isn't accurate here, all hope is lost. There can be pre-EQ/insert and post-EQ/insert solo buttons. Check these to verify the signal before and after it has gone through the mixer EQ circuitry or an outboard processor. The other common solo points are before and after the final channel fader.

Mutes

A Mute button is an off button. A *channel mute* turns the channel off. Use the mutes instead of the faders to turn a channel down, especially when setting up a mix or setting levels for a tracking session. Beginning recordists often pull the faders down instead of using the mutes. Once you have a channel level set in relation to the other channels, you'll save time by simply muting and unmuting. The levels will remain the same and you'll avoid continual rebalancing.

Illustration 1-29
Bouncing Tracks

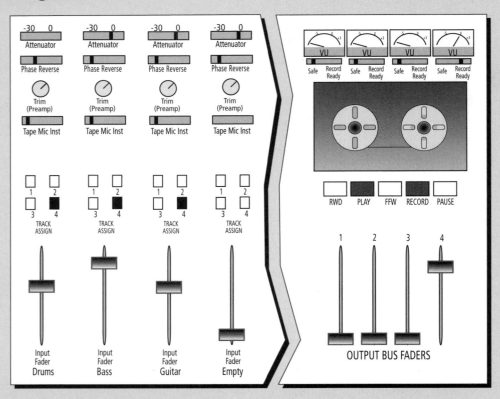

- Notice tracks 1, 2 and 3 are set to Tape on the Tape-Mic-Inst selector.
- Notice channels 1, 2 and 3 are assigned to track 4, and a mix of the three instruments is set up. This mix is what will be recorded onto track 4.
- Notice track 4 is set to Record Ready on the Safe-Record Ready selector and that Output Bus Fader #4 is up. This is the fader that sets the record level (to track 4) of the mix sent by input faders 1, 2 and 3.

The Equalizer

The equalizer or EQ section is usually located at about the center of each channel and is definitely one of the most important sections of the mixer. EQ is also called tone control; highs and lows; or highs, mids and lows. Onboard EQ typically has an in/out or bypass button. With the button set to in, your signal goes through the EQ. With the button set to out or bypass, the EQ circuitry is not in the signal path. If you're not using EQ, it is best to bypass the circuit rather than just set all of the controls to *flat* (no boost and no cut). Anytime you bypass a circuit, you eliminate one more possibility for coloration or distortion.

From a purist's standpoint, EQ is to be used sparingly, if at all. Before you use EQ, use the best mic choice and technique. Be sure the instrument you're miking sounds its best. Trying to mike a poorly tuned drum can be a nightmare. It's a fact that you can get wonderful sounds with just the right mic in just the right place on just the right instrument. That's the ideal.

From a practical standpoint, there are many situations where using EQ is the only way to a great sound on time and on budget. This is especially true if you don't own all of the right choice mics. During mixdown, proper use of EQ can be paramount to a really outstanding sound.

Proper control of each instrument's unique tone (also called its timbre) is one of the most musical uses of the mixer, so let's look more closely at equalization.

There are several different types of EQ on the hundreds of different mixers available. What we want to look at are some basic principles that are common to all kinds of boards.

We use EQ for two different purposes: to get rid of (cut) part of the tone that we don't want and to enhance (boost) some part of the tone that we do want.

Hertz

When we use the term *Hertz* or *frequency* we're talking about a musical waveform and the number of times it completes its cycle, with a crest and a trough, per second (Illustration 1-30).

As a reference, the human ear can hear a range of frequencies from about 20Hz at the low end to about 20,000Hz at the high end. 20,000Hz is also called 20 kilohertz or 20kHz.

The ability to hear the effect of isolating these frequencies provides a point of reference from which to work. Try to learn the sound of each frequency and the number of Hertz that goes with that sound.

To understand boosting or cutting a frequency, picture a curve with its center point at that frequency (Illustration 1-31).

Listen to the effect that cutting and boosting certain frequencies has on Audio Examples 1-27 to 1-35.

Audio Example 1-27 starts out flat (meaning no frequencies are cut or boosted). Notice a boost at 60Hz followed by a cut at 60Hz.

Audio Example 1-27 60Hz
CD-1: Track 13

Audio Example 1-28 demonstrates a boost then a cut at 120Hz.

Audio Example 1-28 120Hz
CD-1: Track 13

Audio Example 1-29 demonstrates a boost then a cut at 240Hz.

Audio Example 1-29 240Hz
CD-1: Track 13

Audio Example 1-30 demonstrates a boost then a cut at 500Hz.

Audio Example 1-30 500Hz
CD-1: Track 13

Illustration 1-30
Amplitude, Frequency, Length and Speed

Four important characteristics of sound waves are: amplitude, frequency, length and speed.

Amplitude expresses the amount of energy in a waveform (the amount of air being moved). In our graphic representation of the sine wave, the amplitude is indicated by the height of the crest and the depth of the trough. Wave B has twice the amplitude of Wave A and, therefore, moves twice the amount of air.

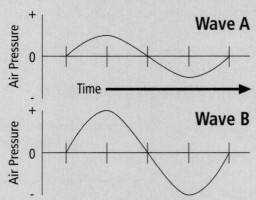

Frequency is the number of times the wave completes its 360° cycle in one second. This is expressed as hertz, abbreviated Hz. One thousand Hz is expressed in kilohertz and is abbreviated kHz. A frequency like 12,000Hz is abbreviated 12kHz or is simply expressed as 12k.

Each frequency has its own length (the number of feet sound travels while it completes one 360° cycle). Wavelength can be mathematically calculated as the speed of sound (approximately 1130 feet per second) divided by the frequency of the waveform in Hz (i.e., wavelength = 1130 ÷ Hz).

28Hz = 40.36 feet (lowest note on the piano)
100Hz = 11.3 feet
1kHz = 1.13 feet
4186Hz = .27 feet or 3.24 inches (highest note on the piano)
10kHz = .113 feet or 1.36 inches
20kHz = .0565 feet or .678 inches

Audio Example 1-31 demonstrates a boost then a cut at 1kHz.

Audio Example 1-31 1kHz
CD-1: Track 13

Audio Example 1-32 demonstrates a boost

then a cut at 2kHz.

Audio Example 1-32 2kHz
CD-1: Track 13

Audio Example 1-33 demonstrates a boost then a cut at 4kHz.

Audio Example 1-33 4kHz
CD-1: Track 13

Audio Example 1-34 demonstrates a boost then a cut at 8kHz.

Audio Example 1-34 8kHz
CD-1: Track 13

Audio Example 1-35 demonstrates a boost then a cut at 16kHz.

Audio Example 1-35 16kHz
CD-1: Track 13

Our goal in understanding and recognizing these frequencies is to be able to create sound pieces that fit together. The frequencies in Audio Examples 1-27 to 1-35 represent most of the center points for the sliders on a 10-band graphic EQ.

If the guitar track has many different fre-

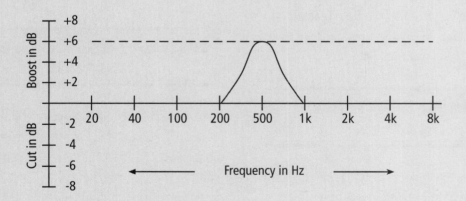

Illustration 1-31
Equalization Curve

Boosting or cutting a particular frequency also boosts or cuts the frequencies nearby. If you boost 500Hz on an equalizer, 500Hz is the center point of a curve being boosted. Keep in mind that a substantial range of frequencies might be boosted along with the center point of the curve. The exact range of frequencies boosted is dependent upon the shape of the curve.

quencies, it might sound great all by itself. If the bass track has many different frequencies, it might sound great all by itself. If the keyboard track has many different frequencies, it might sound great all by itself. However, when you put these instruments together in a song, they can get in each other's way and cause problems for the overall mix.

Ideally, we'll find the frequencies that are unnecessary on each track and cut those and then locate frequencies that we like on each track and enhance, or boost, those. If we keep the big picture in mind while selecting frequencies to cut or boost, we can use different frequencies on the different instruments and fit the pieces together.

For instance, if the bass sounds muddy and needs to be cleaned up by cutting at about 250Hz and if the high end of the bass could use a little attack at about 2500Hz, that's great. When we EQ the electric guitar track, it's very possible that we could end up boosting the 250Hz range to add punch. That works great because we've just filled the hole that we created in the bass EQ. Audio Example 1-36 demonstrates a bass recorded without EQ (flat).

Audio Example 1-36 Bass (Flat)
CD-1: Track 14

Listen to Audio Example 1-37 as I turn down a frequency with its center point at 250Hz. It sounds much better because I've turned down the frequency range that typically clouds the sound.

Audio Example 1-37 Bass (Cut 250Hz)
CD-1: Track 14

Audio Example 1-38 demonstrates a guitar recorded flat.

Audio Example 1-38 Guitar (Flat)
CD-1: Track 15

Audio Example 1-39 demonstrates the guitar with a boost at 250Hz. This frequency is typical for adding punch to the guitar sound.

Audio Example 1-39 Guitar (Boost 250Hz)
CD-1: Track 15

Audio Example 1-40 demonstrates the guitar and bass blending together. Notice how each part becomes more understandable as the EQ is inserted.

Audio Example 1-40 Guitar and Bass Together
CD-1: Track 16

In a mix, the lead or rhythm guitar doesn't generally need the lower frequencies below about 80Hz. You can cut those frequencies substantially (if not completely), minimizing interference of the guitar's low end with the bass guitar.

If the guitar needs a little grind (edge, presence, etc.) in the high end, select from the 2 to 4kHz range. Since you have already boosted 2.5kHz on the bass guitar, the best choice is to boost 3.5 to 4kHz on guitar. If these frequencies don't work well on the guitar, try shifting the bass high-end EQ slightly. Find different frequencies to boost on each instrument—frequencies that work well together and still sound good on the individual tracks. If you avoid equalizing each instrument at the same frequency, your song will sound smoother and it'll be easier to listen to on more systems.

Definition of Frequency Ranges

As I stated before, the range of frequencies that the human ear can hear is roughly from 20Hz to 20kHz. Individual response may vary, depending on age, climate and how many rock bands the ears' owner might have heard or played in. This broad frequency range is broken down into specific groups. It's necessary for us to know and recognize these ranges.

Listen to Audio Examples 1-41 to 1-51. I'll isolate these specific ranges.

Audio Example 1-41 Flat
CD-1: Track 17

Audio Example 1-42 Highs (Above 3.5kHz)
CD-1: Track 17

Audio Example 1-43 Mids (250Hz to 3.5kHz)
CD-1: Track 17

Audio Example 1-44 Lows (Below 250Hz)
CD-1: Track 17

These are often broken down into more specific categories. See Illustration 1-32 for a visual reference of these ranges.

Listen to each of these more specific ranges.

Audio Example 1-45 Flat (Reference)
CD-1: Track 18

Audio Example 1-46 Brilliance
CD-1: Track 18

Audio Example 1-47 Presence
CD-1: Track 18

Audio Example 1-48 Upper Midrange
CD-1: Track 18

Audio Example 1-49 Lower Midrange
CD-1: Track 18

Audio Example 1-50 Bass
CD-1: Track 18

Audio Example 1-51 Sub-bass
CD-1: Track 18

Some of these ranges may be more or less audible on your system, though they're recorded at the same level. Even on the best system, these won't sound equally loud because of the uneven frequency response of the human ear.

Bandwidth

Bandwidth has to do with pinpointing how much of the frequency spectrum is being adjusted. A parametric equalizer has a bandwidth control. Most equalizers that don't have a bandwidth control cut or boost a curve that's about one octave wide. A one-octave bandwidth is specific enough to enable us to get the job done but not so specific that we might create more problems than we eliminate. Bandwidth is sometimes referred to as the Q (Illustration 1-33).

A wide bandwidth (two or more octaves) is good for overall tone coloring. A narrow bandwidth (less than half an octave) is good for finding a problem frequency and cutting it.

Personal 4-track Multitrack

A simple, personal 4-track multitrack might only have adjustment for highs and lows. These are each centered on one frequency. Highs are usually between 8 and 10kHz, lows around 100Hz.

This type of EQ can be of some help. For instance, it can help on the guitar track to cut the lows in order to stay out of the way of the

Illustration 1-32
Frequency Ranges

The range of frequencies that the human ear can hear is roughly from 20Hz to 20kHz. This broad frequency range is broken down into specific groups. It's necessary to know and recognize these ranges.

- **highs** - above 3.5kHz
- **mids** - between 250Hz and 3.5kHz
- **lows** - below 250Hz

These are often broken into more specific categories:

- **brilliance** - above 6kHz
- **presence** - 3.5–6kHz
- **upper midrange** - 1.5–3.5kHz
- **lower midrange** - 250Hz–1.5kHz
- **bass** - 60–250Hz
- **sub-bass** - below 60Hz

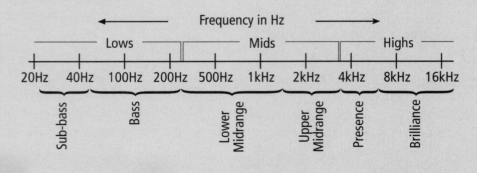

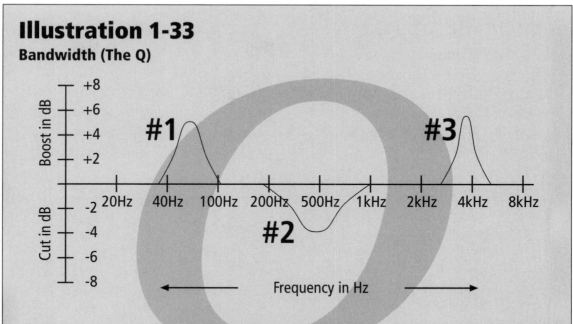

Illustration 1-33
Bandwidth (The Q)

Many equalizers let you control the width of the curve being manipulated. Notice the differing bandwidths in this illustration. Refer to bandwidth in octaves or fractions of an octave.

- Band #1 is about one octave wide.
- Band #2 is about two octaves wide.
- Band #3 is about half an octave wide.

bass guitar. Also, on the cymbals you can boost the highs for added brilliance.

If you only have two bands of EQ, consider buying a decent outboard graphic or parametric EQ. This isn't as flexible as having great EQ built in to your mixer, but with preplanning of your arrangement and instrumentation, it is possible to get lots of mileage out of one good EQ. In the 4-track world, preplanning is the answer to nearly all problems.

Some EQs cut or boost just one fixed frequency. A button near the cut/boost knob can select between two predetermined frequencies (Illustration 1-34).

Sweepable EQ

A lot of mixers have sweepable EQ (also called *semiparametric EQ*). Sweepable EQ dramatically increases the flexibility of sound shaping. There are two controls per sweepable band:

1. A cut/boost control to turn the selected frequency up or down
2. A frequency selector that lets you sweep a certain range of frequencies

This is a very convenient and flexible EQ. With the frequency selector, you can zero in on the exact frequency you need to cut or boost. Often, the kick drum has one sweet spot where the lows are warm and rich or the attack on the guitar is at a very specific frequency. With

Illustration 1-34
Selectable Frequencies

Two bands of EQ are available on each knob, enabling access to eight frequency bands. Pressing the Frequency Select button determines which frequency is boosted or cut. Each knob adjusts one frequency or the other, not both at the same time.

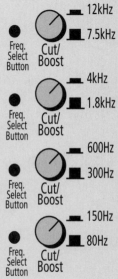

Parametric EQ

This is the most flexible type of EQ. It operates just like a sweepable EQ but gives you one other control: the bandwidth, or Q (Illustration 1-36).

With the bandwidth control, you choose whether you're cutting or boosting a large range of frequencies or a very specific range of frequencies. For example, you might boost a four-

Illustration 1-35
Sweepable EQ

A sweepable equalizer has a cut/boost control to determine the severity of EQ. The frequency selector lets you slide the band throughout a specific range.

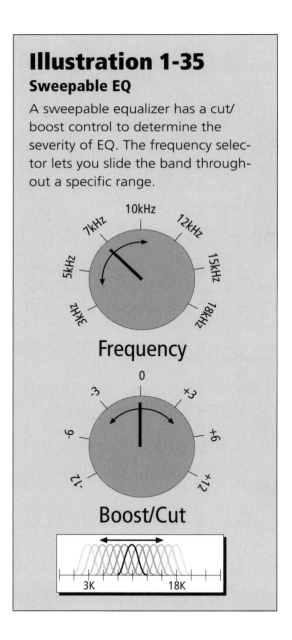

sweepable EQ, you can set up a boost or cut, then dial in the frequency that breathes life into your music.

Mixers that have sweepable EQ almost always have three separate bands on each channel: one for highs, one for mids and one for lows. Sometimes the highs and lows are fixed-frequency equalizers but the mids are sweepable (See Illustration 1-35).

octave band centered at 1000Hz, or you might cut a very narrow band of frequencies, a quarter of an octave wide, centered at 1000Hz.

With a tool like this, you can create sonic pieces that fit together like a glove (Illustration 1-37). A parametric equalizer is a great addition to your home studio. They are readily available in outboard configurations and some of the more expensive consoles even have built-in parametric equalization.

Graphic EQ

This is called a graphic equalizer because it's the most visually graphic of all EQs. It's obvious, at a glance, which frequencies you've boosted or cut.

A graphic equalizer isn't appropriate to include in the channels of a mixer, but it is a standard type of outboard EQ. The graphic EQs that we use in recording have 10, 31 or sometimes 15 individual sliders that each cut or boost a set frequency with a set bandwidth. The bandwidth on a 10-band graphic is one octave. The bandwidth on a 31-band graphic is one third of an octave (Illustration 1-38).

Other Types of EQ

Notch Filter

A notch filter is used to seek and destroy problem frequencies, like a high-end squeal, ground hum or possibly a noise from a heater, fan or camera.

Notch filters have a very narrow bandwidth and are often sweepable. These filters generally cut only.

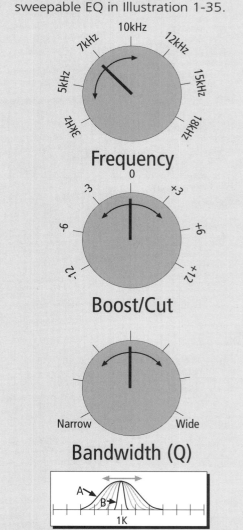

Illustration 1-36
Parametric EQ

The width of the selected frequency band is controlled by the Q adjustment (also called bandwidth). Curve A (below) is a very broad tone control. Curve B is a very specific pinpoint boost. The Q can vary infinitely from its widest bandwidth to its narrowest. Frequency and Boost/Cut operate like the sweepable EQ in Illustration 1-35.

Frequency

Boost/Cut

Bandwidth (Q)

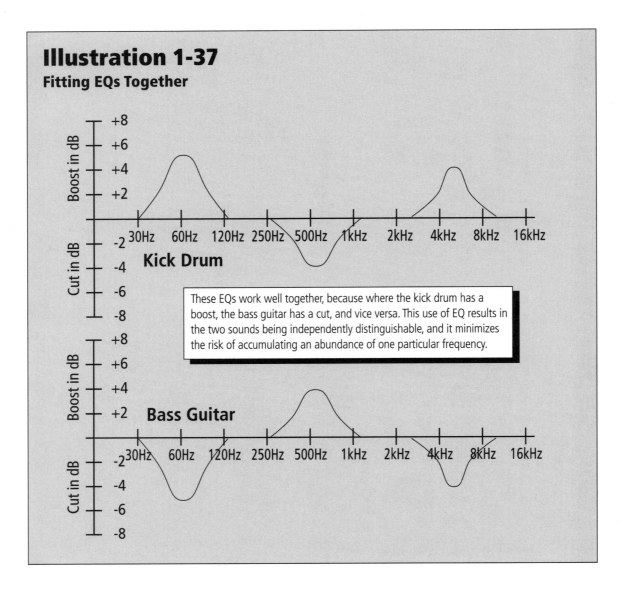

Illustration 1-37
Fitting EQs Together

Kick Drum

These EQs work well together, because where the kick drum has a boost, the bass guitar has a cut, and vice versa. This use of EQ results in the two sounds being independently distinguishable, and it minimizes the risk of accumulating an abundance of one particular frequency.

Bass Guitar

Highpass Filter

A highpass filter lets the high frequencies pass through unaffected but cuts the low frequencies, usually below about 80Hz. A highpass filter can help minimize 60-cycle hum on a particular track by filtering, or turning down, the fundamental frequency of the hum.

Highpass filters function very well when you need to eliminate an ambient rumble, like a furnace in the background or street noise that leaks into a vocal mic.

Lowpass Filter

A lowpass filter lets the low frequencies pass through unaffected and cuts the highs, usually above about 8 to 10kHz. These filters have many uses. For instance, a lowpass filter can help minimize cymbal leakage onto the tom tracks, filter out a high buzz in a guitar amp or filter out string noise on a bass guitar track.

Highpass and lowpass filters are a specific type of equalizer called a shelving equalizer. A *shelving EQ* leaves all frequencies flat to a cer-

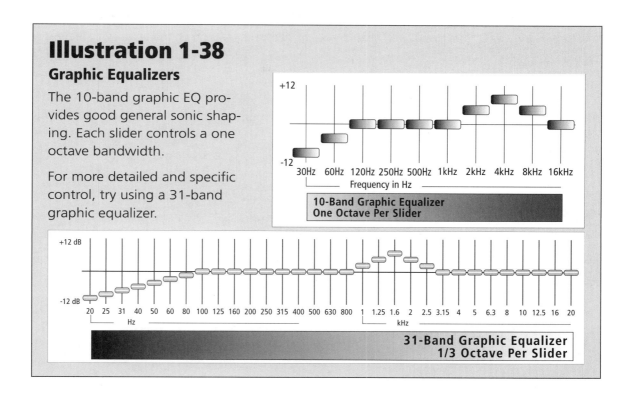

Illustration 1-38
Graphic Equalizers

The 10-band graphic EQ provides good general sonic shaping. Each slider controls a one octave bandwidth.

For more detailed and specific control, try using a 31-band graphic equalizer.

10-Band Graphic Equalizer
One Octave Per Slider

31-Band Graphic Equalizer
1/3 Octave Per Slider

tain point, then turns all frequencies above or below that point down or up at a rate specified in dB per octave. Most high- and lowpass filters roll off the highs or lows at a rate between 6 and 12dB per octave.

Shelving equalizers are useful when trying to get rid of unnecessary frequencies on the individual tracks. For example, on a bass guitar or kick drum track, the frequencies above 8k or so are typically useless. Applying the lowpass filter here could help get rid of any tape noise or leakage in the high frequencies on these tracks.

Use of these filters might be barely noticeable. That's good because it indicates that we're keeping the part of the signal we want and filtering out the frequencies that we don't need. Some mixers include sweepable shelving EQ (adjustable high- and lowpass filters). With

sweepable shelving EQ, you can carve away at the highs and lows of each track to totally eliminate unnecessary frequency conflicts. Be sure, though, that you're not robbing your music of life-giving upper harmonics.

Remember, even with the multitude of equalizers available, don't use EQ first to shape your sounds. First, get as close to the sound you want using mic choice and mic technique, then use EQ if it's necessary.

The Monitor Section

Some mixers have what is called the monitor section, which lets you listen to either the main outputs of the mixer or the tape tracks as they're coming back to the mixer from the multitrack. The switch that selects where each control hears from usually has two positions, bus and tape, or sometimes, input and tape.

This monitor section is used only for monitoring volumes and is totally separate from the recording level controls to the multitrack. Therefore, you can set exact levels to tape with the input faders, then turn their listening volume up or down in the monitor section.

Control Room Monitor Selector

The monitor selector is a very useful control center. It lets you listen to different buses or tape recorders in your setup simply by pressing the appropriate button on the board. This feature is usually located to the right of the channel faders.

If your mixdown recorder is normally connected to your mixer at a tape in point, if you have a CD player in your setup and if you have one or more aux buses available, the monitor selector is a particularly valuable tool.

The monitor selector on most mixers lets you listen to different buses without affecting what's going on in the other buses, including the signal path to tape. While recording a band's basic tracks, you can eavesdrop on the head-

Illustration 1-39
Monitor Selector

The monitor selector lets you listen to the different buses or tape recorders in your setup simply by pressing the appropriate button on the board. This feature is usually located to the right of the channel faders. Your mixer might have some or all of these options available.

Mix will let you hear the main mix from the main faders. This can also be labeled *MON, Program, Stereo out, MAIN,* or *2 Mix.* Your mixer might even have a different variation or abbreviation of these.

Tape 1 lets you hear whatever tape recorder has its outputs connected to the tape 1 input of the mixer.

Tape 2 lets you hear whatever tape recorder has its outputs connected to the tape 2 input of the mixer.

Aux 1 lets you hear whatever mix is going out of the Aux 1 output.

Aux 2 lets you hear whatever mix is going out of the Aux 2 output.

Spare lets you listen to another tape machine, CD or DAT that has its outputs patched into your mixer's spare input. The spare option is not on all monitor selectors.

Phono In lets you listen to a record player that's patched into the Phono Input of the mixer. Phono In has a separate and unique preamp and EQ curve developed for the record player itself. It does not work well to patch another player, like a CD, DAT or cassette into a Phono In.

phone bus, just to get an idea of what the mix sounds like, or you can listen to an effects bus to verify which instruments are being sent to a reverb or delay. See Illustration 1-39 for more of the specific options you might encounter in the monitor selector section.

Stereo to Mono

The Stereo/Mono switch does just what it says. It lets you listen to your song in whatever stereo image you've created with the pan controls, or it can take your stereo mix and combine it all into one mono mix (meaning that exactly the same thing comes from both the left and right speakers).

This is very useful, especially if you suspect that your song will be played on a mono system at any time. Mono is standard for AM radio, television and live sound reinforcement. If you'll be playing your band's demo tape as break music at a performance, be absolutely sure that the demo sounds great even in mono. Audio Example 1-52 demonstrates a simple stereo mix.

Illustration 1-40
Specific Considerations of Stereo to Mono

If your mix doesn't sound good in mono, it's often the result of a chorus, flanger or delay that might be part of the mix. These are common effects on background vocals, guitars and keyboards. Sound modules with stereo outputs frequently use chorusing.

Adjust some of the delay length parameters of the effect until the track sounds good in mono. This will solve the problem, and your track will still sound good in stereo.

Sometimes having instruments panned hard right and or hard left can sound wide and impressive in stereo, but in mono these instruments become hidden or lost. Try panning instruments a little closer to center to achieve better translation from stereo to mono.

Also, phase problems can accentuate a difficulty in going from stereo to mono. Try reversing the phase of suspicious tracks to help smooth things out in mono.

Suspicious tracks include:

- Any instrument that was miked with more than one microphone (like a drum set)
- Any instrument with a chorus or phase shifter
- Any stereo output from a keyboard or sound module
- Any track that has been doubled *live* (such as background vocals)
- Any track that has been doubled *electronically,* especially with short delay times
- Any track recorded using microphones and cables that might have been wired incorrectly

---

Audio Example 1-52 Simple Stereo Mix
CD-1: Track 19

Audio Example 1-53 uses the same mix, this time in mono.

Audio Example 1-53 Stereo Mix in Mono
CD-1: Track 19

Notice the change in sound between Audio Examples 1-52 and 1-53. With some changes in panning and delay times, this mix can work well in stereo *and* mono. We'll cover this transition from stereo to mono in detail later. See Illustration 1-40 for some specific considerations of stereo-to-mono comparisons.

Stereo Master

The stereo master control is the final level adjustment out of the mixer going to the mixdown recorder or power amp. The level adjustment to the mixdown recorder is very important. A good mix for a commercial-sounding song, in most styles, should be fairly constant in its level. The ideal setting for the overall mix is at about 0VU, with an occasional +1 or +2 reading at the peaks.

Mixes work best if there aren't long sections with very low levels (around -7 to -10). These sections tend to get buried or covered up when they're heard in a noisy environment, like a car. With levels that low, tape noise becomes more and more apparent. That's bad!

Talkback/Communications

The talkback button lets you talk to someone listening to the headphone bus. Communication with musicians through the headphones is essential to efficient recording. A small microphone is often mounted on the mixer for this purpose. Some mixers have a separate mic input for a handheld or stand-mounted talkback mic.

Talkback can also be sent onto tape to add a verbal reference, like the song title, date or artist. This verbal reference is called a *slate*. If a button has the word slate on it there's typically a low frequency (around 40Hz) that's sent to tape with your voice. In fast rewind or fast forward, this low frequency tone is heard as a beep, because the playback head picks up the magnetization as the tape speeds past the slate points. The slate beep is used to locate different songs on a reel.

Test Tones

Your mixer might have a section marked *tones, test tones, osc* or *oscillator*. This section contains a frequency generator that produces different specific frequencies in their purest form—a sine wave (Illustration 1-12). These frequencies are used to adjust input and output levels of your mixer, recorders and outboard equipment.

Consider the stereo master output from your mixer to the mixdown recorder. Raise the level of the reference tone (between 500 and 1000Hz) until the VU meter reads 0VU on the stereo output of the mixer. Do this with the stereo master output faders set at the point where your mix level is correct. Adjust the tones level to the meters with the tones output control.

Fine-tune the left/right output balance. If one side reads slightly higher than the other, from the same 1kHz tone send, balance the two sides. Most mixers have separate level controls for left and right stereo outs. Proper adjustment of the left/right balance ensures the best accuracy in panning and stereo imaging. We'll cover this procedure in depth during our study of mixdown.

Reference Tones

One thousand Hz is the most common reference tone. A *reference tone* is an accurate representation of the average recording level. Therefore, if your mix level is correct and peaks at 0VU or +1 or so, then this 1k tone at 0VU is an accu-

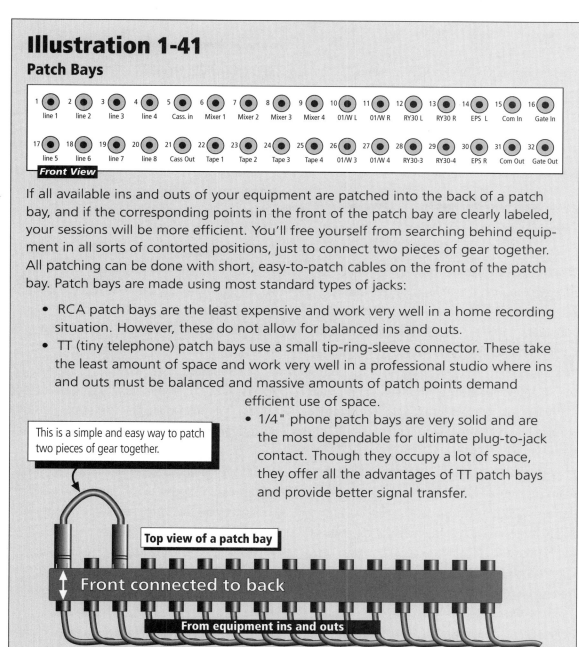

Illustration 1-41
Patch Bays

| 1 line 1 | 2 line 2 | 3 line 3 | 4 line 4 | 5 Cass. in | 6 Mixer 1 | 7 Mixer 2 | 8 Mixer 3 | 9 Mixer 4 | 10 01/W L | 11 01/W R | 12 RY30 L | 13 RY30 R | 14 EPS L | 15 Com In | 16 Gate In |

| 17 line 5 | 18 line 6 | 19 line 7 | 20 line 8 | 21 Cass Out | 22 Tape 1 | 23 Tape 2 | 24 Tape 3 | 25 Tape 4 | 26 01/W 3 | 27 01/W 4 | 28 RY30-3 | 29 RY30-4 | 30 EPS R | 31 Com Out | 32 Gate Out |

Front View

If all available ins and outs of your equipment are patched into the back of a patch bay, and if the corresponding points in the front of the patch bay are clearly labeled, your sessions will be more efficient. You'll free yourself from searching behind equipment in all sorts of contorted positions, just to connect two pieces of gear together. All patching can be done with short, easy-to-patch cables on the front of the patch bay. Patch bays are made using most standard types of jacks:

- RCA patch bays are the least expensive and work very well in a home recording situation. However, these do not allow for balanced ins and outs.
- TT (tiny telephone) patch bays use a small tip-ring-sleeve connector. These take the least amount of space and work very well in a professional studio where ins and outs must be balanced and massive amounts of patch points demand efficient use of space.
- 1/4" phone patch bays are very solid and are the most dependable for ultimate plug-to-jack contact. Though they occupy a lot of space, they offer all the advantages of TT patch bays and provide better signal transfer.

This is a simple and easy way to patch two pieces of gear together.

Top view of a patch bay

Front connected to back

From equipment ins and outs

rate gauge for setting levels for duplication of this particular song.

Patch the output of the mixer to the mixdown recorder and adjust the input level of the mixdown recorder to read 0VU while the mixer is showing 0VU from the 1kHz tone. We can now be sure that the level on the board matches the level on the mixdown machine.

Once these levels match, go ahead and record some of the 0VU so that when you make copies you can use this as a reference tone to set the input levels of the duplicating machine. Tones are used for electronic calibration and level setting, whereas pink and white noise are used for acoustical adjustments.

Patch Bays

One tool that's essential to any setup is a patch bay—nothing more than a panel with jacks in the front and jacks on the back (Illustration 1-41). Jack #1 on the front is connected to Jack #1 on the back, #2 on the front to #2 on the back and so on.

If all available ins and outs for all of your equipment are patched into the back of a patch bay and the corresponding points in the front of the patch bay are clearly labeled, you'll never need to search laboriously behind equipment again just to connect two pieces of gear together. All patching can be done with short, easy-to-patch cables on the front of the patch bay (Illustration 1-42).

Patch bays are used for line level patches like channel ins and outs, tape recorder line ins and outs, sound module outputs and any signal processor ins and outs. **Don't use the patch bay for powered outputs, like the speaker outputs of your power amplifiers.**

The concept of easy and efficient patching becomes obvious when it's explained, and once you've made the move to include a patch bay in your setup, you'll never go back, because you'll be able to accomplish more, faster and more efficiently.

Session Procedures

Use this procedure as a starting point for your sessions. Start each session with your studio clean and all equipment adjusted to a predetermined typical level. Starting clean prevents problems resulting from unknown buttons being pushed in unknown places on the mixer.

Basic Procedure
- Move all channel faders to 0.
- Set input gain (preamp) and attenuator to lowest level.
- If you have only a mic/line switch, set it to line.
- Pan all channels to center.
- Set all EQ to flat (no boost or cut). If there is an EQ in/out switch, set it to out.
- Turn any auxiliary sends, effects sends or reverb sends all the way down or off.
- Set VU meters to allow monitoring of the final stereo output to the mixdown machine. If available, set other VU meters to monitor levels of aux buses to effects.
- Make sure there are no track assignments selected.
- Be sure there are no solo buttons selected.
- Be sure there are no mutes selected.
- If your mixer has a tone generator or frequency oscillator, turn it on, select a frequency

Illustration 1-42
Patch Bay With Easy Patches

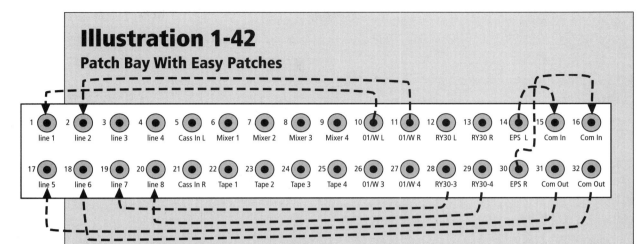

Patch bays are used for line level patches like channel ins and outs, tape recorder line ins and outs, sound module outputs and any signal processor ins and outs. **Don't use the patch bay for powered outputs, like the speaker outputs from your power amplifiers.** Patch bays are for line level signals. Only in very special cases will patch bays carry mic level signals, but they almost never contain powered signals.

If all the line ins to each channel on your mixer are connected to the back of a patch bay and all the outputs of all of your synthesizers and sound modules are connected to the back of the same patch bay, the task of patching any keyboard into any channel becomes very simple, fast and efficient.

If all channel inserts, sends and returns are patched to a patch bay, it becomes simple and fast to patch an EQ, compressor, gate or any other piece of signal processing into any channel.

When I mentioned channel inserts, I used the term normalled to indicate that the insert jacks (send and return) were normally connected until you plugged into them. Plugging in breaks the circuit, or the normal. In order to hear your signal, you must re-complete the circuit by sending to and returning from a processor. In order to use a patch bay with your mixer's channel inserts, use a patch bay in which one row of jacks is normalled to another row, so that the circuit is completed within the patch bay until you patch in a signal processor (Illustration 1-21A and 1-21B).

Not all budgets can justify buying enough patch bays to get *all* equipment inputs and outputs to the patch bay. Start small if you must and build from there. Patch bays are commonly available in 32-point and 64-point configurations for home use. A 32-point bay has 32 jacks in front and 32 corresponding jacks in back. Most are rack mountable, which makes for clean and simple installation in an effects rack.

Commercially made, high-quality patch cables are a bit expensive, but in the long run they're well worth the cost. They're much more durable and dependable than inexpensive or homemade cables.

between 500Hz and 1000Hz, and raise the level on the mixdown master VUs on the mixer until they read 0VU.

- Patch the mixdown master output from your mixer to the line inputs of your mixdown recorder.
- Set mixdown machine to record ready and, if available, select monitoring of the input or source.
- Now adjust record levels to read 0VU from the tone being generated at the mixer. This should ensure that the levels on the mixer will match the levels on your mixdown recorder. It's convenient and standard procedure in the recording industry to actually record this tone onto your mixed master tape at the beginning of the reel. This is called a reference tone.

If your master will be duplicated by a professional duplication facility, these tones let them adjust the level of their equipment to match yours. Following this procedure should result in a better, cleaner and more accurate copy. The standard frequencies to record at the beginning of a master tape are 100Hz, 1kHz and 10kHz. These frequencies represent lows, mids and highs. Giving the duplicator these references helps them compensate for any inherent problems in your system or mixing environment.

Conclusion

We've covered a lot of material in this chapter. We have seen and heard how important it is for you, the operator, to be aware of the proper techniques for adjusting levels at the different stop-off points along the signal path.

You should be starting to think in terms of shaping sounds with EQ, so that the different parts work well together. You've probably learned some new terminology. Begin to use these words in your vocabulary.

Being well versed in the recording world is the only way you'll be able to communicate with other enlightened musicians and engineers, and that constant communication can inspire your individual growth and possibly open doors into the business world of music and recording.

The mixer can be your most flexible means of achieving the musical sounds that you want. Go to your own setup and find what kind of controls you have. Review this material thoroughly and apply each point, deliberately, to your own setup.

A thorough understanding of the information in this chapter is necessary as a foundation for upcoming chapters. We'll build on this foundation in a methodical, easy-to-follow way. Each chapter is structured, using combined media, to closely resemble a private lesson.

If you do the assignments and study the CDs, text and illustrations, you'll see a marked difference in your recording skills and end results.

The first two chapters of *The AudioPro Home Recording Course* provide a very solid informational base. Combine your musical skill with these practical recording techniques to open the door for many new areas of fun and profit in the music industry.

Chapter 2 Signal Processing

Intro to Signal Processors

Since there are so many types and manufacturers of signal processing equipment, it would be overwhelming at this point to cover every piece of gear available. Right now it's most important to know the basics of signal processing.

You need to recognize the sounds of these basic tools, *and* you need to know how to adjust their settings to fit each unique musical situation. It's surprisingly simple to learn the controls on most processors. Once you know how to use these controls, you possess knowledge that lets you operate similar units with minimal stress and maximum efficiency.

Slang/Terminology

As we continue to build knowledge and skill, we'll see that each processor has many different and creative uses. For now we'll cover the basic units and their basic uses.

According to my *Funk & Wagnall's Standard Dictionary*, *process*, when used as a verb, means to treat or prepare by a special method. A signal processor is doing just that to our music: treating and preparing it in order to form an appealing and intelligible blend of textures.

My thesaurus shows that synonyms for process are *filter* and *sift*. These, too, give an accurate image of what signal processors do. If we can filter our music like we can filter light, we can start with one color and end up with another. In the music and recording industry, musical textures are often referred to as colors.

Describing music and sounds verbally is a necessary skill. In the middle of a session, you will come up with some great ideas, and the more experienced you become, the more easily the ideas will flow. Your ideas are worthless if you can't verbalize them to the other musicians you're with. See Illustration 2-1 for some terminology that is unique to describing musical sounds, feelings and idiosyncrasies. You don't need to use the most current jargon for a session to go well, but you must be sincere, proficient and easy to get along with. Music is fundamentally a form of emotional expression and communication. Be involved enough in your pursuits to walk the walk and talk the talk in a way that is sincere and easily understood. Notice that we consistently describe what we hear with terms normally used for things that we see, feel or taste. Describing the emotional impact of music involves describing far more than just what we hear. Good music communicates to all feelings and senses.

Signal Processor Basics

A signal processor changes your musical signal for two basic reasons: to enhance an existing

Illustration 2-1
Slang

There is some slang terminology that you should become familiar with when speaking about some of the colors and textures. This is really the language of musicians and producers. No matter how schooled you become and how familiar you are with the specific settings on a compressor, for example, you must be able to verbally communicate what you do.

As an example, you might recognize a signal that's been compressed with a 20:1 ratio, resulting in up to 20dB of gain reduction with an extremely fast attack time of about 100 microseconds and a release time of 1.5 seconds or so, but until you can translate that to the word *squashed,* you are out of the musical communication loop.

big - Containing a broad range of frequencies with ample clarity and sparkle in the highs and plenty of punch and thump in the lows. Usually contains large-sounding reverbs or large amounts of interesting reverb effects. Very impressive. Synonyms: *huge, gigantic, large, monstrous, very big.*

cold - Cooler than cool. See *cool.*

cool - The definition of *cool* changes with musical style. Very impressive, in a stylistically sophisticated way.

dry - Without reverb or effect.

edge - Upper frequencies of a sound that have a penetrating and potentially abrasive effect (typically 3–8kHz). Used in moderation, these are the frequencies that add clarity and understandability.

honk - See *squawk.*

lush - Very smooth, pleasing texture. Often used in reference to strings that use wide voicings and interesting (although not extremely dissonant) harmonies. Typically includes a fair amount of reverb or concert hall.

moo - Smooth, rich and creamy lows.

open - Uncompressed, natural and clean with a wide dynamic range—a sound that can be heard through, or seen through to use a visual analogy. In a musical arrangement, a situation where there is a lot of space (places in the arrangement where silence is a key factor). Each part is important and audible, and the acoustical sound of the hall can be appreciated.

continued…

Illustration 2-1

...continued

raunchy - Often slightly distorted (especially in reference to a guitar). A sound that doesn't include the very high frequencies or the very low frequencies. Earthy and bluesy. When referring to musical style, indicates a loose and simple but soul wrenching performance.

shimmer - Like *sparkle* in frequency content. Often includes a high frequency reverberation or some other type of lengthened decay.

sizzle - See *sparkle*. Can also include the airy-sounding highs.

sparkle - The upper frequencies of a sound. Includes the high bell-like sounds and upper cymbal frequencies from approximately 8–20kHz. These are very high frequencies that add clarity and excitement.

squawk - Midrange accentuation (approximately 1kHz). Sounds a lot like a very small, cheap transistor radio.

squashed - Heavily compressed. Put into a very narrow dynamic range.

sweet - Similar to *lush* in that it is smooth and pleasing and includes a fair amount of reverb. Generally in a slightly higher register (above middle C). Pleasantly consonant.

syrupy - Sweet, consonant sounds with ample reverberation. Often very musically and stylistically predictable.

thump - Low frequencies. Especially, the lows that can be felt as well as heard (about 80–150Hz).

transparent - Nonintrusive. A sound that has a broad range of frequencies but doesn't cover all the other sound around it. A sound that silence can be heard through.

verb - Reverberation.

wash - Lots of reverb that runs from one note to the next. This is common on string pads, where the reverb becomes an interesting part of the pad texture. A producer will often ask the engineer to bathe the strings in reverb, so the engineer gives the producer a wash of reverb.

wet - Reverb. Doesn't include the direct, original sound. To say something is very *wet* indicates that it's heard with a lot of reverb and not too much of the original, nonreverberated sound. Sometimes used in reference to other effects as well.

sound and to compensate for an inherent problem with a sound.

This section of *The AudioPro Home Recording Course* covers the three main categories of signal processors:

- Dynamic range processors
- Equalizers
- Effects processors (which include delays, reverberation and multi-effects processors)

Listen to Audio Examples 2-1 to 2-9. They are broken into four categories: reverberation effects, delay effects, dynamic processing and equalization. These examples demonstrate the processors used most in professional studios. The same music is run through all of the processors to help you evaluate the subtleties of each sound.

Audio Examples 2-1 to 2-3 demonstrate some reverberation effects.

Audio Example 2-1 Hall Reverb
CD-1: Track 20

Audio Example 2-2 Plate Reverb
CD-1: Track 20

Audio Example 2-3 Gated Reverb
CD-1: Track 20

Audio Examples 2-4 to 2-9 demonstrate delay effects.

Audio Example 2-4 Slapback
CD-1: Track 21

Audio Example 2-5 Echo
CD-1: Track 22

Audio Example 2-6 Doubling
CD-1: Track 23

Audio Example 2-7 Chorus
CD-1: Track 24

Audio Example 2-8 Flanging
CD-1: Track 25

Audio Example 2-9 Phase Shifting
CD-1: Track 26

The dynamic range processors are a little more subtle in the effect they have on a musical sound, and in most situations, the listener shouldn't be aware that anything out of the ordinary is going on.

The vocal track on Audio Examples 2-10 and 2-11 was simultaneously recorded onto two different tracks—one with a compressor and one without. Notice the difference between the soft and the loud parts of each track.

Audio Example 2-10 Vocal Without Compression
CD-1: Track 27

Audio Example 2-11 Vocal With Compression
CD-1: Track 27

Illustration 2-2

Assignment: Perception Chart

Review Audio Examples 2-1 to 2-12 (the dynamic range processors, effects and EQ). Below, write down your perception of their sounds. Use words like warm, airy, soft, harsh, red, blue, full, rich or wild.

Really think about this, and use as many descriptive terms and phrases as you can come up with.

The purpose of this assignment is to increase your understanding of these sounds while improving your ability to verbally communicate about them.

hall reverb:

plate reverb:

gated reverb:

slapback:

echo (regenerated slapback):

double:

chorus:

flange:

phase shifter:

lows:

mids:

highs:

We've covered several aspects of equalization. Be sure that you're familiar with the sound of the different frequency ranges (highs, mids, lows, brilliance, presence, upper mids, lower mids, bass and sub-bass).

Remember that parametric equalizers have a bandwidth control and are able to sweep a range of frequencies. Audio Example 2-12 demonstrates the sound of sweeping frequencies using a parametric equalizer.

Audio Example 2-12 Parametric EQ
CD-1: Track 28

If you aren't already totally familiar with what each of the effects sound like, review the Audio Examples until you have each sound memorized. As we move into using effects and specific techniques, it becomes more and more important to train our ears *and* our minds to recognize the sounds and the emotion surrounding each.

Complete the assignment in Illustration 2-2. Fill in the chart with your own description of the characteristics for each of the types of effects listed.

Recall (from Chapter 1) that processors are typically connected to your system in one of only a few ways:
- Channel inserts
- Aux sends
- Direct patch from instrument

The channel insert on the mixer is an individual patch point on a channel. A piece of gear connected here becomes part of the signal from that point on. This patch point works very well for dynamic processors (Illustration 2-3).

Another common tool for sending to ef-

Illustration 2-3
Using the Insert

The compressed signal inserts back into the signal path. Past the insert we only have the signal in its processed (compressed) form.

If your mixer provides optional insert points in the signal path (like preamp out, pre fader, post fader, etc.), choose the insert point closest to the source. The best insert point when compressing a miked signal is directly out of the preamp.

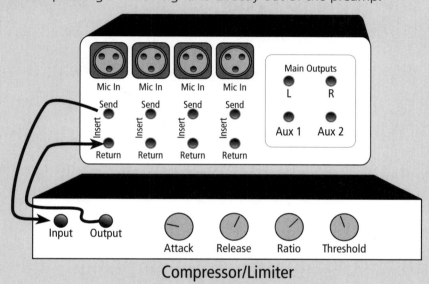

Compressor/Limiter

fects processors is the auxiliary bus. Plug the output of the aux bus into the input of the effects processor, then patch the output of the effects processor into an available channel or effects return. Always try to keep the effects return separate from the original dry track so that you can select the appropriate effect and balance for the final mix.

Using an aux bus for an effects send and returning the affected sound to a channel is the most flexible system for reverb and delay effects. In this way you can send multiple instruments, in varying levels, to one effects processor (Illustration 2-4).

It's also common to simply plug an instru-ment directly into the processor itself, then patch the complete sound into the mixer or tape re-corder.

Once you can recognize these processors when you hear them, and you're feeling com-fortable with the options for patching them in, you can move on. Let's get into some of the nuts and bolts of how they work.

Dynamic Processors

The dynamic processors (compressors, limiters, gates and expanders) all work in a very similar way and have very similar, if not identical, con-

Illustration 2-4
Patching the Aux Bus

There'll be many situations in recording where some unforeseen factor will dictate the use of almost any equipment in a nonstandard or possibly even substandard way. It is my goal to show you the proper ways to use these processors. Experiment with each of these methods, and expand on each of them. When you set out to shape a sound, envision it first in your mind, then try to achieve the sound. This is the best approach. Sometimes, we all get stuck and uninspired, and a little knob twiddling *can* trigger a stroke of genius, but this should become the exception instead of the rule. Strive to hear the sound first and *then* produce it!

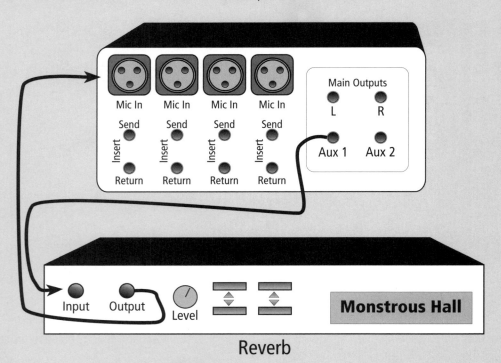

Reverb

About the VCA

When the VCA is turned all the way up, your signal will be at whatever level it would've been if the VCA were not in the circuit. When a circuit puts out exactly the same level of signal that it receives at the input, it's called *unity gain*. Ideally, the VCA will be at unity gain when it turns itself all the way up. A common phrase that refers to unity gain is same in-same out. To understand the operation of compressors, limiters, gates and expanders, you must realize that these units change the distance in level between loud and soft by turning the loud down in relation to the soft or by turning the soft down in relation to the loud.

trols from unit to unit. The task for any dynamic processor is to change the distance, in volume, from the softest sound to the loudest sound or to alter the dynamic range.

The VCA

The central operator in each of the dynamic processors is the VCA. *VCA* stands for voltage controlled amplifier. Its name is almost its definition. Inside each processor is an amplifying circuit that turns up and down as it senses more or less voltage—it's a voltage controlled amplifier. The changing levels in your musical signal determine the amount of voltage.

In the dynamic range processors I'll cover in this chapter, the VCA only turns your signal down and then back up to its original level. As we go through each dynamic processor, you'll

see just how the VCA is able to help.

Dynamic range processors are typically patched into the signal path of the microphone, instrument or tape track. This is accomplished at the channel insert (on the mixer or the patch bay) or from the mic or instrument. See Illustrations 2-5A to 2-5C for different patching schemes.

Compressor/Limiter

The *compressor* is an automatic volume control that turns loud parts of the musical signal down. When the VCA senses the signal exceeding a certain level, it acts on that signal and turns it down.

Imagine yourself listening to the mix and every time the vocal track starts to get too loud and read too hot on the meter, you turn the fader

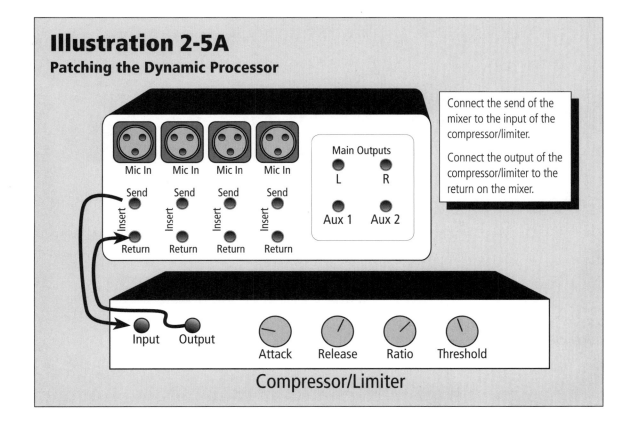

Illustration 2-5A
Patching the Dynamic Processor

Mic In   Mic In   Mic In   Mic In

Main Outputs
L   R

Send   Send   Send   Send

Aux 1   Aux 2

Insert

Return   Return   Return   Return

Connect the send of the mixer to the input of the compressor/limiter.

Connect the output of the compressor/limiter to the return on the mixer.

Input   Output

Attack   Release   Ratio   Threshold

Compressor/Limiter

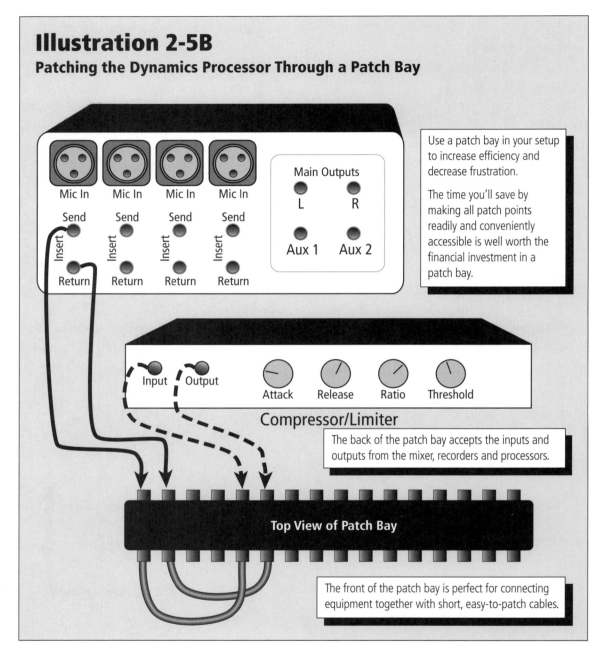

Illustration 2-5B
Patching the Dynamics Processor Through a Patch Bay

Mic In Mic In Mic In Mic In

Main Outputs
L R
Aux 1 Aux 2

Send Send Send Send

Insert Insert Insert Insert

Return Return Return Return

Use a patch bay in your setup to increase efficiency and decrease frustration.

The time you'll save by making all patch points readily and conveniently accessible is well worth the financial investment in a patch bay.

Input Output Attack Release Ratio Threshold

Compressor/Limiter

The back of the patch bay accepts the inputs and outputs from the mixer, recorders and processors.

Top View of Patch Bay

The front of the patch bay is perfect for connecting equipment together with short, easy-to-patch cables.

down and then back up again for the rest of the track. That is exactly what a compressor does.

This is an essential tool for recording instruments that have very loud louds and very soft softs. A compressor is almost always used on vocals and bass and is often used on instruments with wide dynamic ranges.

Again, the VCA in a compressor only turns down in response to a signal and then turns back up again; it doesn't turn up beyond the original level.

Why do we need a compressor? We need a compressor to protect against overly loud sounds that can overdrive electronic circuitry or

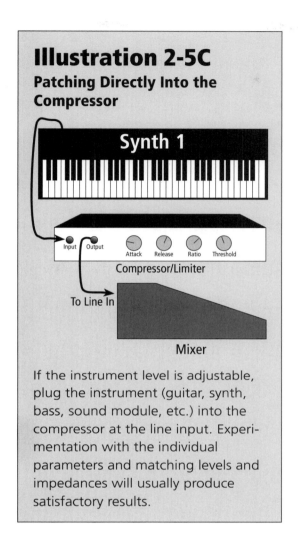

Illustration 2-5C
Patching Directly Into the Compressor

Synth 1

Input Output Attack Release Ratio Threshold
Compressor/Limiter

To Line In

Mixer

If the instrument level is adjustable, plug the instrument (guitar, synth, bass, sound module, etc.) into the compressor at the line input. Experimentation with the individual parameters and matching levels and impedances will usually produce satisfactory results.

oversaturate magnetic tape. In Chapter 1, we heard the result of overdriving mixer circuitry (distortion). When tape is oversaturated, it receives more signal than it can handle, and the magnetic particles aren't arranged in a way that can accurately reproduce the signal. This is also distortion.

A compressor can also help even out the different ranges of an instrument. Instruments like brass, strings, vocals and guitars can have substantially different volumes and impact in different pitch ranges. These ranges can disappear, then suddenly jump out in a mix. A highly skilled

and very focused engineer might catch many of these variations in level, but a compressor is often more reliable and less intrusive. A compressor can also even out volume differences created by an artist changing their distance from the mic.

Since we've put a lid on the loud passages and can therefore print the entire track with a stronger signal to tape, we are able to move the overall signal away from the tape noise. This gives us a better signal-to-noise ratio.

Does the compressor detract from the life and depth of the original sound? When used correctly, compression doesn't detract from the life of the original sound. In fact, it can be the one tool that helps that life and depth to be heard and understood in a mix.

Think about a vocal track. Singers perform many nuances and licks that define their individual style. Within the same second, they may jump from a subtle, emotional phrase to a screaming loud, needle-pegging, engineer-torturing high note. Even the best of us aren't fast enough to catch all of these changes by simply riding the input fader. In this situation, a compressor is needed to protect against levels that will distort on tape.

This automatic level control gives us a very important by-product. As the loudest parts of the track are turned down, we are able to bring the overall level of the track up. In effect, this brings the softer sounds up in relation to the louder sounds (Illustrations 2-6A to 2-6C). The subtle nuance becomes more noticeable in a mix, so the individuality and style of the artist is *more* easily recognized, plus the understandability and audibility of the lyrics is greatly increased.

There are four controls common to all compressors: threshold, attack time, release time

Illustration 2-6A
The Uncompressed Signal

A compressor can turn the loud parts down automatically as soon as it senses their levels. Once the signal passes the user-set threshold, the VCA acts on the signal according to the ratio setting.

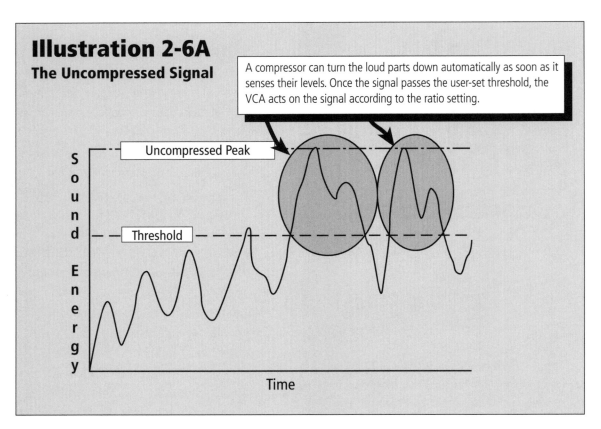

Uncompressed Peak

Threshold

Sound Energy

Time

Illustration 2-6B
The Compressed Signal

This graph represents the compression of the wave in Illustration 2-6A. Everything below the threshold is unaffected. Everything above the threshold is reduced in level according to the ratio control.

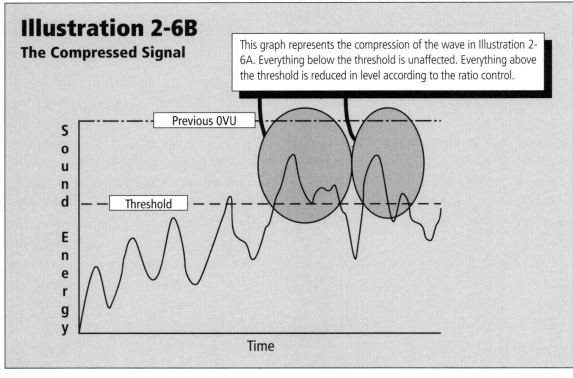

Previous 0VU

Threshold

Sound Energy

Time

Illustration 2-6C
Readjusting the Compressed Signal to Read 0VU

The gray line represents the level of the compressed signal from Illustration 2-6B. Once the compressor has turned the loudest part of the track down, the entire track can be turned up so the overall level still reaches 0VU. The black line represents the new level. Notice that the softest parts of the track are louder (consequently easier to hear in the mix) as the entire level increases.

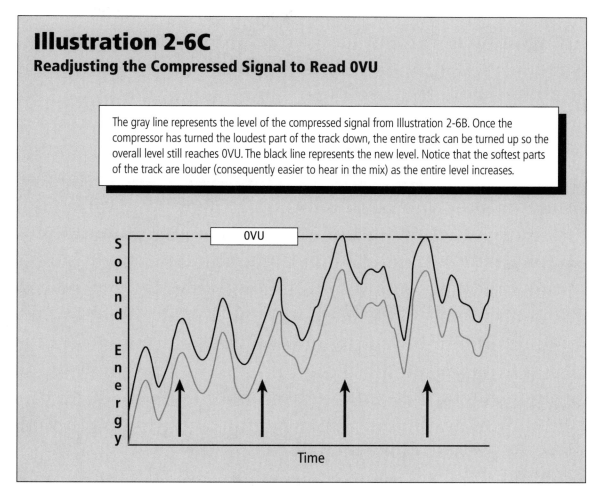

and ratio.

Once you see how these work, you can operate any compressor, anywhere, anytime. To make it even better, these controls are easy to understand and they do just what they say they do.

Threshold

The threshold is the point where the compressor begins to recognize the signal. Once the compressor recognizes the signal, it begins to act in a way that is determined by adjustment of the attack time, release time and ratio controls. A threshold is an entrance point where the signal enters to be compressed.

Two different ways that compressors deal with the threshold control:

1. Picture yourself in a room with an opening in the ceiling directly overhead. You represent the signal, with your head being the loudest sounds. The opening represents the threshold of the compressor. Imagine that the floor moves up and you begin to go through the opening. That's the way that some compressors move the signal into the threshold: They turn it up until it goes through the threshold.

2. Picture yourself in the same room with an opening directly overhead, but now the ceiling moves down until you're through the opening. This is the other way the threshold

control can work: The signal level stays the same but the threshold moves down into the peaks.

Once the signal is through the threshold, the compressor turns down just the part of the signal that's gone through. It will leave the rest of the signal unaffected (Illustration 2-7). The portion that's above the threshold will be turned down according to how you have set the remaining controls (attack time, release time and ratio).

Attack Time

The *attack time* is just that. It controls the amount of time it takes the compressor to turn

the signal down once it's passed the threshold. If the attack time is too fast, the compressor will turn down the transients. This can cause an instrument to lose life and clarity (refer to Chapter 1 for a description of transients). On a vocal, for instance, if the attack time is too fast, all of the "t" and "s" sounds will start to disappear.

Audio Example 2-13 S's and T's
CD-1: Track 29

On the other hand, if the attack time is too slow and the vocal is very compressed, the t's and s's will fly through uncompressed and

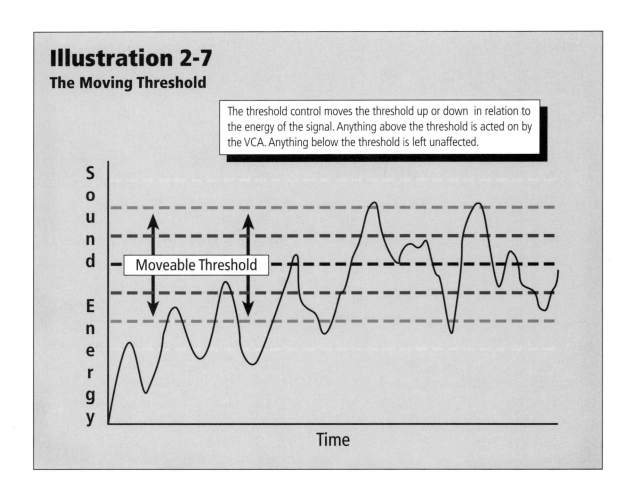

Illustration 2-7
The Moving Threshold

The threshold control moves the threshold up or down in relation to the energy of the signal. Anything above the threshold is acted on by the VCA. Anything below the threshold is left unaffected.

Sound Energy

Moveable Threshold

Time

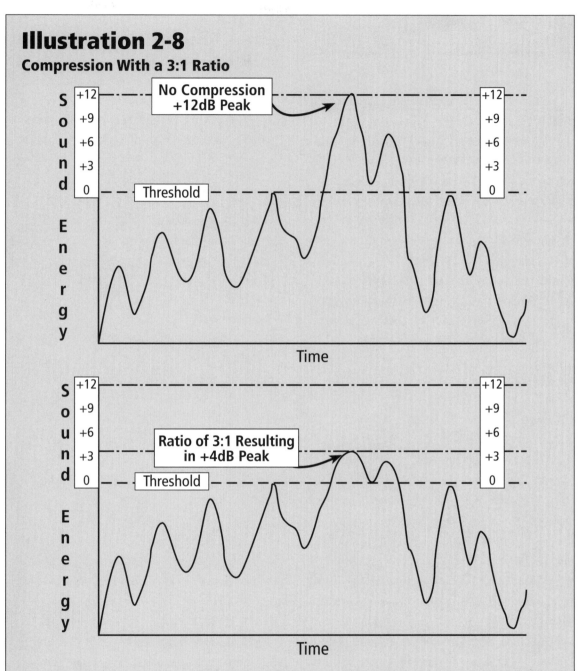

Illustration 2-8

Compression With a 3:1 Ratio

The threshold in the top graph is set so that the peak sound energy level exceeds the threshold by 12dB. The VCA turns the signal (above the threshold) down according to the ratio. With the ratio set at 3:1, the VCA only allows 1dB of increase for every 3dB that exceed the threshold. The original signal exceeded the threshold by 12dB (with no compression), but the compressor only allows a 4dB peak when the ratio is set at 3:1 (bottom graph).

sound exaggerated.

Audio Example 2-14 S's and T's
CD-1: Track 29

As we progress through this series, we'll see several examples of how to specifically adjust all of these controls for individual situations.

The attack times on different compressors will vary. One characteristic of the more expensive compressors is that they have faster attack times. The attack times on compressors range from as fast as 100 microseconds down to about 20 milliseconds. A microsecond is a millionth of a second, and a millisecond is a thousandth of a second. Also, some compressors have the attack time fixed for a specific purpose, like vocals.

Release Time

Release time is the time that it takes for the compressor to let go, or turn the signal back up, once it is out of the threshold. The release time might be as fast as 5/100 of a second or as slow as two or three seconds. Longer release times, of a second or so, typically work the best and produce the most natural and smooth sound.

If the release time is too fast, the VCA turns down and up so fast that it actually follows the crest and trough of each low frequency waveform. This produces an undesirable type of distortion. The VCA level changes might produce their own warble sound or even a pitch.

For vocals and bass, the release time will typically be set between a half a second and 2 seconds, depending on the tempo and style of music.

Ratio

Once the compressor starts acting on the signal, there's one more control that determines how extreme that action will be. This is called the ratio.

The *ratio* is simply a comparison between what goes through the threshold and the output of the compressor. If you adjust the threshold so that the loudest note of the song exceeds the threshold by 3dB (and the ratio is 3:1), the 3dB peak *in* will come *out* of the compressor as a 1dB peak. Using that same 3:1 ratio, if you had a 12dB peak, the unit would put out a 4dB peak—still a ratio of 3:1 (Illustration 2-8).

Summary

The *threshold* is what we adjust to determine how much of the signal the VCA acts on. It might only compress the very loudest parts of the signal, or it might be compressing almost all the time.

Attack and release control the amount of time it takes the unit to react to (or turn down) the signal once it senses it at the threshold, as well as the amount of time it takes the unit to release (or turn up) the signal once it stops seeing it at the threshold.

Ratio controls the severity of gain reduction once the signal is past the threshold.

Gain Reduction

Compressors either have a series of LEDs or a VU meter to indicate how much gain reduction is happening at any given time. *Gain reduction* refers to the amount that the VCA has turned the signal down once it crosses the threshold. Typically, the LEDs light up from right to left, indicating how far the unit has turned your musical signal down. Each LED represents two or

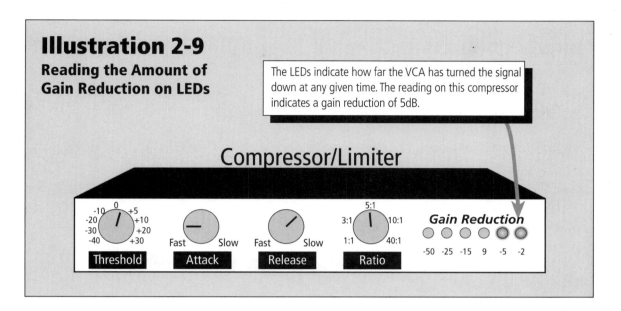

Illustration 2-9
Reading the Amount of Gain Reduction on LEDs

The LEDs indicate how far the VCA has turned the signal down at any given time. The reading on this compressor indicates a gain reduction of 5dB.

Compressor/Limiter

Threshold | Attack | Release | Ratio | Gain Reduction

more dB of gain reduction (Illustration 2-9).

If your compressor has a VU meter, a reading of 0VU indicates no gain reduction. In fact, 0VU is the normal (rest) position on a meter used to indicate no gain reduction. As the compressor turns down, the needle moves backwards from 0 to indicate the amount of gain reduction. A -5 reading on the VU indicates 5dB of gain reduction (Illustration 2-10).

What's the difference between a compressor and a limiter? Most compressors are labeled compressor/limiter. The only difference between a compressor and a limiter is where you set the ratio control. The range of adjustment on the ratio control can go from 1:1 up to 60:1, 100:1, or, on some units, even ∞:1. A compressor uses any ratio between 1:1 and 10:1. A limiter uses any ratio from 10:1 to ∞:1. It's that simple. A *limiter* is a very extreme compressor.

Limiters are used to record a sound source that might suddenly blast out but is usually fairly constant in level. A bass guitar that plays normally on the verse but plays an occasional thump, slap or snap on the chorus is a good example of where a limiter is needed. The difference in level from the normal playing to the snaps can be dramatic, but the level of the recorded bass track should stay fairly constant to provide a solid foundation for the rest of the arrangement. If left unchecked, these louder notes could cause oversaturation and distortion on tape.

Limiters mean business. At 100:1, your signal could exceed the threshold by 100dB, and the limiter would only let a 1dB peak out of the output. That's extreme (Illustration 2-11)!

Proper Use of the Compressor/ Limiter

There should be several times during the track where there is no gain reduction. If there is always gain reduction, the VCA is always working, and you begin to lose the clarity and integrity of the original signal. An experienced engineer tries to eliminate unnecessary amplifying circuits in the signal path. That's our approach here. You only want the VCA to act when it's needed, not all of the time.

Illustration 2-10
Compressors With VU Meters

Some compressor/limiters use a VU meter instead of LEDs to indicate gain reduction. Normal position for the needle is 0VU. 0VU indicates no gain reduction. As the VCA turns the signal down, the VU meter reads negative numbers according to the amount of gain reduction. The meter in this illustration indicates 7dB of gain reduction.

Remember, VU meters indicate average levels, whereas LEDs indicate peak levels. A compressor with LEDs indicating gain reduction and a compressor with VU meters indicating gain reduction might have the exact same attack time, but the LEDs will give a quicker, more accurate picture of what is really happening. As an operator, you can adjust quickly to either metering system, as long as you understand their differences.

Compressor/Limiter

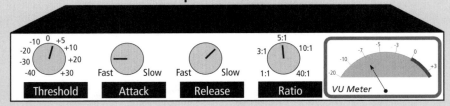

Methodical Approach to Setting Up the Compressor/Limiter

- **Determine the ratio.** Most natural sounding compression typically has a ratio setting of between 3:1 and 7:1. Limiting uses a ratio greater than 10:1.
- **Adjust the attack and release times.** A good general approach is to start with the attack time around 1ms and the release time of 1/2–1 second. We'll talk about techniques for specific situations as we progress through this course.
- **Adjust the threshold for the amount of gain reduction that you want.** You should typically have 3–6dB of reduction at the strongest part of the track, and there should be times when there is no gain reduction. This is the text book approach for the most natural and least audibly conspicuous compression.

If you've achieved 6dB of gain reduction you're able to boost your overall level to tape by 6dB over what it would have been without the compressor. With the entire track boosted we can hear the nuances and softer passages more clearly. As an additional bonus, the complete track (including the soft passages) will be 6dB further away from the tape noise floor than they were before compression.

Compressors are essential tools for making professional sounding audio recordings. If you are involved in audio for video and television, compressors are essential because of the limited dynamic range in these mediums.

Illustration 2-11
Limiting

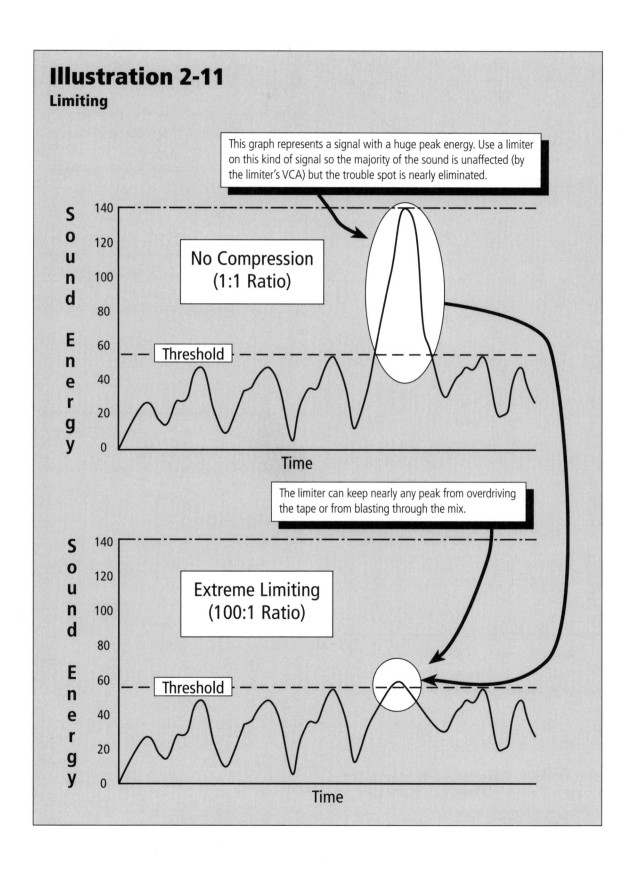

This graph represents a signal with a huge peak energy. Use a limiter on this kind of signal so the majority of the sound is unaffected (by the limiter's VCA) but the trouble spot is nearly eliminated.

No Compression
(1:1 Ratio)

Threshold

Sound Energy

Time

The limiter can keep nearly any peak from overdriving the tape or from blasting through the mix.

Extreme Limiting
(100:1 Ratio)

Threshold

Sound Energy

Time

Compressors and limiters are generally used while recording tracks as opposed to during mixdown, since one of the main benefits in compressing the signal is that you can get a more consistently hot signal on tape.

Compressing on mixdown can result in more apparent noise on a track. The compressor is putting a lid on the loud passages. That lets the soft passages come up in level relative to the loud passages, so they're heard more easily. When the VCA turns the tape track back up during the soft passages, the tape noise is audibly increased, too. We hear this noise turning up and down as the signal crosses the threshold, and the VCA reacts by turning up and down. This is one of the adverse effects of compression. The sound of the noise turning up and down is called *pumping* or *breathing*.

Listen to the different versions of the exact same vocal performance in Audio Examples 2-15 to 2-19. I've adjusted the level so that the peak of each version is at +1VU on the meter. The only difference is the amount of compression. Pay special attention to the understandability of each word, the apparent tape noise and the overall feel of each track.

Audio Example 2-15 demonstrates no compression.

Audio Example 2-15 No Compression
CD-1: Track 30

Audio Example 2-16 demonstrates compression with 3dB of gain reduction.

Audio Example 2-16 3dB Gain Reduction
CD-1: Track 30

Audio Example 2-17 demonstrates compression with 6dB of gain reduction.

Audio Example 2-17 6dB Gain Reduction
CD-1: Track 30

Audio Example 2-18 demonstrates compression with 9dB of gain reduction.

Audio Example 2-18 9dB Gain Reduction
CD-1: Track 30

Audio Example 2-19 includes tape noise with the vocal. Listen to the compressor turning up and down (pumping and breathing).

Audio Example 2-19 Pumping and Breathing
CD-1: Track 30

Gate/Expander

The gate and expander are in the same family as the compressor/limiter. They're also centered around a VCA, and the VCA still turns the signal down. When the VCA is all the way up, the signal is at the same level as if the VCA weren't in the circuit.

When the compressor/limiter senses the signal passing the threshold in an upward way, it turns down the signal that's above the threshold. The amount of gain reduction is determined by the ratio control. In contrast, when the *gate/expander* senses the signal passing the threshold in a downward way, the VCA turns the signal down even further. In other words, everything that's below the threshold is turned down

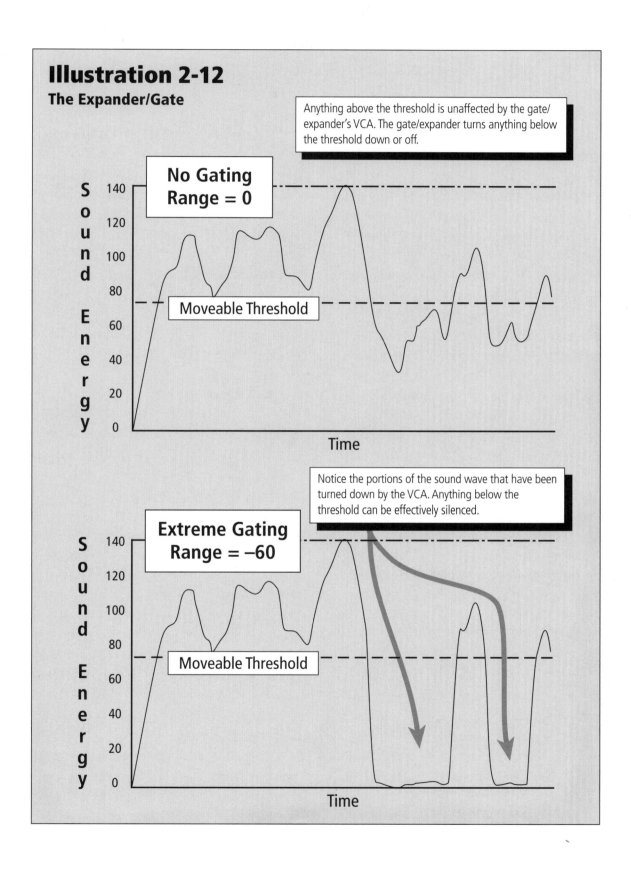

Illustration 2-12
The Expander/Gate

Anything above the threshold is unaffected by the gate/expander's VCA. The gate/expander turns anything below the threshold down or off.

**No Gating
Range = 0**

Sound Energy

Moveable Threshold

Time

Notice the portions of the sound wave that have been turned down by the VCA. Anything below the threshold can be effectively silenced.

**Extreme Gating
Range = –60**

Sound Energy

Moveable Threshold

Time

(Illustration 2-12).

What are the controls on a gate/expander? The controls on the gate/expander are essentially the same as the controls on a compressor/limiter. The threshold is the control that determines how much of the signal is acted on by the unit, as indicated in Illustration 2-12. The attack and release times do the same thing here that they did on the compressor: They control how quickly the unit acts once the signal has passed the threshold and how fast the unit turns the signal back up once the signal is no longer below the threshold.

The range control on the expander/gate correlates to the ratio control on the compressor/limiter. In fact, some multifunction dynamic processors use the same knob to control both ratio and range. The ratio on a compressor determines how far the VCA turns the signal down once it passes the threshold in an upward direction. The range on a gate/expander determines how far down the VCA will turn the signal once it passes the threshold in a downward direction.

When the signal gets below the threshold and the range setting tells the VCA to turn all the way off, the unit is called a gate. When the signal is below the threshold, the gate is closed. The gate closes behind the sound and doesn't open again until the signal is above the threshold.

The range can also be adjusted so that the VCA only turns down the signal part of the way once it gets below the threshold. In this case, the unit is called an expander.

A gate is called a gate because it opens and closes when it senses the signal come and go across the threshold.

An expander is called an expander because it expands the dynamic range of the music. It creates a bigger difference between the softer and the louder sound by turning the softer parts down.

The most common type of expander doesn't turn the louder parts up; it just seems to in relation to the softer parts. Specifically, an expander that turns the softer sounds down is called a *downward expander*. There is also an *upward expander* which turns the louder part up even louder. Upward expanders aren't very common and are somewhat noisy and difficult to control in a medium such as magnetic tape. Unless I specify otherwise, I'll refer to a downward expander throughout this course simply as an expander.

Gates vs. Expanders

Gates are especially useful in getting rid of noise, either from an instrument like a noisy electric guitar or from tape. If the threshold is set just above the noise floor, as the signal fades to the noise, the gate will simply continue the fade to silence. An expander can do exactly the same thing, but it will turn the noise down rather than off. Gates and expanders can really clean up a recording by getting rid of noise between the musical segments of each track.

Some units have a separate button to select the gate or the expander. Both the gate and the expander have the same controls, including full use of the range control. I've found that expanders are usually smoother in their level changes and are typically more musical and glitch free than gates.

Expanders are useful for restoring dynamic range to a signal that has been severely compressed. If the compressor reduced the loud parts by 9dB, then, in theory, if the signal is expanded and the range control is adjusted to turn the soft parts down by 9dB, we should have a pretty reasonable facsimile of our original dynamic range.

Gates and expanders are usually used on mixdown, rather than when recording tracks. If the gate or expander threshold were set incorrectly, some softer notes might not get printed to tape because they couldn't open the gate. If this happens, these softer notes are gone forever. Thus, the safest approach is to use gates and expanders on mixdown. During mixdown, the threshold can be adjusted without destroying any of the notes.

In a small setup, we often need to gate as we're recording (if we're going to gate at all) because of a lack of tracks and gates. This can work just fine, but more care must be taken in setting the processor, and the musical performance must be more consistent and predictable.

For instance, a noisy guitar track is often gated during recording because the noise is consistent and it's easy to set the threshold so that the guitar sound comes through fine and the noise never touches tape.

So, a gate and an expander are really the same tool. The gate is an extreme version of an expander, with the gate turning the soft parts off where the expander just turns them down.

Audio Example 2-20 Guitar: No Gate
CD-1: Track 31

Audio Example 2-21 Guitar: Gated
CD-1: Track 31

Illustration 2-13A
Assignment: Dynamic Range Processors

- Practice shaping sounds with all of the dynamic range processors.
- Practice running several different types of sounds through the dynamic processors. Try using vocal, instrumental or recorded sound sources. Also, practice on complete songs from tapes or CDs.
- When adjusting each unit, go to extremes. Be sure you hear and see the processor working. Change the sound as much as you can. Try all of the controls, then make them sound as natural as possible.

You'll end up using these processors in a subtle way, more often than not. The goals in controlling the dynamic range of your tracks are:

- Protect the tape from signals that are too hot. Strong signals can oversaturate the tape with magnetism. Oversaturation usually results in distortion.
- Produce a track that is always understandable, even in the subtle nuance of artistic expression.
- Increase (gate/expand) or decrease (compress/limit) the difference in level between the loudest part of a track and the softest part of a track.

Illustration 2-13B
Assignment: External Inputs and Keys

There is probably a switch on the processor to choose whether the VCA sensing circuit hears from the regular input or from an external input. This switch might be labeled key, trigger, external input, external, side chain or insert.

- Experiment with the external input. This input can receive any sound source, live or recorded.
- Set up a pattern on a drum machine, and patch the snare into the external input. Patch a record, tape or CD in and out of the normal jacks. Set the internal/external (key) switch to external or key.
- See what kind of different effects you can create. The snare will trigger the VCA to act. There are a lot of possibilities that can grow out of this experiment. Use your imagination and see what kind of clever uses you can invent, or reinvent, for this technique. As this course advances, we'll find some interesting applications for this feature.

Many dynamic processors currently available contain all of the features we've just used. If you're shopping, try to find a single processor that has many different features. This will save money and space. You should be able to find a unit that has a compressor, limiter, gate and expander all in one box.

Audio Example 2-22 Hi-hat: No Expander
CD-1: Track 32

Audio Example 2-23 Hi-hat: Expander
CD-1: Track 32

These dynamic range processors are all very useful, and often essential, in creating professional sounds. Each unit offers many creative and musical possibilities. As we study the individual instruments and their unique sound schemes, we'll use these processors, time and again. See Illustration 2-13A for an assignment on dynamic processors. See Illustration 2-13B for an assignment on keys and external triggers.

More About Equalizers

We covered a lot about equalization and its principles in Chapter 1. We know that EQ is tone control, and when we boost or cut a frequency we're really boosting or cutting a curve that has width around a center point.

Listen to Audio Example 2-24. The entire track is run through a semiparametric EQ. The bandwidth is about one octave, and the frequency selector sweeps a boost from 50Hz to 500Hz.

Audio Example 2-24 Sweeping 50 to 500Hz
CD-1: Track 33

Audio Example 2-25 uses the same setup, sweeping the frequencies between 100Hz and 5kHz.

Audio Example 2-25 Sweeping 100Hz to 5kHz
CD-1: Track 33

Notice how different instruments stick out in the mix as we sweep through the frequency spectrum. This shows the usefulness of sweepable EQ for finding specific ranges to highlight or hide.

Audio Example 2-26 sweeps from 2.5kHz to 15kHz. Notice the edge, clarity and brilliance of the different instruments.

Audio Example 2-26 Sweeping 2.5 to 15kHz
CD-1: Track 33

In Audio Example 2-27, we switch to a fully parametric EQ, narrow the bandwidth down to about 1/5 of an octave, then sweep. Notice how the sweeping curve takes on the pitch of the curve's center point.

Audio Example 2-27
Sweeping a Narrow Bandwidth
CD-1: Track 33

An EQ like this is best used for finding a problem frequency, like high frequency squeal, that you want to cut. One of the best ways to find the frequency of the problem area is to set up a boost and then sweep the spectrum until that problem sounds its loudest. Once you've located the frequency, change the boost to an extreme cut, and the problem is at least easier to live with. Used like this, a parametric EQ is acting like a notch filter. A notch filter has a very narrow bandwidth and is used to cut problem frequencies.

Effects Processors

Now we come to the effects processors. All of the effects (echoes, reverbs and chorus effects) revolve around one thing: the delay.

Delay Effects

A *delay* does just what its name says: it hears a sound and then waits for a while before it reproduces it. Current delays are simply digital recorders that digitally record the incoming signal and then play it back with a time delay selected by the user. This time delay can vary from unit to unit, but most delays have a range of delay length from a portion of a millisecond up to one or more seconds. This is called the delay time or delay length and is variable in milliseconds.

Almost all digital delays are much more than simple echo units. Within the delay are all of the controls you need to produce slapback, repeating echo, doubling, chorusing, flanging, phase shifting, some primitive reverb sounds and any hybrid variation you can dream up. See Illustration 2-14 for considerations about patching effects processors into your system.

Slapback Delay

The simplest form of delay is called a slapback. The *slapback delay* is a single repeat of the signal. Its delay time is anything above about 35ms. Any single repeat with a delay time of less than

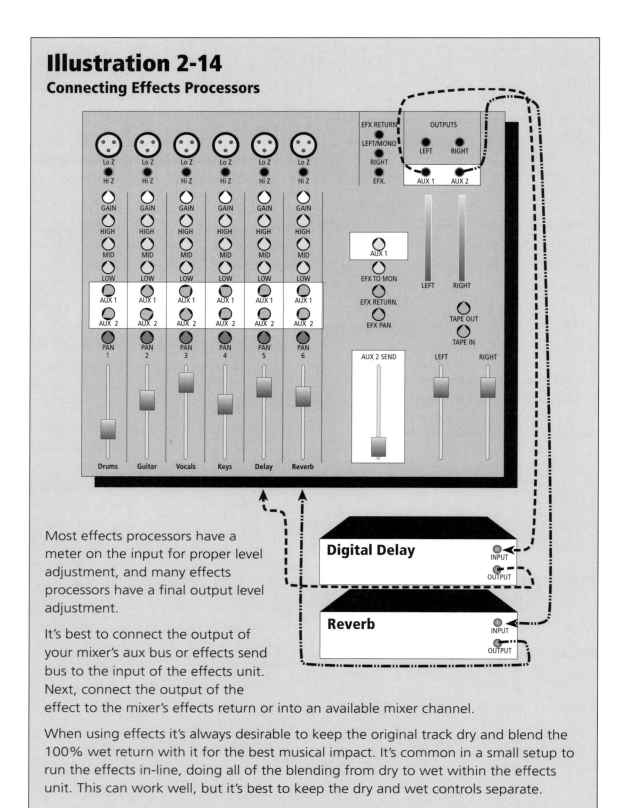

Illustration 2-14
Connecting Effects Processors

Most effects processors have a meter on the input for proper level adjustment, and many effects processors have a final output level adjustment.

It's best to connect the output of your mixer's aux bus or effects send bus to the input of the effects unit. Next, connect the output of the effect to the mixer's effects return or into an available mixer channel.

When using effects it's always desirable to keep the original track dry and blend the 100% wet return with it for the best musical impact. It's common in a small setup to run the effects in-line, doing all of the blending from dry to wet within the effects unit. This can work well, but it's best to keep the dry and wet controls separate.

35ms is called a *double*.

To achieve a slapback from a delay, simply adjust the delay time and turn the delayed signal up, either on the return channel or on the mix control within the delay.

For a single slapback delay, feedback and modulation are set to their off positions. Slapback delays of between 150ms and about 300ms are very effective and common for creating a big vocal or guitar sound.

Audio Example 2-28 demonstrates a track with a 250ms slapback delay.

Audio Example 2-28 250ms Slapback
CD-1: Track 34

Slapback delays between 35 and 75ms are very effective for thickening a vocal or instrumental sound.

Audio Example 2-29 demonstrates a track with a 50ms delay.

Audio Example 2-29 50ms Slapback
CD-1: Track 34

Slapback delay can be turned into a repeating delay. This smooths out the sound of a track even more and is accomplished through the use of the regeneration control. This is also called *feedback* or *repeat*.

This control takes the delayed signal and feeds it back into the input of the delay unit, so we hear the original, the delay and then a delay of the delayed signal. The higher you turn the feedback up, the more times the delay is repeated. Practically speaking, anything past about three repeats gets too muddy and does more

musical harm than good.

The vocal track in Audio Example 2-30 starts with a simple single slapback, then the feedback raises until we hear three or four repeats.

Audio Example 2-30 Repeating Delays
CD-1: Track 35

Why does a simple delay make a track sound so much bigger and better? Delay gives the brain the perception of listening in a larger, more interesting environment. As the delays combine with the original sound, the harmonics of each part combine in interesting ways. Any pitch discrepancies are averaged out as the delay combines with the original signal. If a note was sharp or flat, it's hidden when heard along with the delay of a previous note that was in tune. This helps most vocal sounds tremendously and adds to the richness and fullness of the mix.

The human brain gets its cue for room size from the initial reflections, or repeats, that it hears off surrounding surfaces. Longer delay times indicate, to the brain, that the room is larger. The slapback is really perceived as the reflection off the back wall of the room or auditorium as the sound bounces back (slaps back) to the performer. Many great lead vocal tracks have used a simple slapback delay as the primary or only effect. Frequently, this delay sounds cleaner than reverb and has less of a tendency to intrusively accumulate.

Slapback delay is typically related in some way to the beat and tempo of the song. The delay is often in time with the eighth note or sixteenth note, but it's also common to hear a slapback in time with the quarter note or some triplet sub-

Illustration 2-15
Delay Calculations in Milliseconds

Tempo in Beats per Minute	Quarter Note	Eighth Note	Sixteenth Note	Quarter-Note Triplets	Eighth-Note Triplets
20.00	3000.00	1500.00	750.00	2000.00	1000.00
25.00	2400.00	1200.00	600.00	1600.00	800.00
30.00	2000.00	1000.00	500.00	1333.33	666.67
35.00	1714.29	857.14	428.57	1142.86	571.43
40.00	1500.00	750.00	375.00	1000.00	500.00
45.00	1333.33	666.67	333.33	888.89	444.44
50.00	1200.00	600.00	300.00	800.00	400.00
55.00	1090.91	545.45	272.73	727.27	363.64
60.00	1000.00	500.00	250.00	666.67	333.33
65.00	923.08	461.54	230.77	615.38	307.69
70.00	857.14	428.57	214.29	571.43	285.71
75.00	800.00	400.00	200.00	533.33	266.67
80.00	750.00	375.00	187.50	500.00	250.00
85.00	705.88	352.94	176.47	470.59	235.29
90.00	666.67	333.33	166.67	444.44	222.22
95.00	631.58	315.79	157.89	421.05	210.53
100.00	600.00	300.00	150.00	400.00	200.00
105.00	571.43	285.71	142.86	380.95	190.48
110.00	545.45	272.73	136.36	363.64	181.82
115.00	521.74	260.87	130.43	347.83	173.91
120.00	500.00	250.00	125.00	333.33	166.67
125.00	480.00	240.00	120.00	320.00	160.00
130.00	461.54	230.77	115.38	307.69	153.85
135.00	444.44	222.22	111.11	296.30	148.15
140.00	428.57	214.29	107.14	285.71	142.86
145.00	413.79	206.90	103.45	275.86	137.93
150.00	400.00	200.00	100.00	266.67	133.33
155.00	387.10	193.55	96.77	258.06	129.03
160.00	375.00	187.50	93.75	250.00	125.00
165.00	363.64	181.82	90.91	242.42	121.21
170.00	352.94	176.47	88.24	235.29	117.65
175.00	342.86	171.43	85.71	228.57	114.29
180.00	333.33	166.67	83.33	222.22	111.11
185.00	324.32	162.16	81.08	216.22	108.11
190.00	315.79	157.89	78.95	210.53	105.26
195.00	307.69	153.85	76.92	205.13	102.56

division. The delay time can add to the rhythmic feel of the song. A delay that's in time with the eighth note can really smooth out the groove of the song, or if the delay time is shortened or lengthened just slightly, the groove may feel more aggressive or relaxed. Experiment with slight changes in delay time.

Refer to the table in Illustration 2-15 for specific delay times, tempos and note values. It's easy to find the delay, in milliseconds, for the quarter note in your song, especially when you're working from a sequence and the tempo is already available on screen. Simply divide 60,000 by the tempo of your song (in beats per minute). **60,000 ÷ bpm = delay time per beat in milliseconds** (typically the quarter note).

Doubling

A single delay of less than 35ms is called a double. This short delay can combine with the original track to sound like two people (or instruments) on the same part. Often, performers will actually record the same part twice to achieve the doubled sound, but sometimes the electronic double is quicker, easier and sounds more precise. Audio Example 2-31 demonstrates an 11ms delay (with no feedback and no modulation) combined with the original vocal. At the end of the example, the original and the delayed double pan apart in the stereo spectrum. This can be a great sound in stereo, but is a potential problem when summing to mono.

Audio Example 2-31 11ms Vocal Delay
CD-1: Track 35

When doubling, use prime numbers for delay times. You'll hear better results when your song is played in mono. A prime number can only be divided by one and itself (e.g., 1, 3, 5, 7, 11, 13, 17, 19, 23, 29 and so on).

Modulation

The modulation control on a delay is for creating chorusing, flanging and phase shifting effects. The key factor here is the *LFO* (low frequency oscillator); its function is to continually vary the delay time. The LFO is usually capable of varying the delay from the setting indicated by the delay time to half of that value and back. Sometimes the LFO control is labeled modulation.

As the LFO is slowing down and speeding up the delay, it's speeding up and slowing down the playback of the delayed signal. In other words, modulation actually lowers and raises the pitch in exactly the same way that a tape recorder does if the speed is lowered and raised. Audio Example 2-32 demonstrates the sound of the LFO varying the delay time. This example starts subtly, with the variation from the original going down slightly, then back up. Finally, the LFO varies dramatically downward, then back up again.

Audio Example 2-32 The LFO
CD-1: Track 36

On most usable effects, these changes in pitch are slight and still within the boundaries of acceptable intonation, so they aren't making the instrument sound out of tune. In fact, the slight pitch change can have the effect of smoothing out any pitch problems on a track.

As the pitch is raised and lowered, the sound waves are shortened and lengthened. When we talked about waveforms combining, in Chapter 1, we noticed that when two waveforms follow the same path, they sum together. The result is twice the amount of energy. We also noticed that when two waveforms are out of phase, they work against and cancel each other, either totally or partially.

When the modulation is lengthening and shortening the waveform and the resulting sound is combined with the original signal, the two waveforms continually react together in a changing phase relationship. They sum and cancel at varying frequencies. The interaction between the original sound and the modulated delay can simulate the sound we hear when several different instrumentalists or vocalists perform together. Even though each member of a choir tries their hardest to stay in tune and together rhythmically, they're continually varying pitch and timing. These variations are like the interaction of the modulated delay with the original track. The *chorus* setting on an effects processor is simulating the sound of a real choir by combining the original signal with the modulated signal.

The speed control adjusts how fast the pitch raises and lowers. These changes might happen very slowly, taking a few seconds to complete one cycle of raising and lower the pitch, or they might happen quickly, raising and lowering the pitch several times per second.

Audio Example 2-33 demonstrates the extreme settings of speed and depth. It's obvious when the speed and depth controls are changed here. Sounds like these aren't normally used, but when we're using a chorus, flanger or phase shifter, this is exactly what is happening, in moderation.

Audio Example 2-33 Extreme Speed and Depth
CD-1: Track 36

Phase Shifter

Now that we're seeing what all these controls do, it's time to use them all together. Obviously, the delay time is the key player in determining the way that the depth and speed react. If the delay time is very, very short, in the neighborhood of 1ms or so, the depth control will produce no pitch change. When the original and affected sounds are combined, we hear a distinct sweep that sounds more like an EQ frequency sweeping the mids and highs. With these short delay times, we're really simulating wave-

forms, moving in and out of phase, unlike the larger changes of singers varying in pitch and timing. The phase shifter is the most subtle, sweeping effect, and it often produces a swooshing sound.

Audio Example 2-34 demonstrates the sound of a phase shifter.

Audio Example 2-34 Phase Shifter
CD-1: Track 37

Flanger

A flanger has a sound similar to the phase shifter, except it has more variation and color. The primary delay setting on a flanger is typically about 20ms. The LFO varies the delay from near 0ms to 20ms and back, continually. Adjust the speed to your own taste.

Flangers and phase shifters work very well on guitars and Rhodes-type keyboard sounds. See Illustration 2-16 for some musical considerations when using a phase shifter or flanger.

Audio Example 2-35 demonstrates the sound of a flanger.

Audio Example 2-35 Flanger
CD-1: Track 37

Chorus

The factor that differentiates a chorus from the other delay effects is, again, the delay time. The typical delay time for a chorus is about 15 to 35ms, with the LFO and speed set for the richest effect for the particular instrument voice or song. With these longer delay times, as the LFO

Illustration 2-16
Flanger Speed

Since you hear a sweep of EQ with phase shifters and flangers (as opposed to the chorus effect), you'll get good results when the speed of the LFO matches the tempo of the song in some way. For example, a complete LFO cycle could take one complete measure, two beats, or even two complete measures. I've also had great results when the LFO speed didn't relate to the tempo. Experiment. Let the music guide your final choice when you adjust any sound altering parameter.

Why Is a Flanger Called a Flanger? In the early recording days, an engineer was trying to get two separate tape recorders to play the same song in time with each other, in sync. To slow one machine down as they got closer to being in sync, he actually had to press on one of the reels. When the machines were nearly in sync and the engineer pressed on the reel he began to hear the very interesting and rich sound that we call flanging. It was caused by the varying time delay between the two machines.

A tape reel has different names for the different parts of the reel. The center part is the hub. The top and bottom are called the flanges. Since the engineer pressed on the flange of one of the machines to get this rich and interesting effect, this sound became known as *flanging*.

varies, we actually hear a slight pitch change. The longer delays also create more of a difference in attack time. This also enhances the chorus effect. Since the chorus gets its name from the fact that it's simulating the pitch and time variation that exist within a choir, it might seem obvious that a chorus works great on background vocals. It does. Chorus is also an excellent effect for guitar and keyboard sounds.

Audio Example 2-36 demonstrates the sound of a chorus.

Audio Example 2-36 Chorus
CD-1: Track 37

Phase Reversal and Regeneration

The regeneration control can give us multiple repeats by feeding the delay back into the input so that it can be delayed again. This control can also be used on the phase shifter, chorus and flange. Regeneration, also called *feedback,* can make the effect more extreme or give the music a sci-fi feel. As you practice creating these effects with your equipment, experiment with feedback to find your own sounds.

Most units have a phase reversal switch that inverts the phase of the affected signal. Inverting the phase of the delay can cause very extreme effects when combined with the original signal (especially on phase shifter and flanger effects). This can make your music sound like it's turning inside out.

Audio Example 2-37 starts with the flanger in phase. Notice what happens to the sound as the phase of the effect is inverted.

Audio Example 2-37 Inverting Phase
CD-1: Track 37

Stereo Effects

The majority of effects processors are stereo, and with a stereo unit, different delay times can be assigned to the left and the right sides. If you are creating a stereo chorus, simply set one side to a delay time between 15 and 35ms, then set the other side to a different delay time, between 15 and 35ms. All of the rest of the controls are adjusted in the same way as a mono chorus. The returns from the processor can then be panned apart in the mix for a very wide and extreme effect. Listen as the chorus in Audio Example 2-38 pans from mono to stereo.

Audio Example 2-38 Stereo Chorus
CD-1: Track 37

For a stereo phase and flange, use the same procedure. Simply select different delay times for the left and right sides. See Illustration 2-17 for a chart of the suggested delay times for the different effects.

Understanding what is happening within a delay is important when you're trying to shape sounds for your music.

Sometimes it's easiest to bake a cake by simply pressing the Bake Me a Cake button, but if you are really trying to create a meal that flows together perfectly, you might need to adjust the recipe for the cake. That's what we need to do when building a song, mix or arrangement; we must be able to custom fit the pieces.

Reverberation Effects

As we move from the delay effects into the reverb effects, we must first realize that reverb is just a series of delays. Reverberation is simulation of sound in an acoustical environment, like

Illustration 2-17
Suggested Delay Times for Different Effects

Effect	Delay A	Delay B (Stereo)	LFO	Speed	Regeneration	Phase
Slapback	35–350ms		No	No	No	No
Echo (Repeats)	35–350ms		No	No	2–10	No
Simulated Reverb	15-35ms	15-35ms	No	No	Several	No
Doubling	1-35ms		No	No	No	No
Tripling	1-35ms	1-35 ms	No	No	No	No
Phase Shifter	0.5-2ms	0.5-2 ms	Yes	Low	Medium	Yes/No
Flanger	10-20ms	10-20ms	Yes	Low	Medium	Yes/No

a concert hall, gymnasium or bedroom.

No two rooms sound exactly alike. Sound bounces back from all the surfaces in a room to the listener or the microphone. These bounces are called *reflections*. The combination of the direct and reflected sound in a room creates a distinct tonal character for each acoustical environment. Each one of the reflections in a room is like a single delay from a digital delay. When it bounces around the room, we get the effect of regeneration. When we take a single short delay and regenerate it many times, we're creating the basics of reverberation. Audio Example 2-39 demonstrates the unappealing sound of simulated reverb, using a single delay.

Audio Example 2-39 Simulated Reverb
CD-1: Track 38

Reverb must have many delays and regenerations combining at once to create a smooth and appealing room sound, as in Audio Example 2-41. Audio Example 2-40 demonstrates the smooth quality created by many delays working together in the proper balance.

Audio Example 2-40 Reverberation
CD-1: Track 38

If you can envision thousands of delays bouncing (reflecting) off thousands of surfaces in a room and then back to you, the listener, that's what's happening in the reverberation of a concert hall or any acoustical environment. There are so many reflections happening in such a complex order that we can no longer distinguish individual echoes. See Illustration 2-18 for a visual reference of a simple slapback delay and reverb in a room.

Our digital simulation of this process is accomplished by a digital reverb that produces enough delays and echoes to imitate the smooth sound of natural reverb in a room. The reason different reverb settings sound unique is because of the different combinations of delays and regenerations.

A digital reverb is capable of imitating a lot of different acoustical environments and can do so with amazing clarity and accuracy. The many different echoes and repeats produce a rich and full sound. Digital reverbs can also shape many special effects that would never occur acoustically. In fact, these sounds can be so fun to listen to that it's hard not to overuse reverb.

Keep in mind that sound perception is not just two dimensional, left and right. Sound perception is at least three dimensional, with the third dimension being depth (distance). Depth is created by the use of delays and reverb. If a sound (or a mix) has too much reverb, it loses the feeling of closeness or intimacy and sounds like it's at the far end of a gymnasium. Use enough effect to achieve the desired results, but don't overuse effects.

Most digital reverbs have several different reverb sounds available. These are usually labeled with descriptive names like halls, plates, chambers, rooms, etc.

Hall Reverb

Hall indicates a concert hall sound. These are the smoothest and richest of the reverb settings. Audio Example 2-41 demonstrates a Hall Reverb .

Illustration 2-18
Slapback Delay and Reflections

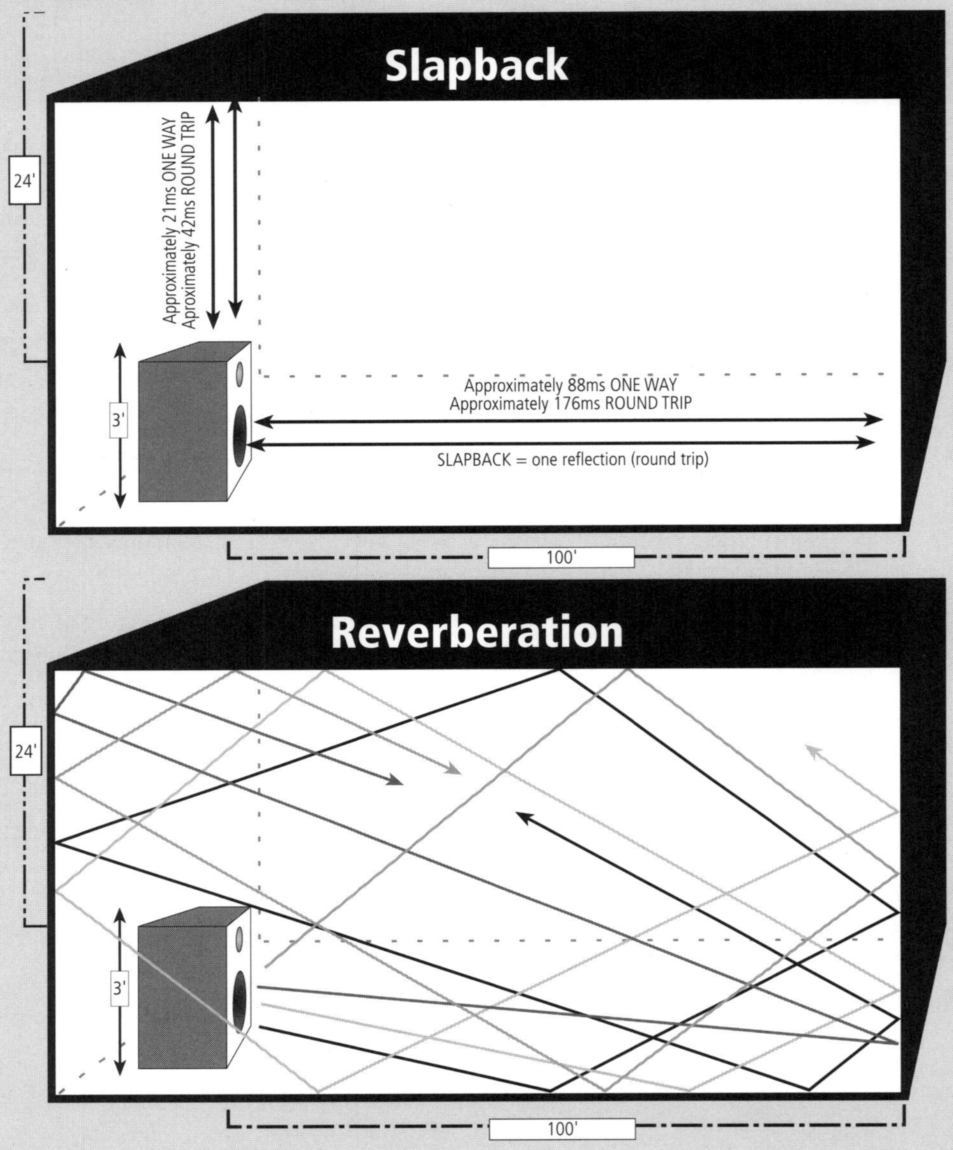

Slapback

24'

Approximately 21ms ONE WAY
Aproximately 42ms ROUND TRIP

3'

Approximately 88ms ONE WAY
Approximately 176ms ROUND TRIP

SLAPBACK = one reflection (round trip)

100'

Reverberation

24'

3'

100'

Sound travels at the rate of about 1130 ft./sec. To calculate the amount of time (in seconds) it takes for sound to travel a specific distance, divide the distance (in feet) by 1130 (ft./sec.): time = distance (ft.) ÷ speed (1130 ft./sec.).

In a 100' long room, sound takes about 88ms to get from one end to the other (100÷1130). A microphone at one end of this room wouldn't pick up the slapback until it completed a round trip (about 176ms after the original sound).

Audio Example 2-41 Hall Reverb
CD-1: Track 39

Chamber Reverb

Chambers imitate the sound of an acoustical reverberation chamber, sometimes called an echo chamber. Acoustical chambers are fairly large rooms with hard surfaces. Music is played into the room through high-quality, large speakers, and then a microphone in the chamber is patched into a channel of the mixer as an effects return. Chambers aren't very common now that technology is giving us great sounds without taking up so much real estate. The sound of a chamber is smooth, like the hall's, but has a few more mids and highs.

Audio Example 2-42 demonstrates the sound of a chamber reverb.

Audio Example 2-42 Chamber Reverb
CD-1: Track 39

Plate Reverb

Plates are the brightest sounding of the reverbs. These sounds imitate a true plate reverb. A *true plate* is a large sheet of metal (about 4' by 8') suspended in a box and allowed to vibrate freely. Sound is induced onto the plate by a speaker attached to the plate itself. Two contact microphones are typically mounted on the plate at different locations to give a stereo return to the mixer. The sound of a true plate reverb has lots of highs and is very clean and nonintrusive.

A digital simulation of the plate is also full of clean highs. Audio Example 2-43 demon-

strates a plate reverb sound.

Audio Example 2-43 Plate Reverb
CD-1: Track 39

Room Reverb

A room setting can imitate many different types of rooms that are typically smaller than the hall/chamber sounds. These can range from a bedroom to a large conference room or a small bathroom with lots of towels to a large bathroom with lots of tile.

Rooms with lots of soft surfaces have little high-frequency content in their reverberation. Rooms with lots of hard surfaces have lots of high-frequency in their reverberation.

Audio Example 2-44 demonstrates some different room sounds.

Audio Example 2-44 Room Reverb
CD-1: Track 39

Reverse Reverb

Most modern reverbs include *reverse* or *inverse reverb*. These are simply backwards reverb. After the original sound is heard, the reverb swells and stops. It is turned around. These can actually be fairly effective and useful if used in the appropriate context.

Audio Example 2-45 demonstrates reverse reverb.

Audio Example 2-45 Reverse Reverb
CD-1: Track 39

Illustration 2-19
Diffusion

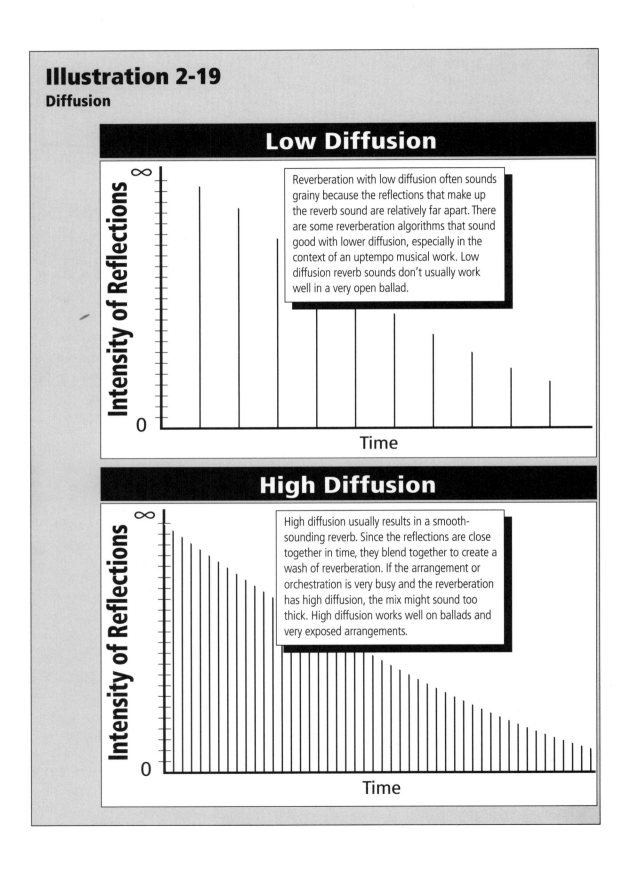

Low Diffusion

Reverberation with low diffusion often sounds grainy because the reflections that make up the reverb sound are relatively far apart. There are some reverberation algorithms that sound good with lower diffusion, especially in the context of an uptempo musical work. Low diffusion reverb sounds don't usually work well in a very open ballad.

High Diffusion

High diffusion usually results in a smooth-sounding reverb. Since the reflections are close together in time, they blend together to create a wash of reverberation. If the arrangement or orchestration is very busy and the reverberation has high diffusion, the mix might sound too thick. High diffusion works well on ballads and very exposed arrangements.

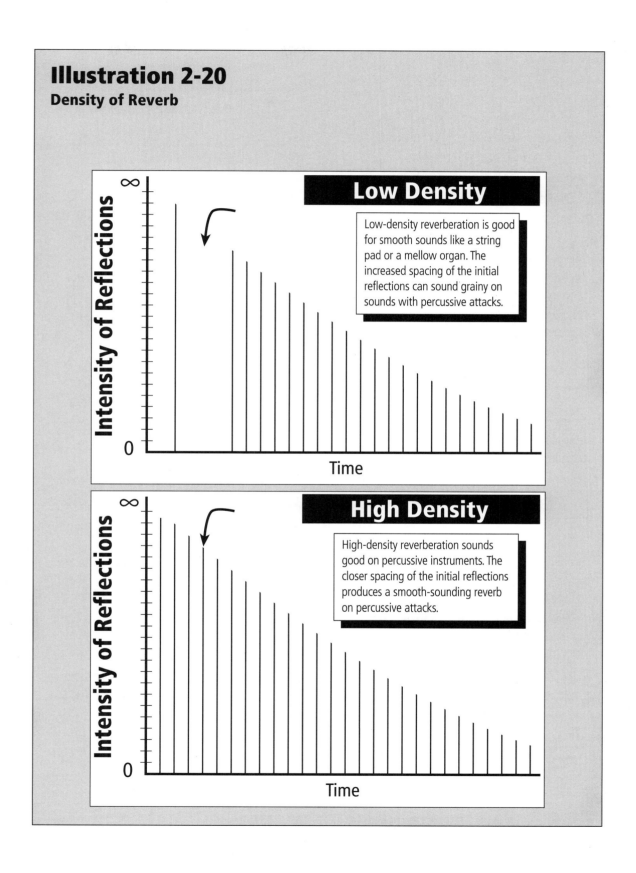

Illustration 2-20
Density of Reverb

Low Density

Low-density reverberation is good for smooth sounds like a string pad or a mellow organ. The increased spacing of the initial reflections can sound grainy on sounds with percussive attacks.

High Density

High-density reverberation sounds good on percussive instruments. The closer spacing of the initial reflections produces a smooth-sounding reverb on percussive attacks.

Gated Reverb

Gated reverbs have a sound that is very intense for a period of time, then closes off quickly. This has become very popular because it can give an instrument a very big sound without overwhelming the mix, because the gate keeps closing it off.

Though this is a trendy, popular sound, the technique has been around for a long time. The assignment on dynamic range processors (Illustration 2-13) can shed some light on how this sound evolved technically. Audio Example 2-46 demonstrates a gated reverb sound.

Audio Example 2-46 Gated Reverb
CD-1: Track 39

There are many variations of labels for reverb. You might see bright halls, rich plates, dark plates, large rooms, small rooms, or bright phone booth, but they can all be traced back to the basic sounds of halls, chambers, plates and rooms.

These sounds often have adjustable parameters. They let us shape the sounds to our music so that we can use the technology as completely as possible to enhance the artistic vision. We need to consider these variables so that we can customize and shape the effects.

Predelay

Predelay is a time delay that happens before the reverb is heard. This can be a substantial time delay (up to a second or two) or just a few milliseconds. The track is heard clean (dry) first, so the listener can get a more upfront feel; the reverb comes along shortly thereafter to fill in the holes and add richness. Listen to Audio Example 2-47 as the predelay setting is changed.

Audio Example 2-47 Predelay
CD-1: Track 40

Diffusion

Diffusion controls the space between the reflections (Illustration 2-19).

A low diffusion can be equated with a very grainy photograph. We might even hear individual repeats in the reverb.

A high diffusion can be equated with a very fine grain photograph, and the sound is a very smooth wash of reverb.

Listen to the reverberation in Audio Example 2-48 as the change is made from low diffusion to high diffusion.

Audio Example 2-48 Diffusion
CD-1: Track 41

Decay Time

Reverberation time, reverb time and decay time all refer to the same thing. Traditionally, reverberation time is defined as: *The time it takes for the sound to decrease to one-millionth of its original sound pressure level.* In other words, it's the time it takes for the reverb to go away.

Decay time can typically be adjusted from about 1/10 of a second up to about 99 seconds. We have ample control over the reverberation time. Audio Example 2-49 demonstrates a constant reverb sound with a changing decay time.

Audio Example 2-49 Decay Time
CD-1: Track 42

Density

The density control adjusts the initial short delay times. Low density is good for smooth sounds like strings or organ. High density works best on percussive sounds (Illustration 2-20).

In the recording world of yesteryear the only way to adjust reverberation time was to dampen or undampen the springs in the spring reverb tanks or physically move a bar that moved a felt pad onto, or off of, the plate reverb. Trying to control reverb time in a true reverberation chamber is even more difficult. Current technology provides a myriad of variables when shaping reverb sounds. In fact, when you consider the number of possible options, it can be mind boggling. We can design unnatural hybrids like a large room with a very short decay time and plenty of high frequency, or any other natural or unnatural effect.

Each parameter is important, and as we deal with individual guitar, drum, keyboard and vocal sounds, reverb is a primary consideration. If you expect to have professional-sounding recordings, you must use a digital reverb or, better yet, a multi-effects processor. A multi-effects processor contains many different reverb, delay and chorus sounds. These can usually be used separately or chained together to form thousands of interesting effects.

Conclusion

We have just covered the basic signal processors. There are more options to deal with as we expand our knowledge and skill base, but having a good working relationship of the dynamic range processors, delay effects, EQ and reverbs is essential. If you can operate these fundamental tools, you can shape and mold your own unique sounds.

If all this is new to you, then you have a lot of work ahead of you. There's a lot to absorb, so please review these chapters as many times as it takes to get a solid grasp of the information. If you understand (and apply) these principles and techniques, you're building an excellent foundation for recording your music.

Chapter 3 Microphones

Microphones: Our Primary Tools

The study of microphones is a complete course of its own. For our purposes, we must understand some basic principles and techniques in order to be functional in the recording industry. This chapter will familiarize you with basic principles and terminology. There are many other excellent sources available that cover the study of microphones in depth, but this chapter of *The AudioPro Home Recording Course*, along with the practical applications throughout, will provide a solid foundation for you.

The microphone is your primary tool in the chain from sound source to audio storage medium. There's much more to mic choice than finding a trusted manufacturer that you can stick with. There's much more to mic placement than simply setting the mic close to the sound source. The difference between mediocre audio recordings and exemplary audio recordings is quite often defined by the choice and placement of microphones.

As we cover techniques for recording different instruments, we'll consistently need to consider microphone choice and technique. The MIDI era led us away from the art of acoustic recording but as time has proceeded, acoustic recordings of drums, guitars, strings, brass, percussion and sound effects have returned. There is a kind of life to an acoustic recording that can only truly exist through recording real instruments played by real people in an acoustical environment.

We can increase the life in our MIDI sounds by running them into an amplification system, then miking that sound. We might or might not need to include the direct sound of the MIDI sound module.

Using a mic to capture sound is not as simple as just selecting the best mic. There are two critically important factors involved in capturing sound using a microphone:

- Where we place the mic in relation to the sound source
- The acoustical environment in which we choose to record the sound source

As you'll see in the audio examples in this course, the sound of the acoustical environment plays a very important role in the overall sound quality.

Although there are hundreds of different microphones available from a lot of manufacturers, they essentially all fit into three basic categories: condenser, moving-coil and ribbon. Condenser and moving-coil mics are the most common of these three, although they may all be used in recording, as well as live, situations.

There are other types of microphones with operating principles that differ from what we will cover in this course, and each type of microphone has its own individual personality. Mic types other than condenser, moving-coil and ribbon are usually selected for a special effect in a situation where the music needs a unique sound that enhances the emotional impact of the song.

Condenser Microphones

Condenser microphones are the most accurate. They respond to fast attacks and transients more precisely than other types, and they typically add the least amount of tonal coloration. The large vocal mics used in professional recording studios are usually examples of condenser mics. Condenser mics also come in much smaller sizes and interesting shapes. Some popular condenser mics are:

- Neumann U87, U89, U47, U67, TLM170, KM83, KM84, KM184, TLM193
- AKG 414, 451, 391, 535, C1000, 460, C3000, C-12, The Tube
- Electro-Voice BK-1
- Sennheiser MKH 40, MKH 80
- B&K 4011
- Shure SM82, BG4.0
- Audio-Technica 4033, 4050, 4051, 853
- Milab DC96B
- Schoeps CMC 5U
- Groove Tube MD-2, MD-3
- Sanken CU-41
- Crown PZM-30D

Use a condenser microphone whenever you want to accurately capture the true sound of a voice or instrument. Condensers are almost always preferred when recording:

- acoustic guitar
- acoustic piano
- vocals
- real brass
- real strings
- woodwinds
- percussion
- acoustic room ambience

Condenser microphones (especially in omni configuration) typically capture a broader range of frequencies from a greater distance than the other mic types. In other words, you don't need to be as close to the sound source to get a full sound. This trait of condenser microphones is a great advantage in the recording studio because it enables us to record a full sound while still including some of the natural ambience in a room. The further the mic is from the sound source, the more influential the ambience is on the recorded sound.

Condenser microphones that work wonderfully in the studio often provide poor results in a live sound reinforcement situation. Since they have a flat frequency response, these condenser mics tend to feed back more quickly than microphones designed specifically for live sound applications (especially in the low-frequency range). There are many condenser mics designed for sound reinforcement, and there are many condenser mics that work very well in either setting. Condenser mics often have a low-frequency roll-off switch that lets you decrease low-frequency sensitivity. In a live audio situation, the low-frequency roll-off is effective in reducing low-frequency feedback.

Operating Principle of the Condenser Mic

If you possess the basic understanding of each mic type and if you have a grasp on how each type works, you'll be able to make very good microphone selections. The microphone you select for your specific recording situation makes a big difference on the sound of the final recording. It's almost pathetic how easy it is to get great sounds when you've selected the right mic for the job and you've run the mic through a high quality preamp.

Condenser mics operate on a fairly simple premise. A charged (positive or negative) electrical current is applied to a metal-coated piece of plastic. The plastic is a little like the plastic wrap you keep on your leftover food. The metallic coating is thin enough to vibrate in response to sound waves. Its function is to provide conductivity for the electrical charge while not inhibiting the flexibility of the plastic membrane. The ingredients of the alloy vary from manufacturer to manufacturer, but the key factor is conductivity—it must be able to carry an electrical charge.

The metal-coated plastic will vibrate when it's subjected to an audio wave because of sympathetic vibration. The principle of *sympathetic vibration* says, if it is possible for a surface to vibrate at a specific frequency, it will vibrate when it is in the presence of a sound wave containing that frequency. The metal-coated plastic membrane in a condenser microphone should be able to sympathetically vibrate when in the presence of any audio wave in our audible frequency spectrum.

This metal-coated piece of plastic is positioned close to a solid piece of metallic alloy. The electrical charge starts to accumulate between the two metallic surfaces. As the crest and trough of a sound wave meet the thinly coated plastic, the plastic vibrates sympathetically with the sound wave. As the plastic vibrates, the area between the solid metal surface and the moveable metal surface changes. These changes in the space between the surfaces create a dis-

charge of electrical current. This discharge exactly represents the changing energy in the sound wave. In other words, you have an electrical version of the acoustic energy you started with at the sound source (Illustration 3-1).

Since there is very little mass in the condenser microphone's metal-coated membrane, it responds very quickly and accurately when in the presence of sound. Therefore, the condenser capsule is very good at capturing sounds with high transient content as well as sounds with interesting complexities.

The signal that comes from the capsule is very weak and must be amplified to mic level. Then, once the signal from the mic reaches the mixer, it's boosted to line level at the input preamp.

Phantom Power

The capsule of a condenser microphone requires power to charge the metal-coated membrane. Power is also required to amplify the signal from the capsule up to microphone level.

It's a technical fact that each condenser microphone needs power to operate. The source of power for a condenser mic can come from a power supply in the mixer (called phantom power) that sends power up the mic cable, from an external phantom power supply or from a battery within the mic. If you use batteries to power a condenser mic, always be sure the batteries are fresh and that they're supplying sufficient voltage to optimally run the microphone's circuitry. Phantom power is the best way to supply power to a condenser microphone because it's constant and predictable.

Phantom power is sent to the microphone from the mixer or external phantom power supply through the mic cable. There is little electri-

Illustration 3-1
The Condenser Mic Capsule

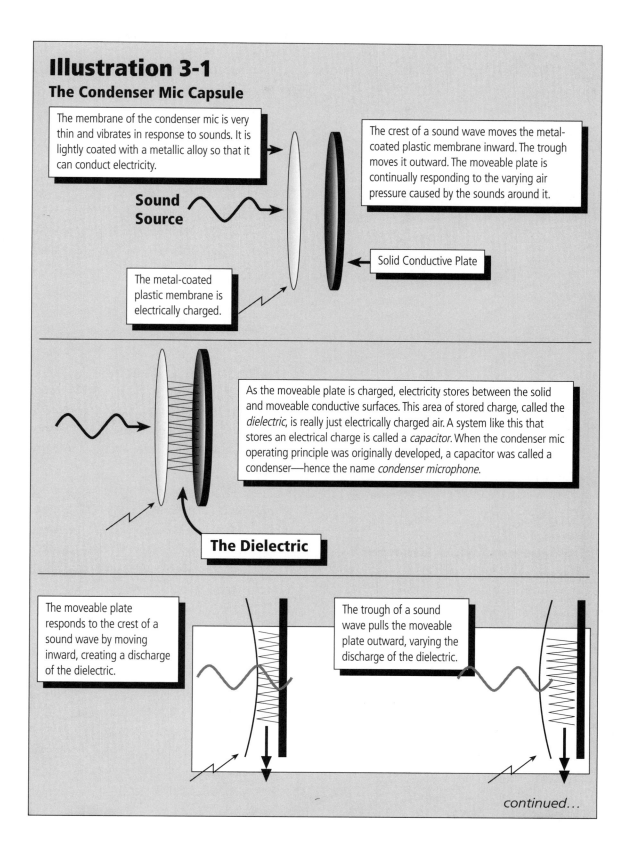

The membrane of the condenser mic is very thin and vibrates in response to sounds. It is lightly coated with a metallic alloy so that it can conduct electricity.

The crest of a sound wave moves the metal-coated plastic membrane inward. The trough moves it outward. The moveable plate is continually responding to the varying air pressure caused by the sounds around it.

Sound Source

The metal-coated plastic membrane is electrically charged.

Solid Conductive Plate

As the moveable plate is charged, electricity stores between the solid and moveable conductive surfaces. This area of stored charge, called the *dielectric*, is really just electrically charged air. A system like this that stores an electrical charge is called a *capacitor*. When the condenser mic operating principle was originally developed, a capacitor was called a condenser—hence the name *condenser microphone*.

The Dielectric

The moveable plate responds to the crest of a sound wave by moving inward, creating a discharge of the dielectric.

The trough of a sound wave pulls the moveable plate outward, varying the discharge of the dielectric.

continued...

Illustration 3-1
...continued

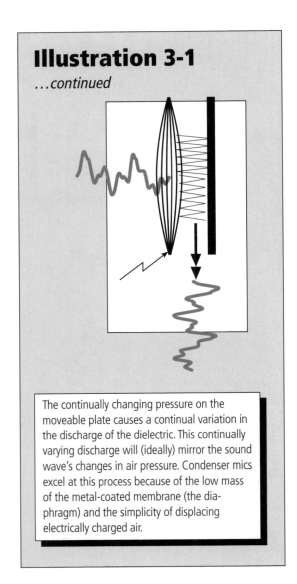

The continually changing pressure on the moveable plate causes a continual variation in the discharge of the dielectric. This continually varying discharge will (ideally) mirror the sound wave's changes in air pressure. Condenser mics excel at this process because of the low mass of the metal-coated membrane (the diaphragm) and the simplicity of displacing electrically charged air.

cal danger to the user since phantom power is low voltage and very low amperage DC current. In addition, phantom power has no adverse effect on the audio signal being carried by the mic cable.

Moving-coil Mics

Moving-coil mics are the standard choice for most live situations, but they are also very use-ful in the studio. Here are some examples of popular and trustworthy moving-coil microphones:

- Shure SM57, SM58, SM7
- Electro-Voice RE20
- Sennheiser 421, 441
- Audio-Technica ATM25, Pro-25
- AKG D12, D112, D3500, D1000E
- Beyer M88

Moving-coil mics are the most durable of all the mic types. They also withstand the most volume before they distort within their own circuitry.

A moving-coil mic typically colors a sound more than a condenser mic. This coloration usually falls in the frequency range between about 5kHz and 10kHz. As long as we realize that this coloration is present, we can use it to our advantage. In our studies on EQ, we've found that this frequency range can add clarity, presence and understandability to many vocal and instrumental sounds.

Moving-coil mics have a thin sound when they are more than about a foot from the sound source. They're usually used in close-mic applications, with the mic placed anywhere from less than an inch from the sound source up to about 12 inches from the sound source.

Since moving-coil mics can withstand a lot of volume, they sound the best in close-mic applications; and since they add high-frequency edge, they're good choices for miking electric guitar speaker cabinets, bass drum, snare drum, toms or any loud instrument that benefits from close-mic technique. Use them when you want to capture lots of sound with lots of edge from a close distance and aren't as concerned about subtle nuance and literal accuracy of the original waveform.

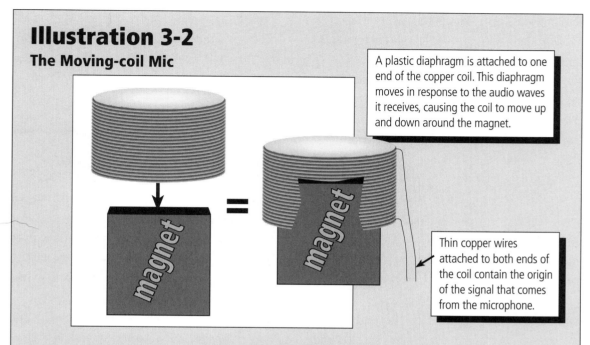

Illustration 3-2
The Moving-coil Mic

A plastic diaphragm is attached to one end of the copper coil. This diaphragm moves in response to the audio waves it receives, causing the coil to move up and down around the magnet.

Thin copper wires attached to both ends of the coil contain the origin of the signal that comes from the microphone.

Copper wire is wrapped into a cylinder. This cylinder is then suspended around a magnet. The copper coil moves up and down in response to pressure changes caused by sound waves.

The crest of the audio wave moves the coil down, causing a change in the coil magnetism. The trough of the audio wave moves the coil up, again causing a change in the coil magnetism.

As the coil moves around the magnet it receives a continually varying magnetic image. The continually varying magnetism will ideally mirror the changing air pressure from the sound wave. This continually varying magnetism is the origin of the signal that arrives at the mixer's mic input.

Moving-coils are also used in live performances for vocals. They work well in close miking situations, add high-frequency clarity and are very durable.

Operating Principle of the Moving-coil Mic

A moving-coil microphone operates on a completely magnetic principle in contrast to the electrical complexities of the condenser mic. When an object that can be magnetized is moved around a magnet, there is a change in the energy within the magnet. There is also a continual variation in the magnetic status of the object moving in relation to the magnet. The moving-coil microphone uses this fact to transfer the changing air pressure, produced by an audio waveform, into a continually varying flow of electrons that can be received by the mic preamp.

In a moving-coil mic, a coil of thin copper wire is suspended over a magnet, enabling the coil to move up and down around the magnet.

A thin mylar plastic diaphragm closes the top of the coil and serves to receive the audio waves. As the crests and troughs of the continually varying audio waveform reach the diaphragm, the coil is forced to move around the magnet. The movement of the copper coil around the magnet is what causes the changing flow of electrons that represent the sound wave (Illustration 3-2).

The moving-coil microphone uses a much more mechanical process than the delicately sensitive condenser mic. Since there's a larger mass to move than in the condenser operating principle, it makes sense that the moving-coil microphone doesn't respond as quickly to transients as the condenser mic and that the moving-coil microphone doesn't catch all of the subtle nuances that the condenser microphone excels in.

Though moving-coil mics don't excel in capturing transients and subtleties, you can still take advantage of their tendencies and characteristics. And, since moving-coil mics operate on a magnetic principle, they don't require power to operate.

Ribbon Mics

Ribbon mics are the most fragile of all the mic types. This one factor makes them less useful in a live sound reinforcement application, even though ribbon mics produced within the last 10 or 15 years are much more durable than the older classic ribbon mics.

These mics are like moving-coil mics in that they color the sound source by adding a high-frequency edge, and they generally have a thin sound when used in a distant miking setup. When used as a close-mic, ribbon microphones

Illustration 3-3
The Ribbon Mic

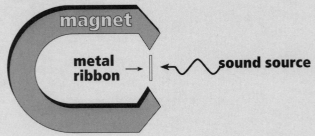

A thin metal ribbon suspended between two poles of a magnet vibrates in response to each crest and trough of a sound wave. As the ribbon moves in the magnetic field, it continually varies in its magnetism. These changes of magnetism are the origin of the signal that is sent to the mic input of your mixer.

The signal produced by the ribbon is typically weaker than the signal produced by the moving-coil. In practical terms, that means you'll usually need more preamplification at the mic input to achieve a satisfactory line level signal.

Illustration 3-4
Cardioid Pickup Pattern

A microphone with a cardioid pickup pattern hears sound best from the front and actively rejects sounds from behind. With its heart-shaped pickup pattern, you can point the mic toward the sound you want to record and away from the sound you don't want to record.

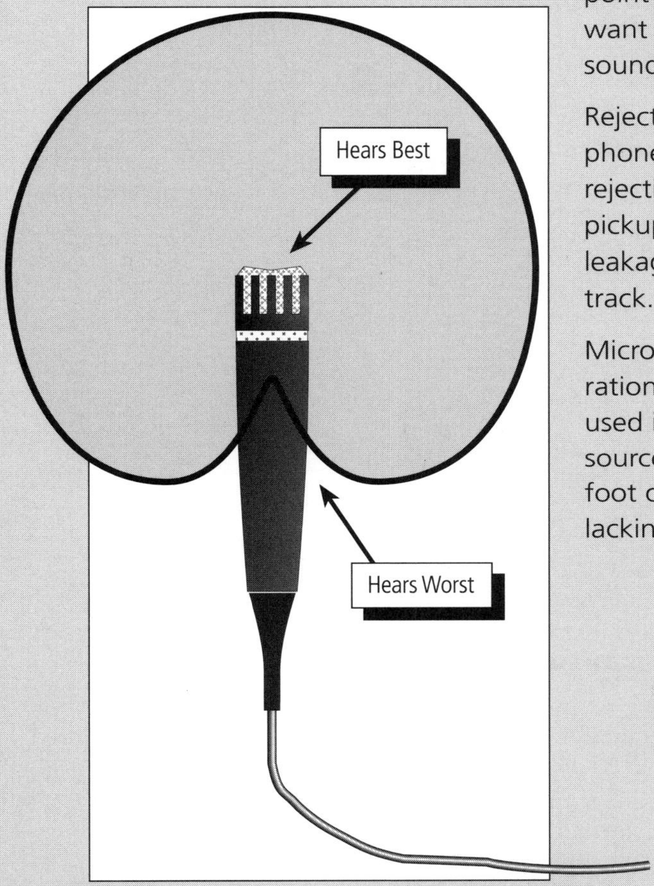

Rejection of sound behind the microphone isn't complete or total, but the rejection characteristic of a cardioid pickup pattern can help minimize leakage of unwanted sounds onto a track.

Microphones with this pickup configuration are typically most accurate when used in close proximity to the sound source. From a distance of more than a foot or so, they usually sound thin, lacking low-frequency content.

Hears Best

Hears Worst

can have a full sound that is often described as being warmer and smoother than a moving-coil.

There are some great sounding ribbon microphones available. Some of the commonly used ribbon microphones are:
• Beyer M160, M500

• RCA 77-DX, 44 BY, 10001

Ribbon mics are fragile and need to be used in situations where they won't be dropped or jostled. If you use a ribbon mic to record drums and the drummer hits the mic too many times with his stick, the ribbon will break. Repairs like this can be costly. After breaking a couple of these mics, I decided it might be best if I stuck to one of the tried and true, very durable choices. I still tend to use the Beyer M160 ribbon a lot when I'm recording drum samples because I like the sound, but sampling is a very controlled mic usage, and I'm usually the only one around with a drum stick.

Operating Principle of the Ribbon Mic

A ribbon microphone operates on a magnetic principle like the moving-coil. A metallic ribbon is suspended between two poles of a magnet.

As the sound wave vibrates the thin ribbon, the magnetic flow changes in response, causing a continually varying flow of electrons. As the ribbon moves between the poles of the magnet, it is being magnetized in varying degrees of north and south magnetism, in direct proportion to the changes in amplitude produced by the sound wave. This continually varying flow of electrons is the origin of the signal that reaches the microphone input of your mixer (Illustration 3-3).

Since ribbon mics operate on a magnetic principle, they don't require a power source to operate.

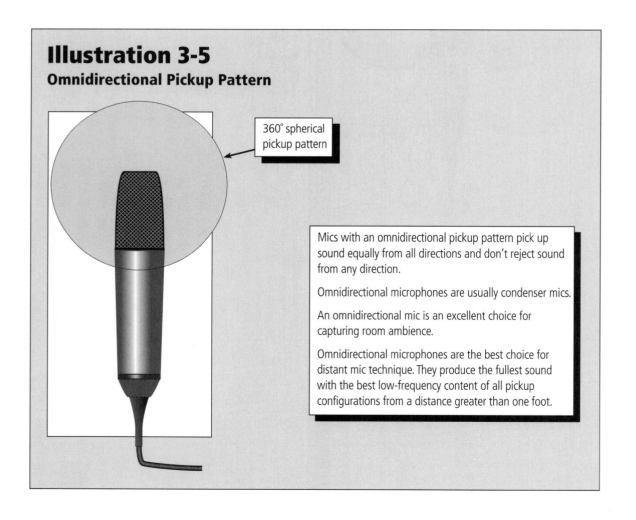

Illustration 3-5
Omnidirectional Pickup Pattern

360° spherical pickup pattern

Mics with an omnidirectional pickup pattern pick up sound equally from all directions and don't reject sound from any direction.

Omnidirectional microphones are usually condenser mics.

An omnidirectional mic is an excellent choice for capturing room ambience.

Omnidirectional microphones are the best choice for distant mic technique. They produce the fullest sound with the best low-frequency content of all pickup configurations from a distance greater than one foot.

Pickup/Polar Patterns

Cardioid

Most microphones have what is called a cardioid pickup pattern. This is also called a unidirectional or heart-shaped pickup pattern. The unidirectional mic is most sensitive (hears the best) at the part of the mic that you sing into. It is least sensitive (hears the worst) at the side opposite the part you sing into (Illustration 3-4). The advantage to using a microphone with a cardioid pickup pattern lies in the ability to isolate sounds. You can point the mic at one instrument while you're pointing it away from another instrument. The disadvantage to a cardioid pickup pattern is that it will typically only give you a full sound from a close proximity to the sound source. Once you're a foot or two away from the sound source a cardioid pickup pattern produces a very thin-sounding rendition of the sound you're miking.

In a live sound setting, cardioid mics are almost always best because they produce far less feedback than any other pickup pattern.

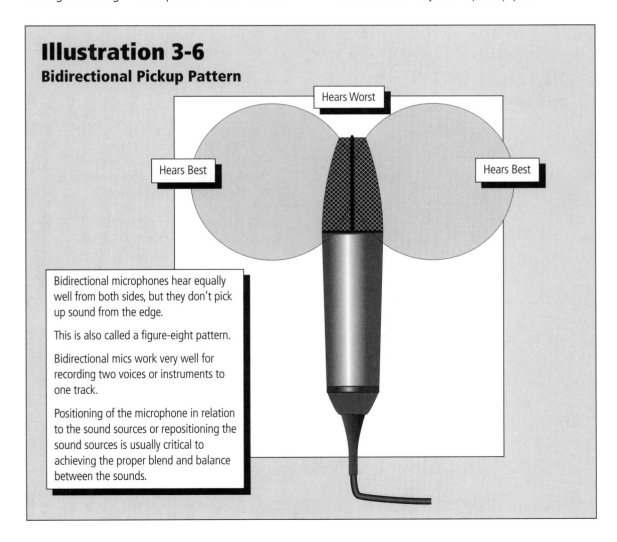

Illustration 3-6
Bidirectional Pickup Pattern

Hears Worst

Hears Best

Hears Best

Bidirectional microphones hear equally well from both sides, but they don't pick up sound from the edge.

This is also called a figure-eight pattern.

Bidirectional mics work very well for recording two voices or instruments to one track.

Positioning of the microphone in relation to the sound sources or repositioning the sound sources is usually critical to achieving the proper blend and balance between the sounds.

We should be familiar with two other basic pickup patterns: omnidirectional and bidirectional.

Omnidirectional

An omnidirectional mic hears equally from all directions. It doesn't reject sound from anywhere (Illustration 3-5). An omnidirectional pickup pattern will give you the fullest sound from a distance. Omni microphones are very good at capturing room ambience, recording groups of instruments that you can gather around one mic and capturing a vocal performance while still letting the acoustics of the room interact with the sound of the voice.

Omnidirectional microphones are usually difficult in a live setting because they produce feedback more quickly than any other pickup pattern.

Bidirectional

Bidirectional microphones hear equally from the sides, but they don't hear from the edges (Illustration 3-6). Bidirectional microphones are an excellent choice for recording two sound sources to one track with the most intimacy and least adverse phase interaction and room sound. Position the mic between the sound sources for

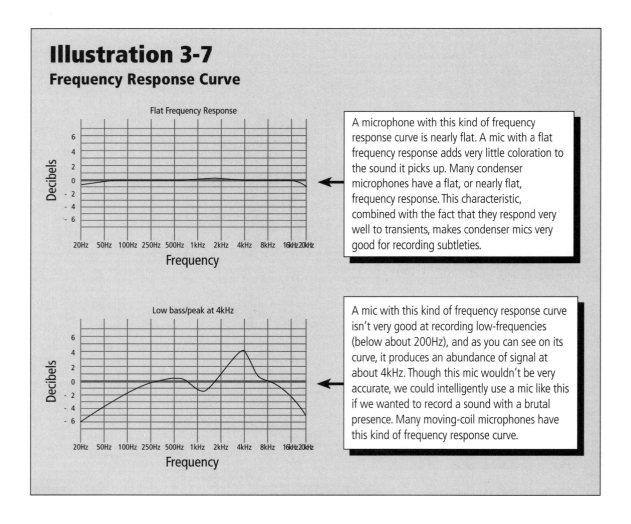

Illustration 3-7
Frequency Response Curve

Flat Frequency Response

A microphone with this kind of frequency response curve is nearly flat. A mic with a flat frequency response adds very little coloration to the sound it picks up. Many condenser microphones have a flat, or nearly flat, frequency response. This characteristic, combined with the fact that they respond very well to transients, makes condenser mics very good for recording subtleties.

Low bass/peak at 4kHz

A mic with this kind of frequency response curve isn't very good at recording low-frequencies (below about 200Hz), and as you can see on its curve, it produces an abundance of signal at about 4kHz. Though this mic wouldn't be very accurate, we could intelligently use a mic like this if we wanted to record a sound with a brutal presence. Many moving-coil microphones have this kind of frequency response curve.

the best blend. Once you've committed the sound to one tape track, there's not much you can do to fix a bad balance or blend.

Frequency Response Curve

Almost any microphone responds to all frequencies we can hear plus frequencies above and below what we can hear. The human ear has a typical frequency response range of about 20Hz to 20kHz. Some folks have high-frequency hearing loss so they might not hear sound waves all the way up to 20kHz, and some small children might be able to hear sounds well above 20kHz.

For a manufacturer to tell us that their microphone has a frequency range of 20Hz to 20kHz tells us absolutely nothing until they tell us how the mic responds throughout that frequency range. A mic might respond very well to 500Hz, yet it might not respond very well at all to frequencies above about 10kHz. If that were the case, the sound we captured to tape with that mic would be severely colored.

We use a frequency response curve to indicate exactly how a specific microphone responds to the frequencies across the audible spectrum (Illustration 3-7). If a frequency response curve shows a peak at 5kHz, we can expect that the mic will color the sound in the highs, likely producing a sound that has a little more aggressive sound than if a mic with a flat response was used. If the frequency response curve shows the low-frequencies dropping off sharply below 300Hz we can expect the mic to sound thin in the low end unless we move it close to the sound source to proportionally increase the lows.

The frequency response curve is one of the most valuable tools to help us predict how a mic will sound. What the frequency response curve doesn't tell us is how the mic responds to transients. We can predict the transient response of a mic based on what we already know about the basic operating principles of the different mic types.

Conclusion

You can cover most home recording situations if you have at least one good moving-coil mic and one good condenser mic. With these two options available, you can fairly consistently achieve professional-sounding results.

This chapter was written with the intent to provide fundamental information that will immediately help you understand the practical applications of the three basic microphone types you use in the studio. It was not written with the intent to be the end-all authority on microphones. The upcoming chapters all present specific microphone applications and techniques as they apply to practical recording situations. Once you've completed the entire course, you'll have a very good working knowledge of specific microphone choice, technique, placement and recording in general.

Chapter 4 Guitars and Guitar Sounds

Recording Guitars

In this chapter, we cover recording techniques for five different types of guitar sounds:

- Electric guitars plugged directly into the mixer
- Electric guitars miked at the amplifier
- Electric acoustic guitars, plugged directly into the mixer
- Acoustic guitars recorded with a microphone
- Guitar samples from a keyboard

Recorded guitar sounds, whether electric or acoustic, can be very dependent on:

- The instrument's condition and intonation
- The technical and artistic ability of the performer
- The microphone used to record the instrument
- The acoustics of the room in which the guitar or amp is recorded
- Choice of dynamic range processing
- Choice of effects processing
- Volume
- EQ
- Panning placement in the mix

We'll evaluate how each of these important factors influence the recorded sounds of the guitar family. Listen to the Audio Examples several times, thoroughly read all text and practice these techniques in your own setup. It'll make a difference in the sound of your recordings.

Let's get started on our study of recording guitars. We'll use everything we've studied so far. In addition, we'll add mic techniques and acoustic considerations.

Direct Electric

When recording an electric guitar, we have the option of using a microphone at the speaker, running directly into the mixer or combining both of these approaches. Each technique offers advantages and disadvantages. Running direct into the mixer produces ultimate separation. If you process the direct guitar sound, you don't risk altering the sound of another instrument since no other instrument has had the opportunity to bleed into a microphone.

Miking the guitarist's speaker cabinet, although allowing for leakage of another instrument into the guitar mic, typically produces the best sound. Using a microphone on the electric guitarist's cabinet captures the essence of the sound the guitarist designed for the part they're playing. Since sound plays such an important role in what and how a guitarist plays, miking the cabinet is often the only way to capture the guitar part in a musically authentic way.

For the sake of understanding some of the more fundamental variables involved in recording the electric guitar, we'll first plug directly into the mixer. When running a guitar directly into the mic input of a mixer, plug the guitar

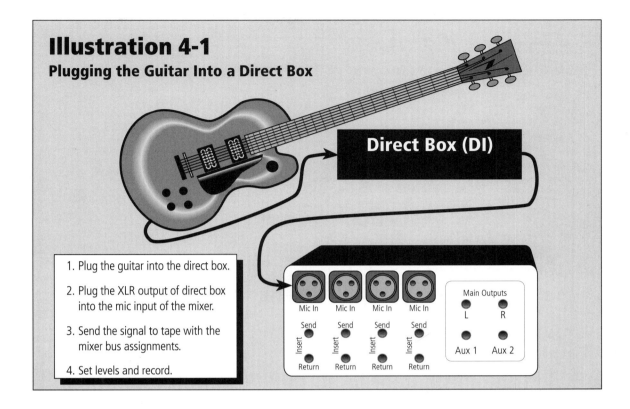

Illustration 4-1
Plugging the Guitar Into a Direct Box

Direct Box (DI)

1. Plug the guitar into the direct box.

2. Plug the XLR output of direct box into the mic input of the mixer.

3. Send the signal to tape with the mixer bus assignments.

4. Set levels and record.

Mic In   Mic In   Mic In   Mic In

Send   Send   Send   Send

Insert   Insert   Insert   Insert

Return   Return   Return   Return

Main Outputs
L   R

Aux 1   Aux 2

into a direct box first, then plug the direct box into the mixer (Illustration 4-1). The signal going into the direct box can come straight from the guitar or from any effect or group of effects that the guitar is plugged into (Illustration 4-2).

As an alternative, simply plug the guitar straight into the line input of the mixer (Illustration 4-3). When using this technique, the level from the guitar might be a little low, especially if you are using a mixer that operates at +4dBm. Plugging a guitar into Line In works best when using a mixer operating at -10dBV. (Refer to Chapter 1 for a description of +4 and -10 operating levels).

Some guitar amps have a line output. Line Out from a guitar amplifier can be plugged directly into the line input of the mixer (Illustration 4-4). This technique lets you capture some of the amplifier's characteristic sound while still keeping the advantages of running direct into the mixer.

Advantages of Running Direct

When you plug directly into the mixer instead of miking the speaker, the recorded track has no leakage from other acoustic instruments that may have been performing at the same time as the guitar. The tracks typically contain less noise than if the amp were miked. Guitar amps have a bad habit of producing their own share of noise. This can be a problem in mixdown.

Sometimes you must run directly into the mixer simply out of consideration for your neighbors. How sensitive are your neighbors to loud guitar amps screaming raucous licks into the wee hours of the morning? Once you've gotten your neighbors angry because of volume, it's all over. It's best to avoid that conflict altogether. If you

Illustration 4-2
Guitar Through Several Effects

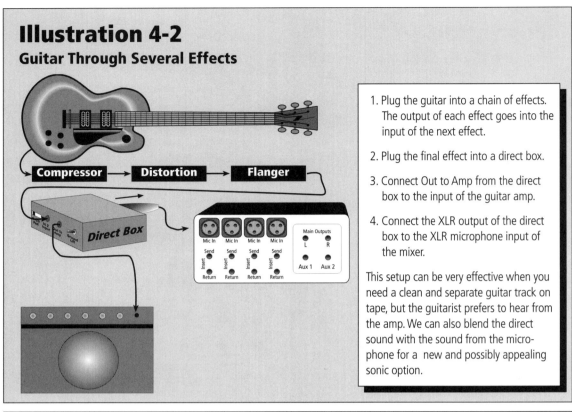

1. Plug the guitar into a chain of effects. The output of each effect goes into the input of the next effect.

2. Plug the final effect into a direct box.

3. Connect Out to Amp from the direct box to the input of the guitar amp.

4. Connect the XLR output of the direct box to the XLR microphone input of the mixer.

This setup can be very effective when you need a clean and separate guitar track on tape, but the guitarist prefers to hear from the amp. We can also blend the direct sound with the sound from the microphone for a new and possibly appealing sonic option.

Illustration 4-3
Guitar and Effects to Line Input

1. Plug the guitar directly into the line input of the mixer or plug the guitar into an effects unit.

2. Plug the output of the effects into the line input of the mixer.

The success of this procedure depends largely on the kind of sound you're recording. Distorted, aggressive sounds are best recorded with a mic on the speaker cabinet. Clean guitar sounds with a little compression, chorus and delay often sound very good when run directly into the mixer.

The strength of the signal produced by the guitar is also a factor. Depending on your guitar, mixer and effects, you might experience difficulty getting enough level from the guitar setup to record at 0VU. If you can't get enough level from this configuration, use the setup in Illustration 4-1.

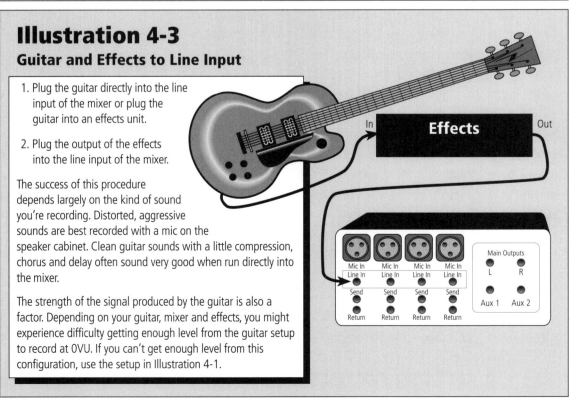

Illustration 4-4
Amplifier Line Output to Mixer Line Input

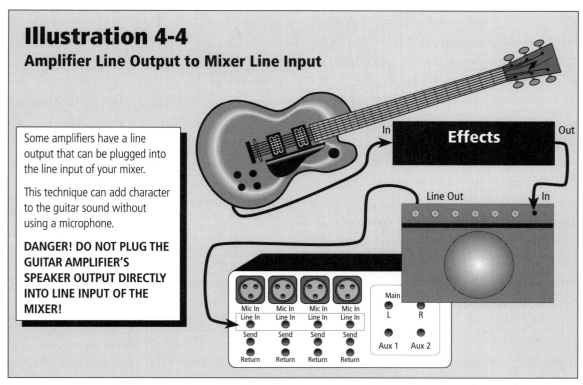

Some amplifiers have a line output that can be plugged into the line input of your mixer.

This technique can add character to the guitar sound without using a microphone.

DANGER! DO NOT PLUG THE GUITAR AMPLIFIER'S SPEAKER OUTPUT DIRECTLY INTO LINE INPUT OF THE MIXER!

Illustration 4-5
Speaker Output Into a Special Direct Box

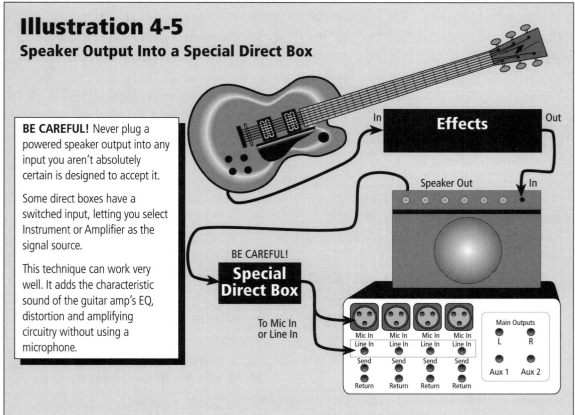

BE CAREFUL! Never plug a powered speaker output into any input you aren't absolutely certain is designed to accept it.

Some direct boxes have a switched input, letting you select Instrument or Amplifier as the signal source.

This technique can work very well. It adds the characteristic sound of the guitar amp's EQ, distortion and amplifying circuitry without using a microphone.

are recording in an apartment or in a compact residential area, you may have no choice but to record all electronic gear direct and monitor at low levels.

If you must run direct into the mixer and you're experiencing difficulty getting a good sound, try using a direct box that will receive a powered signal straight out of the speaker output of the guitar amp. This will give you the most guitar amp sound you can get without using a mic. Be careful!! **Never plug a speaker output into any input until you've been assured by someone whose opinion you trust implicitly that the input is designed to accept a powered output** (Illustration 4-5)**!**

Remember, guitars are high-impedance instruments and the total length of cables between the guitar and the amp or the guitar and the direct box should be less than 25 feet. If the guitarist plugs into several effects chained together, then plugs the output of the last effect into the DI, be sure the cables are all as short as possible. If the cables are too long, you'll hear a lot of noise and radio interference along with the guitar track.

If you get into a situation where the guitarist needs to run a long cable length from the guitar to the amp, try this:

1. Use two direct boxes. Plug the guitar into the high-impedance end of the first direct box.
2. Connect a mic cable to the low-impedance output of that direct box.
3. Connect the other end of this mic cable to the low-impedance end of the second direct box. This requires either a special cable with female XLR connectors on both ends or a female-to-female XLR adapter to plug into the low-impedance end of the second DI.
4. Connect the high-impedance end of the sec-

ond DI to the amp or line in of the mixer.

This procedure lets you take advantage of low impedance within a high-impedance system (Illustration 4-6).

If you're connecting two direct boxes together, be sure to use high quality DIs. Each transformer can rob the signal of life and add noise. This technique requires informed judgment concerning the value of adding cable length versus your need for sonic purity.

Levels

When we record guitars, the VU meter should usually read 0VU at the peaks. There can be a couple of exceptions to this rule.

Distorted guitar sounds are often printed very hot to tape (in the neighborhood of +3 to +5 on the VU meter). Some engineers believe that this adds a little more edge to the part and that the tape being oversaturated has the effect of compressing the sound. This compression helps keep the part in a tighter dynamic range so it can be heard more consistently.

Be careful when recording hot to tape. The signal could become too distorted. You might print so much signal on tape that it begins to spill onto the adjacent tracks as well as onto the track you're trying to record on. The tape recorder and size of tape determine whether or not you can successfully print stronger than normal signals to tape. 8-track cassettes are usually less forgiving than larger formats, like 16 or 24 tracks on 2-inch wide tape.

Transients

If the strings of a guitar are plucked with a hard pick, there are transients in their sound. The extent of the transient depends on the specific instrument, type of guitar pick and the strings.

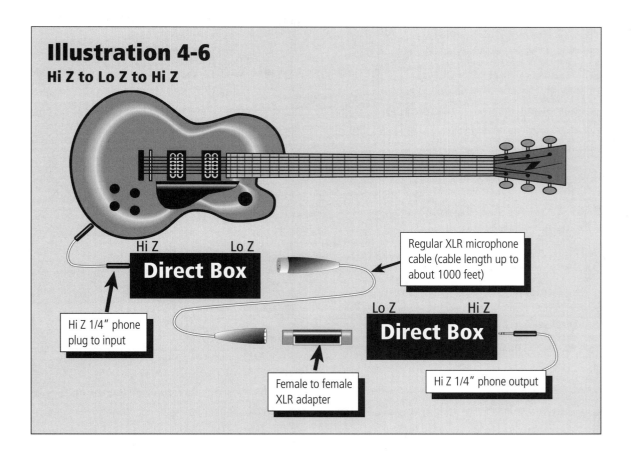

Illustration 4-6
Hi Z to Lo Z to Hi Z

Hi Z   Lo Z

Direct Box

Regular XLR microphone cable (cable length up to about 1000 feet)

Hi Z 1/4" phone plug to input

Lo Z   Hi Z

Direct Box

Female to female XLR adapter

Hi Z 1/4" phone output

Some acoustic guitar parts contain an exaggerated transient because of the way they've been compressed. These parts need to be recorded with especially conservative levels, in order to compensate for the increased transient attack. In Chapter 1 we discovered that transients have an actual level that is higher than the VU reading and that the actual level could be 9dB above the average level.

Even though guitar can have transient content, we don't usually need to be overly cautious in adjusting the record level. Most acoustic parts can be recorded with the loudest part of the track reading at 0VU. An acoustic often has substantial low-frequency content. The lows can actually determine the recording level, so if you record a full sounding guitar up to 0VU you'll usually produce a good sounding track. If the sound doesn't contain much low-frequency energy and has a lot of highs with exaggerated transients, the record level should not read higher than -7 to -5VU.

You must weigh your options. If you record at low levels to capture the most accurate transient, you might end up with a poor signal-to-noise ratio. If you record with hotter levels, you might lose some of the accuracy of the recording, but we'll have a better signal-to-noise ratio. It's up to you, the engineer, to decide which approach to take based on the music you're recording.

Tuning/Instrument Selection

Whenever you record an instrument, your first

consideration should be the status of the instrument. Guitar is definitely no exception to this rule. Does it sound good by itself? Are the strings new or old? Is the instrument in tune? Has the intonation of the neck been fine-tuned? Do the notes stay in tune up and down the neck on all strings? Are the electronics within the instrument operating properly?

A guitar with good electronics that's been set up properly has a definite sound advantage over a guitar that has slid away from its peak performance. Correct tuning and intonation give the instrument a wonderful ability to resonate.

Pickup Types

There are two types of pickups that you'll encounter: single coil and double coil. Single coil pickups have a thin, clean and transparent sound, but they can be noisy, picking up occasional radio interference. These pickups are usually about 3/4-inch wide and 2-1/2 inches long (Illustration 4-7).

Double coil pickups have a thick, meaty sound and are the most noise-free of the pickup types. They get their name from the fact that they have two single coils working together as one pickup. These are wired together in a way that cancels any noise that is picked up. These can also be called humbucking pickups. Double coil pickups are common on most Gibson guitars like the Les Paul (Illustration 4-8).

Many guitars have a combination of single and double coil pickups. It's common for a double coil pickup to have a switch that will turn one of the coils off. This gives the player a choice between single and double coil.

Basic Types of Electric Guitars

There are several different types of guitars available, and each has a characteristic sound. Often, a guitarist will play one type of guitar but ask you to make it sound like another type of guitar. This can be very difficult but not always impossible. It's crucial that you're familiar with these basic guitar sounds.

Even within the basic electric guitar types,

Illustration 4-7
Single Coil Pickup

This is the approximate size of most single coil pickups. Sometimes they're hidden by a plastic or metal cover.

These pickups are common on Fender guitars like the Stratocaster.

Single coil pickups are the most susceptible to noise. If you have a problem with noise when recording a guitar with single coil pickups, try moving the guitarist to a different location in the room. If the noise persists, try having the guitarist face different directions. There's usually somewhere in a 360° radius where the noise and interference is minimal. Keep the guitar away from computers, drum machines or other microprocessor-controlled equipment for minimal noise.

Single Coil Pickup

Illustration 4-8
Double Coil Pickup

This pickup configuration uses two single coil pickups working together as one. They're wired together in a way that minimizes noise and radio interference.

Sometimes both pickups are visible, and sometimes they're hidden by a gold, chrome or plastic cover.

The double coil sound is fuller and less shrill than the single coil sound.

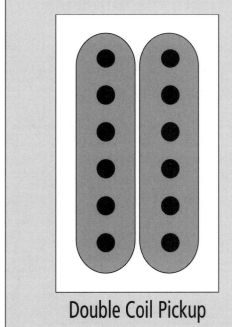

Double Coil Pickup

there are many different combinations of pickups and design configurations. The type of wood, style of body and precision of assembly all play an important part in the sound of the instrument. All considerations aside, we can still break the electric guitar sounds into three recogniz-able categories:

- Stratocaster: single coil
- Les Paul: double coil
- Hollow body electric jazz guitar: double coil

Audio Examples 4-1 to 4-3 demonstrate the sounds of the three fundamental types of electric guitar. These are all recorded direct into the mixer so that you can hear the characteristic tone of each.

Audio Example 4-1 demonstrates the single coil pickups on a Stratocaster. This guitar and its brother, the Telecaster, are very common in the rock, country and pop fields.

Audio Example 4-1 Single Coil
CD-1: Track 43

Audio Example 4-2 demonstrates the double coil sound of the Les Paul. This warm, smooth, punchy sound is a favorite for rock, blues, pop and jazz.

Audio Example 4-2 Double Coil
CD-1: Track 44

Audio Example 4-3 demonstrates the double coil sound of a large hollow-body jazz guitar. This instrument has a pure, rich sound. As a jazz instrument, it's traditionally treated with little or no effect. In fusion and some other jazz or rock styles, we can use any or all effects and techniques to shape the jazz guitar sound.

Audio Example 4-3
Hollow-Body Electric Jazz Guitar
CD-1: Track 45

These guitars have very different sounds and are suited for different types of music. Review these examples, and on a separate sheet of paper, write down as many descriptive adjectives as you can for each instrument. Use words like thin, hollow, round, fat, beefy or chunky. Have friends listen to these examples and list the terms they think describe each guitar sound. Putting a verbal tag on each sound will help you solidify your impression of these instruments. Verbalization will also help you communicate with other musicians about different guitar sounds.

Compressor/Limiter/Gate/Expander

It's very common to use a compressor on an electric guitar. Most guitars have a very wide dynamic range, and many instruments have uneven string volumes due to substandard adjustment of the pickups and string height. A compressor is what gives a guitar that smooth always-in-your-face sound. It puts all the notes and chords into a very narrow dynamic range so there might not be much (if any) volume difference between a single note and a full chord.

An outboard compressor designed for studio use can do a good job on guitar, but it's normal for the boxes made especially for guitar to work best in a player's setup. Most guitarists use a compressor in their setup, so when recording their guitar sounds, you usually don't need to compress much, if at all. When the guitarist has their stuff together, your job as the recordist is pretty simple. Whether you're running direct in or miking the speaker cabinet, your job is to capture the existing sound accurately rather than creating and shaping a new sound. You can put a compressor on the signal that's coming into the mixer if you need to, but ideally, the

guitarist will have a properly adjusted compressor in his kit.

In a guitar setup that uses several effects, the compressor should be the first effect in the chain. This will give the best sounding results and will help guard the rest of the effects from strong signals that might overdrive their inputs.

A compressor can efficiently even out the volume of different notes. This usually makes the guitarist's job easier. With a healthy amount of compression, the guitar will sustain longer, plus each note will be audible (even if the guitarist has sloppy technique). Listen to the difference the compressor makes on the simple guitar sounds in Audio Examples 4-4 and 4-5. Audio Example 4-4 was performed and recorded with no compression.

Audio Example 4-4 No compression
CD-1: Track 46

Audio Example 4-5 demonstrates the same part with a healthy amount of compression. I've used a ratio of 4:1 with about 10dB of gain reduction (refer to Chapter 2 on signal processing if this terminology isn't making sense).

Audio Example 4-5 With Compression
CD-1: Track 46

Distortion is a prime ingredient in many guitar sounds. The type of distortion that's used defines the character of the part and often determines whether the part will blend well in the mix.

There are many different foot pedal distortion boxes for guitar, and they all have different sounds. Some are very buzzy and harsh. Some are very full and warm. Harsh and buzzy distortion sounds are usually best for special effects, but they typically don't work very well in a mix because their sound doesn't blend well in most mixes. The distortion sounds that do mix well in the final product are generally the sounds that are smoother, warmer and less strident.

Audio Examples 4-6 to 4-8 demonstrate totally different distortion sounds. In each case, the guitar is plugged into the distortion unit, then the distortion unit is plugged directly into the mixer.

The box in Audio Example 4-6 has a strident, buzzy distortion and isn't really usable.

Audio Example 4-6 Buzzy Distortion
CD-1: Track 47

The distortion box in Audio Example 4-7 is one manufacturer's attempt at simulating a tube amplifier distorting. This can be a very usable sound on a lot of commercial songs.

Audio Example 4-7 Simulated Tube Distortion
CD-1: Track 47

The distortion box in Audio Example 4-8 is another manufacturer's attempt at simulating the rock stack-type amp. This is a little more aggressive sound and can also work well in many settings.

Audio Example 4-8 Simulated Rock Stack
CD-1: Track 47

Combining these sounds with the sound of a good amp can give them much more life and punch.

Delay

The use of delay on a guitar sound has the effect of placing the sound in a simple acoustical space. In Chapter 2 we discovered that the function of a simple slapback delay was to give the perception of room size. The longer the delay, the larger the room size. Delays of between 250 and 350ms can give a full sound for vocal and instrumental solos (especially on ballads). This is a very popular sound. It's usually most desirable if the delay is in time with the music in some way. See the chart in Chapter 2 (Illustration 1-15) to calculate delay times in relation to the tempo of a song. Audio Example 4-9 was recorded at a tempo of 120bpm. I've added a 250ms delay, which is in time with the eighth note at this tempo.

Audio Example 4-9 The 250ms Delay
CD-1: Track 48

A slapback delay of 62.5ms is in time with the 32nd note, at 120bpm, and gives an entirely different feel to Audio Example 4-10.

Audio Example 4-10 The 62.5ms Delay
CD-1: Track 48

Regenerating a longer delay of about 200 to 400ms can really smooth out a part. All of these effects usually make the guitarist sound like a better player than they really are. Guitarists love that! This enhancement can be advantageous to all concerned, but don't overdo the effects or the part will get lost in the mix. It might lose definition and sound like it's far away.

Should I Print Reverb or Delay to Tape?

There are many different effects that a guitarist can show up with, and most of them sound pretty good. It's tempting to go with whatever sound the guitarist has up at the time and record it to tape. This approach can work well and might be preferred if you don't have much processing gear.

If you have a small 4-track or 8-track setup, most of the time you'll be forced to print whatever reverb, delay or chorus the guitar player is using. Select the proportion that seems to sound good at the time you record the part. If you have a question about the amount of reverb or delay to print to tape, use the least amount that you think you need. If you print too much delay or reverb to tape, it's there forever. Too much delay and reverb can make a part sound like it was recorded from the far end of a gymnasium, especially as the mix develops. The only real way to fix this is to rerecord the part with less effect, which can be costly and is, at the very least, a nuisance. If you record the part a little on the dry side, you can always add whatever reverb is readily available during mixdown to make it sound more distant.

Ideally, have the guitarist get a good sound using whatever compression and distortion is needed for the part, but save the addition of all reverbs, delays and choruses for mixdown. Print the raw sound to tape and finish shaping in the mix. This approach lets you get just the right delay length, delay amount , reverb sound and chorus, after you can hear the part in the con-

text of the rest of the arrangement.

Be flexible. If a guitarist has come up with a great sound that might take you a while to duplicate, and if they want to print the sound to tape, give it a try. Be conservative in the amount of reverb and delay that is included. Conscientious guitarists can come up with great and interesting variations of a sound, and much of the final musical impact depends on how the signal is patched through the effects. They may run the chorus through the distortion or the distortion through the chorus. Both sound different. These routing changes can really result in some unique sounds. Take advantage of the player's diligence. You'll all share the benefit of a great sound. I'll often go ahead and print the chorus, flanger or phase shifter sound, saving the delay and reverb for mixdown, even in a full blown 48-track project.

There are no hard and fast rules when it comes to creating innovative and exciting new sounds, so be open to trying new tricks.

Electronic Doubling

Doubling a guitar part is a very common technique. Doubling can smooth out some of the glitches in the performance and can give the guitar a very wide, bigger-than-life sound. Pan the double apart from the original instrument, and you'll usually get a multidimensional wall of guitar that can sonically carry much of the arrangement. Doubling works well in rock tunes where the guitar must sound very huge and impressive.

This doubling effect can be achieved in a couple of ways. *Electronic doubling* involves patching the instrument through a short delay, then combining that delay with the original instrument. A *live double* simply involves playing the part twice onto different tracks or recording two players (playing the identical part) onto one or two tracks. Both techniques sound great. Experiment! Let the music help you decide.

To set up an electronic double, use a delay time between 0ms and about 35ms. Short doubles, below about 7ms, don't give a very broad-sounding double, but they can produce interesting and full sounds and are definitely worth trying. Pan the original guitar to one side and the delay to the other (Illustration 4-9).

Audio Example 4-11 demonstrates a guitar part doubled electronically using a 23ms

delay and no regeneration.

Audio Example 4-11 The 23ms Double
CD-1: Track 49

Audio Example 4-12 uses the same musical part as Audio Example 4-11, this time with a live double.

Audio Example 4-12 The Live Double
CD-1: Track 49

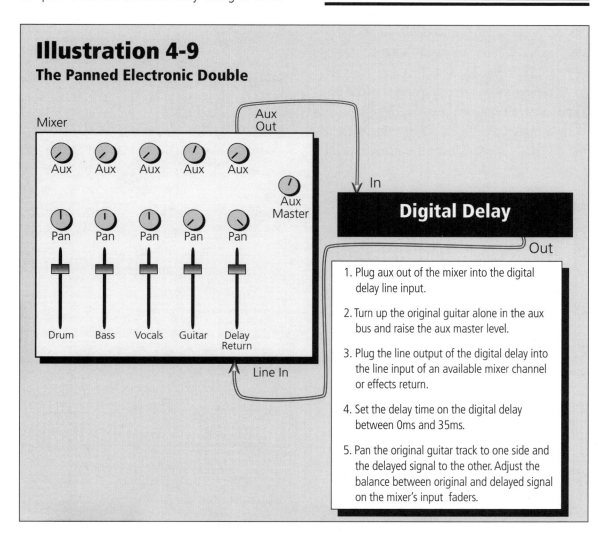

Illustration 4-9
The Panned Electronic Double

Mixer

Aux Out

Aux   Aux   Aux   Aux   Aux

Aux Master

Pan   Pan   Pan   Pan   Pan

Drum   Bass   Vocals   Guitar   Delay Return

Line In

In

Digital Delay

Out

1. Plug aux out of the mixer into the digital delay line input.

2. Turn up the original guitar alone in the aux bus and raise the aux master level.

3. Plug the line output of the digital delay into the line input of an available mixer channel or effects return.

4. Set the delay time on the digital delay between 0ms and 35ms.

5. Pan the original guitar track to one side and the delayed signal to the other. Adjust the balance between original and delayed signal on the mixer's input faders.

Always check a double in mono to make sure the part sounds good in both stereo and mono. Slight changes in delay time can make the part disappear or cut through strong in mono. Find the delay time that works well in stereo *and* mono. If you've panned the original full left and the delay full right, the sounds are very impressive in a stereo mix, but these hard-panned tracks often disappear when the mix is played in mono. Try repositioning the pan adjustments so they are only partially left and partially right.

Multi-effects

The current arsenal of guitar effects includes several units that contain many different, high-quality digital effects. These multi-effects units are relatively inexpensive and can produce excellent premium quality sounds. Take advantage of these effects and the guitarist's diligence in finding great sounds, but be conservative in printing reverb and delay to tape.

Chorus/Flanger/Phase Shifter

Chorus, flanger and phase-shifting effects are very common and important to most styles of electric guitar. A smooth chorus or flange can give a clean guitar sound a ringing tone. It can add richness that's as inspiring to the rest of the musicians as it is to the guitarist. Listen to the chorus on the clean guitar part in Audio Example 4-13.

Audio Example 4-13 Chorus
CD-1: Track 50

A smooth phase shifter can add color to a ballad or interest to a funky rhythm guitar comp.

Notice the interest that's added to Audio Example 4-14 by the phase shifter.

Audio Example 4-14 Phase Shifter
CD-1: Track 51

The chorus effects are often part of a solo guitar sound used together with distortion, compression and delay. The guitar in Audio Example 4-15 is plugged into the compressor first, then the distortion, next the delay and finally the chorus.

Audio Example 4-15 Multiple Effects
CD-1: Track 52

Reverb

Reverb is a useful ingredient in the final mix and is used primarily to smooth out the guitar sound when it must blend into the mix. Too much reverb can spell disaster for the clarity and definition of a good guitar part. On the other hand, reverb can hide many flaws in a marginal guitar part. Adapt to your situation.

Most electric parts sound good with a bright hall reverb sound, a decay time of about 1.5 seconds, a predelay of about 80ms, high diffusion and high density. This kind of setting offers a good place to start in shaping most guitar reverbs. Audio Example 4-16 demonstrates a guitar with this set of effects.

Audio Example 4-16 Hall Reverb
CD-1: Track 53

There are several other types of reverb that can sound great on many different musical parts. Experiment. Often, the sound of the guitar is so interesting with the delay, distortion and chorus that there's really no need for much (if any) reverb. Clean guitar sounds typically benefit the most from interesting and more complex reverb; For instance, slow, open ballads and arena rock projects sound good with hall and chamber reverb using decay times in the range of 1.5–3 seconds. Faster, punchy productions usually work well with plate, inverse and gated reverbs that have a decay time between .5–1.5 seconds.

Try adjusting the predelay to add a different feel to the reverb sound. Longer predelays that match the tempo of the eighth note or quarter note can give both the effect of making the part sound closer to the listener and the effect that it was played in a large room. Listen as I adjust the predelay during Audio Example 4-17.

Audio Example 4-17 Adjusting Predelay
CD-1: Track 54

Panning

There might be two or more separate guitar parts with totally different sounds in the same song. Though this is common, it can cause a bit of a problem during mixdown where each part should be audible and understandable. Panning can play a key role in helping you separate these different sounding parts for the listener's sake. When used along with different EQ settings for each guitar part, panning the instruments to very specific locations can produce excellent results.

When positioning guitars in the left to right spectrum, be sure that you maintain an even balance for the overall mix. It's common for the guitar to be playing the primary harmonic rhythm part. If that part is panned even slightly to one side the entire mix can sound one-sided.

Sometimes the main guitar part gets in the way of the lead vocal or some other instrument that's panned to center. Rather than panning the two parts apart from each other, try leaving the lead vocal in the center, then running the guitar through an electronic double. Pan the original guitar and the double apart from each other. This keeps the presence and aggressive sound of the guitar but lets the vocal be heard and understood better with less interference from the guitar.

Most modern guitar effects are stereo. They accept the single input from the guitar and have stereo outputs. These stereo outputs usually come from a stereo delay, chorus, flanger or phase shifter that is built into the guitar effects processor. If I have enough available tracks I'll usually print both of those outputs to tape. When there aren't many tracks left you generally can't print both outputs from the effect to tape. This is not really a problem. If we need to we can run the guitar through a stereo chorus, flanger or phase shifter during mixdown.

A major problem with multiple guitar parts arises when the mix is played in mono. All those tricky panning positions are laid on top of each other as everything goes to the center. It's crucial that each instrument have unique and different EQ characteristics to maintain some identity in a mono mix. The song in Audio Example 4-18 has three guitar parts. Listen to each part separately and notice that the sound on each is similar. Equalizing like this might sound okay in stereo, but when switched to mono, these parts don't retain much of their identity.

Audio Example 4-18 Conflicting Guitars
CD-1: Track 55

In Audio Example 4-19, first you hear each guitar part separately. Notice that they each have very different sounding EQ. I'll pan them to acceptable positions in the mix. Finally, see if you can still hear all the parts when I switch to mono at the end of the example.

Audio Example 4-19 Equalized for Mono
CD-1: Track 55

Equalizing the Guitar

There are certain EQ ranges that add specific qualities to guitar sounds. Depending on the type of guitar and style of music, EQ changes can have varying results. Here are some good starting points for equalizing a guitar.

100Hz can add a good solid low end to most guitar sounds. Boost this frequency sparingly. It can be appropriate to turn this frequency up, but most of the time a boost here will conflict with the bass guitar. I end up cutting this frequency quite often on guitar. Listen as I turn 100Hz up and down on the guitar sound in Audio Example 4-20.

Audio Example 4-20 Boost and Cut 100Hz
CD-1: Track 56

200Hz tends to be the muddy zone on many guitar sounds. A boost here can make the overall sound of the guitar dull. A cut at 200Hz can expose the lows and the highs so that the entire sound has more clarity and low end punch. Cutting this frequency can help a double coil pickup sound like a single coil pickup. Audio Example 4-21 shows the effect of cutting and boosting 200Hz.

Audio Example 4-21 Boost and Cut 200Hz
CD-1: Track 56

The frequency range from 250Hz to 350Hz can add punch and help the blend of a distorted rock sound. Notice the change in texture of Audio Example 4-22 as I boost and cut 300Hz.

Audio Example 4-22 Boost and Cut 300Hz
CD-1: Track 56

The frequency range from 500 to 600Hz often contains most of the body and punchy character. Try to hear the body of the sound change as I cut and boost 550Hz on the guitar in Audio Example 4-23.

Audio Example 4-23 Boost and Cut 550Hz
CD-1: Track 56

The frequency range from 2.5kHz to about 5kHz adds edge and definition to most guitar sounds. I'll boost and cut 4kHz on the guitar sound in Audio Example 4-24.

Audio Example 4-24 Boost and Cut 4kHz
CD-1: Track 56

Boosting 8kHz to around 12kHz makes many guitar sounds shimmer or sparkle. These frequencies can also contain much of the noise from the signal processors so cutting these frequencies slightly can minimize many noise problems from the guitarist's equipment. Listen as I boost and cut 10kHz on the guitar sound in Audio Example 4-25.

Audio Example 4-25 Boost and Cut 10kHz
CD-1: Track 56

The recording purist's approach to equalization has always been to print the signal to tape without EQ. It's true that recording with a very extreme EQ can cause problems, but with many guitar sounds, you're endeavoring to create different and unique sounds. The tone is almost always a key ingredient in these sounds so it's usually best to go ahead and print the equalized guitar signal.

A word of caution: If the sound is heavy in bass frequency content, it's generally better to print with less lows than you think you'll need in mixdown. These frequencies are easy to turn up in the mix, and you won't lose anything by saving the addition of lows for mixdown. Low frequencies contain the most energy of all the frequencies and virtually control the VU readings. A sound with too many lows will read unnaturally hot on your meters. If you end up needing more high-frequencies in the mix, they can be buried in the mass of lows. When this happens, your tracks become very noisy. As you try to recover the clarity by boosting the highs, you end up boosting processor noise and tape noise.

Amplified Electric

Now let's focus on the miked amplifier/speaker cabinet sound. This is the most popular sound for recorded electric guitar. Guitarists typically think of their guitar amp as a unit that includes the speaker or speaker cabinet. Sometimes people try to literalize the concept of miking the amp to insinuate that you would actually place a mic in front of the power amplifier instead of the speaker. This is obviously not what is implied when someone asks you to mike the guitar amp. It's common to refer to miking the guitar amp, but it actually means to place a mic in front of the guitarist's speaker cabinet.

A guitar going through a direct box straight into the mixer usually sounds too harsh and sterile for most tastes. The guitar amp tends to smooth out the guitar sound so when we record the speaker of the amp, we usually get a sound that blends into the mix better than a direct sound.

When a guitarist chooses equipment, the selections are based almost totally on sound. The other factors to equipment selection are price and features, but I think we can agree that serious guitar players develop their distinct sounds largely through the equipment they choose. The guitar amplifier is one of the key factors in this sound scheme. We usually get the best and most usable sounds when we mic the amp. Different amplifiers have different sounds, especially when they distort.

The effects and sounds we've covered in the previous chapters are still very important to the guitarist's sound. Now we'll be able to add the characteristic sound of the amplifier and speaker cabinet to the picture, plus we can add the acoustic sound of the room that the amp is in.

Listen to the difference in sound between the guitar amplifiers in Audio Examples 4-26 to 4-29.

Audio Example 4-26 demonstrates a small solid-state amp with a clean sound.

Audio Example 4-26 Clean Small Solid-state Amp
CD-1: Track 57

Audio Example 4-27 demonstrates the sound of a large tube amp with a clean sound.

Audio Example 4-27 Clean Large Tube Amp
CD-1: Track 57

Audio Example 4-28 uses the small solid-state amp with the amp distorting.

Audio Example 4-28
Distorted Small Solid-state Amp
CD-1: Track 58

Audio Example 4-29 demonstrates the large tube amp distorting.

Audio Example 4-29 Distorted Large Tube Amp
CD-1: Track 58

For Audio Examples 4-26 to 4-29 I used the same mic and the same EQ through the same board from the same distance. You can tell that the amp is critical to the character of the guitar sound.

Mic Techniques

Using a mic to capture the sound of the guitarist is not as simple as just selecting the best mic. Where we place the mic *and* where we place the amp can be equally influential on the final sound of the instrument. Although there are hundreds of different microphone available from many manufacturers, they essentially all fit into three basic categories: condenser, moving-coil and ribbon. Condenser and moving-coil mikes are the most common of these three, although they may all be used in recording as well as live situations.

It's ideal if you have at least one good moving-coil mic and one good condenser mic for your recordings. With these two options available you can cover most recording situations and achieve professional sounding results. Please refer to Chapter 3 for specifics about microphones and their characteristics.

The Most Common Approach to Miking an Amp

Turn the amp up to a fairly strong level. This doesn't have to be screaming loud, but most amps sound fuller if they're turned up a bit.

Next, place a moving-coil mic about one foot away from the speaker. Most guitar amps will have one or two full range speakers. These speakers are typically 8 to 12 inches in diameter. Moving-coil mics are the preferred choice for close-miking amplifiers because they can handle plenty of volume before they distort the sound. Also, the tone coloration of a moving-coil mic in the higher frequencies can add bite and clarity to the guitar sound.

If the amp you are miking has more than one identical speaker, point the mic at one of the speakers. Point the mic at the center of the speaker to get a sound with more bite and edge. Point the mic more toward the outer rim of the speaker to capture a warmer, smoother sound (Illustration 4-10).

If you're miking a speaker enclosure with separate tweeter, midrange and bass speakers, you'll need to move the mic back two or three feet just to get the overall sound of the cabinet. This gets us into a situation where the room sound becomes an important part of the sound that goes onto the tape.

Audio Example 4-30 demonstrates the sound of an amp with the mic placed six inches

from the speaker and pointed directly at the center of the speaker.

Audio Example 4-30
Mic at the Center of the Speaker
CD-1: Track 59

Audio Example 4-31 demonstrates the sound of the same amp, same guitar and same musical part as Audio Example 4-30. Now the mic is aimed about one inch in from the outside rim of the speaker while maintaining the dis-

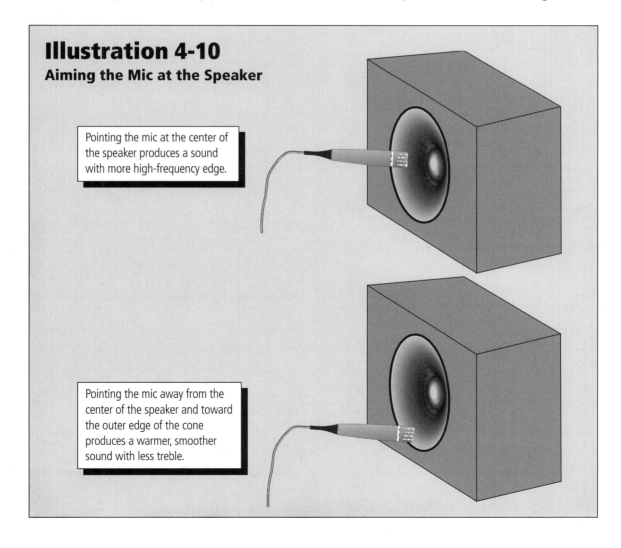

Illustration 4-10
Aiming the Mic at the Speaker

Pointing the mic at the center of the speaker produces a sound with more high-frequency edge.

Pointing the mic away from the center of the speaker and toward the outer edge of the cone produces a warmer, smoother sound with less treble.

tance of six inches from the speaker.

Audio Example 4-31
Mic at the Outer Edge of the Speaker
CD-1: Track 59

When the mic is within a foot of the speaker, the room sound has minimal effect on the sound that goes to tape, especially if the amp volume is fairly strong. If the guitarist hasn't already included reverb and delay in their selection of effects, this approach will give you consistently close-sounding tracks that you can add distance (ambience) to by adding reverb or delay in the mix.

Powerful guitar sounds often include the sound of the immediate space (the room) that the amp is in. This can be accomplished with reverb, but natural ambience can add an unusual and distinct quality to a recording. Try including the sound of the room with the sound of the guitar. This technique often breathes life into an otherwise dull sound.

As we move the mic back more than a couple of feet from any amp, we're using distant miking. The room sound becomes part of the overall sound. We can get great guitar sounds if we put one mic within a foot of the amp and one mic back in the room several feet away from the amp. With this technique, we can blend the sound of the mic closest to the amp with ambient sound captured by the mic farther away. We can combine these two sounds to one track as we record, or if tracks permit, we can print each mic to a separate track and save the blending or panning for mixdown. The effectiveness of this approach is dependent on whether the sound of the room is musically appropriate.

Use a condenser mic to record the most accurate sound of the room. Condensers have a fuller sound from a distance than moving-coil or ribbon mics and they capture the subtleties of the room sound in more detail. In Audio Example 4-32, I've placed a condenser mic about seven feet away from the amp.

Audio Example 4-32
Condenser Mic Seven Feet From the Amp
CD-1: Track 60

Audio Example 4-33 demonstrates the amp in Audio Example 4-32 through a close mic.

Audio Example 4-33 Close-miking the Amp
CD-1: Track 61

In Audio Example 4-34, I blend the sound of the close mic with the sound of the distant mic and then pan the two apart.

Audio Example 4-34
Combining the Close and Distant Mics
CD-1: Track 62

Adding the sound of the room to the close-miked sound usually helps the sound of a distorted guitar blend into the mix better. The guitar part will sound bigger, and the tonal character will be more interesting and unique.

Most people don't have access to a multi-million dollar studio with large rooms that sound great. But even within your own abode lay many interesting acoustical possibilities. Try moving the guitar amp and the mic into the bathroom.

Sometimes it's almost as much fun to play guitar in the shower as it is to sing in the shower. All those hard surfaces and natural reverb can do wonders for a dull sound. Move the mic back a few feet from the speaker and crank it up! In Audio Example 4-35, I have the guitar amp in the bathroom with the mic pointing into the shower. The shower door is partially closed to shield the mic from the direct amp sound. Refer to Illustration 4-11 for a diagram of this setup.

Audio Example 4-35
Miking the Amp in the Shower
CD-1: Track 63

If you want to increase the size of your room sound, place the amp toward one end of

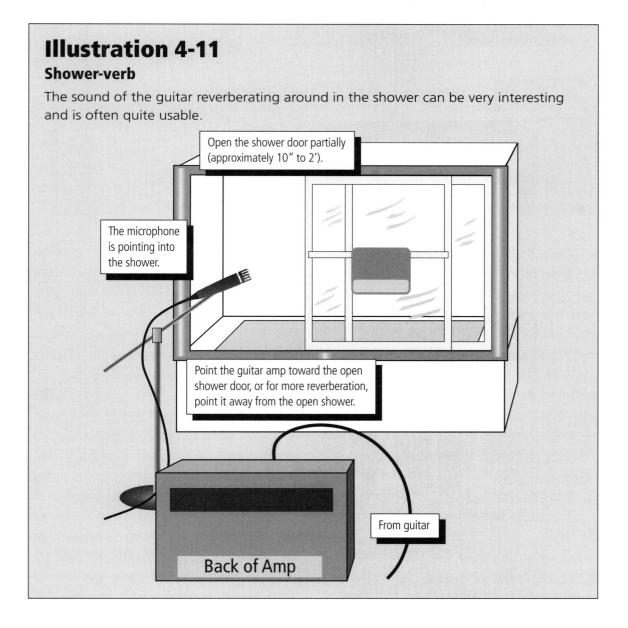

Illustration 4-11
Shower-verb
The sound of the guitar reverberating around in the shower can be very interesting and is often quite usable.

Open the shower door partially (approximately 10" to 2').

The microphone is pointing into the shower.

Point the guitar amp toward the open shower door, or for more reverberation, point it away from the open shower.

From guitar

Back of Amp

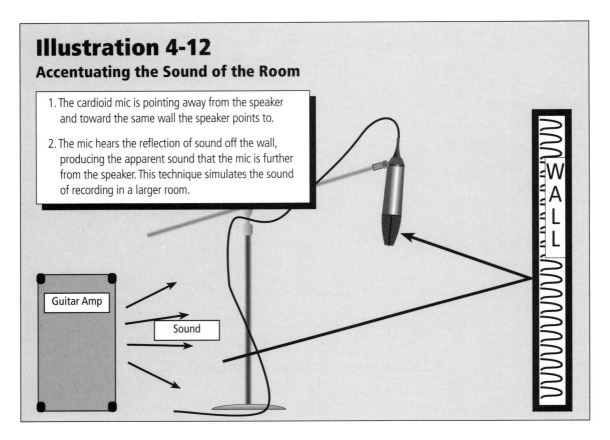

Illustration 4-12

Accentuating the Sound of the Room

1. The cardioid mic is pointing away from the speaker and toward the same wall the speaker points to.

2. The mic hears the reflection of sound off the wall, producing the apparent sound that the mic is further from the speaker. This technique simulates the sound of recording in a larger room.

Guitar Amp

Sound

WALL

the room and place the mic a few feet from the amp. Now instead of pointing the mic at the amp, point it away from the amp. If the microphone has a selectable pickup pattern, select cardioid. Otherwise, select a mic that has a cardioid pickup pattern. Since the mic is pointed away from the amp, it doesn't hear the direct sound from the amp as well. What it does hear is the reflection of the sound off the wall that the speaker and the mic are pointing at. This essentially increases the delay of the initial reflection and makes the room sound larger (Illustration 4-12).

If possible, print the room mic(s) to separate tracks of the multitrack. If you keep them separate, you can choose the proper blend of the direct and reflected sound during the mix. If you must print the close mic and the room mic(s)

to the same track be conservative with the amount of room you include. Too much room sound might cause the track to sound distant in the mix. You can always add a little reverb in the mix if the guitar sound needs more depth, but it's very difficult to take away the sound of the room if your guitar sounds too distant.

If your home has a hallway with bedrooms and/or bathrooms off of it, position the guitar amp at the open end of the hallway. Point the speakers toward the hallway. Now put mics in two of the rooms off the hallway, and open the doors into those rooms. Also, put a mic directly in front of the speaker cabinet. Run all three of the mics into your mixer. If you only have two mics, this technique can still work well—just use one of the rooms off the hallway. Now pan the direct mic center and the room mics hard left and hard right. Turn the amp up to a substantially potent level, have the guitarist play and check out the interesting stereo sound. Blend the center mic and the room mics until you have just enough room and just enough direct sound. Techniques like this can quickly use up several mics and tracks, but this kind of experimentation can produce brilliant sounds that can spark your recording process on to new levels of innovation and excellence.

In Audio Example 4-36, the amp is at the end of a hallway, one mic is eight inches from the speaker, a second mic is in the bathroom off the hallway and a third mic is in a bedroom off

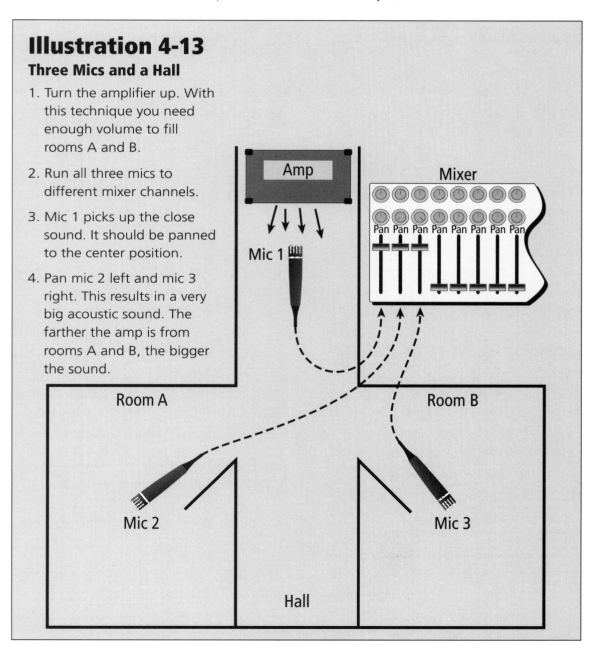

Illustration 4-13
Three Mics and a Hall

1. Turn the amplifier up. With this technique you need enough volume to fill rooms A and B.

2. Run all three mics to different mixer channels.

3. Mic 1 picks up the close sound. It should be panned to the center position.

4. Pan mic 2 left and mic 3 right. This results in a very big acoustic sound. The farther the amp is from rooms A and B, the bigger the sound.

Amp

Mixer

Pan Pan Pan Pan Pan Pan Pan Pan

Mic 1

Room A

Room B

Mic 2

Mic 3

Hall

the hallway. I'll turn each mic up separately, starting with the close mic, then I'll blend them all together and pan the room mics hard left and hard right for a true stereo sound. See Illustration 4-13 for a map of this setup.

Audio Example 4-36 Multiple-Room Miking
CD-1: Track 64

It's often difficult to get that perfectly blended electric guitar sound. Experimentation with microphone techniques can really help solve some problems. The key factors involved in shaping guitar sounds are the raw sound from the instrument, choice of effects and acoustical interaction of the sound in the room. There's much room for creativity here. Start practicing and building your own arsenal of techniques that you like. With the rapid development of affordable technology right now, you'll need to use all available resources to create a new and unique sound that can rise above the masses.

Combining the Miked and Direct Signals

It's possible and common to blend the miked amplifier signal with the direct signal. Plug the guitar into the direct box, then plug into an amplifier from the DIs's out to amp jack. Once this is completed, proceed with miking the amp. From the direct box you can also patch the low-impedance XLR output into the mic input of your mixer. With this setup the direct signal is coming in one channel, and the microphone signal is coming in another channel (Illustration 4-14).

Listen to Audio Example 4-37. I'll turn up the direct signal alone, then I'll turn the miked signal up alone and finally I'll blend the two

sounds and pan them apart.

Audio Example 4-37
Combining Miked and Direct Signals
CD-1: Track 65

Acoustic Guitars

If I have an electric acoustic guitar should I mike it or run it through a direct box? Acoustic guitars with pickups can work well in a live performance situation. Simply plug into the board, an amp or through a direct box. You can get a passable sound and eliminate one microphone in the setup. However, though the sound can be okay for live performances it's hardly ever a great sound for recording. The sound from an electric acoustic pickup typically sounds sterile and small and it doesn't have the broad, full, interesting sound of the acoustic instrument. To run an electric acoustic guitar direct into a mixer, follow the same procedure as with any electric guitar.

Audio Examples 4-38 and 4-39 use the same acoustic steel string guitar. Audio Example 4-38 demonstrates the acoustic guitar run direct into the board from the instrument pickup.

Audio Example 4-38 Acoustic Guitar Direct In
CD-1: Track 66

Audio Example 4-39 is the same guitar as Audio Example 4-38 using a microphone to capture its sound to tape.

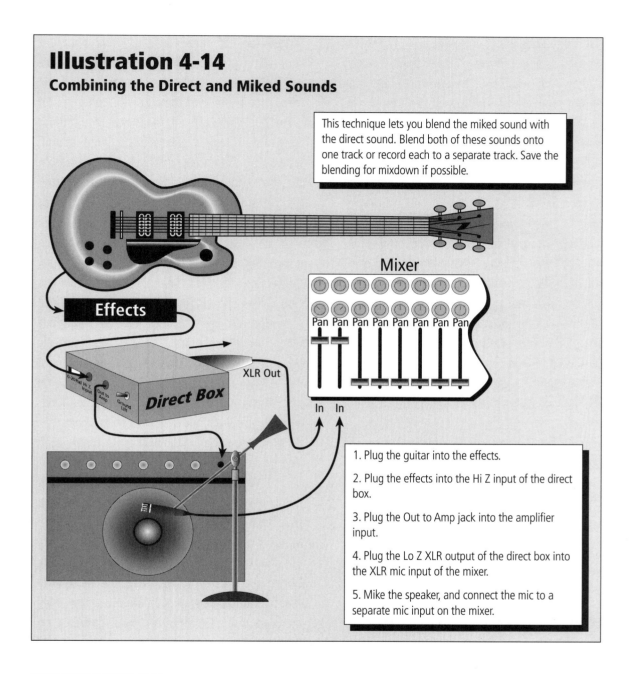

Illustration 4-14
Combining the Direct and Miked Sounds

This technique lets you blend the miked sound with the direct sound. Blend both of these sounds onto one track or record each to a separate track. Save the blending for mixdown if possible.

Mixer

Pan Pan Pan Pan Pan Pan Pan Pan

In   In

Effects

XLR Out

Direct Box

0-20 Pad Hi Z Input   Out to Amp   Ground Lift

1. Plug the guitar into the effects.

2. Plug the effects into the Hi Z input of the direct box.

3. Plug the Out to Amp jack into the amplifier input.

4. Plug the Lo Z XLR output of the direct box into the XLR mic input of the mixer.

5. Mike the speaker, and connect the mic to a separate mic input on the mixer.

Audio Example 4-39 Miking the Acoustic Guitar
CD-1: Track 66

The miked guitar has more tone and character; it sounds better. If you don't want the true sound of the instrument, running direct can pro-duce some unique and usable sounds. There are all sorts of variables that can cause us to record in atypical ways. We need to be open to almost any approach in the interest of finding a new and exciting sound.

Mic Techniques

Typically, the best kind of mic to use on any acoustic guitar is a condenser mic. Condensers capture more of the subtlety of the attack, the sound of the pick on the strings and the nuance of artistic expression. Also, condenser microphones produce a full sound when miking from a distance. Moving-coil mics and ribbon mics can produce passable acoustic guitar sounds, especially if that's all you have, but the accepted mic of choice for acoustic guitars is a condenser.

The steel string acoustic is the most common acoustic guitar. These guitars come in many different shapes, sizes and brands. Each variation has a characteristic sound, but the primary trait of the acoustic guitar is a very clear and full sound. The second most common type of acoustic guitar is the nylon string classical guitar. Classical guitars have a warm, full and mellow sound.

Audio Example 4-40 demonstrates the sound of a steel string acoustic guitar.

Audio Example 4-40
The Steel String Acoustic Guitar
CD-1: Track 67

Audio Example 4-41 demonstrates the sound of a nylon string classical guitar.

Audio Example 4-41
The Nylon String Classical Guitar
CD-1: Track 68

In Audio Examples 4-40 and 4-41, I used a condenser mic about eight inches away from the guitar. With a condenser mic six to eight inches from the guitar, we can potentially get a sound that has too much bass, especially as we move over the sound hole. We can control the frequency content of the acoustic guitar sound dramatically by changing mic placement. If there are too many lows in your acoustic guitar sound, try moving the mic up the neck and away from the sound hole, moving the mic back away from the guitar to the distance of one or two feet or turning the low frequencies down.

One way to turn the low frequencies down is by using the bass roll-off switch. Most condenser microphones have a switch to turn the bass frequencies down. These switches may have a number by them to indicate the frequency where the roll-off starts. The number is typically between 60 and 150. If there's no number, there might be a single line that slopes down to the left. When you use a condenser mic for close-miking, you'll usually need to use the bass roll-off switch to keep a good balance between lows and highs.

If we point a mic at different parts of the acoustic guitar while it's being played, we find that each zone has a different sound. There are all sorts of tricky ways to combine these different sounds from different places on the guitar, but it's usually best to keep it simple. More mics mean more chances of problematic phase interaction and more chance that your great stereo sound will turn to mush when your mix is heard in mono.

I've tried many techniques for miking acoustic guitars, using up to four or five mics. The method that consistently works the best for me uses one good condenser mic placed in the position that gets the sound I need for the track.

There are three common positions to mike the guitar: in front of the sound hole, behind

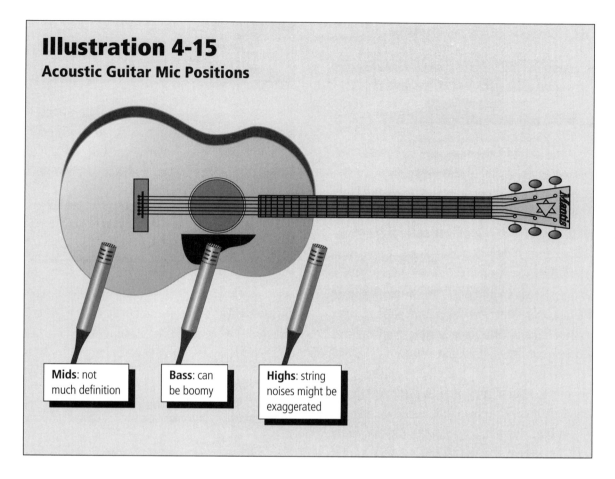

Illustration 4-15
Acoustic Guitar Mic Positions

Mids: not much definition

Bass: can be boomy

Highs: string noises might be exaggerated

the bridge and over the neck. Though each instrument has its own characteristic sound, each of these possible mic positions holds a consistent type of sound from one guitar to the next: Over the neck contains the highs, over the sound hole contains the lows and over the body behind the bridge contains the mids.

We'll use a steel string acoustic for the next set of Audio Examples, but all the techniques are worth trying on any acoustic steel string, nylon string or 12-string guitar (Illustration 4-15).

If you position the mic directly over the sound hole, the sound you'll capture will be bass-heavy and boomy like the sound in Audio Example 4-42.

Audio Example 4-42 The Sound Hole
CD-1: Track 69

If you position the mic over the top and behind the bridge, the sound will be strongest in mids like the sound in Audio Example 4-43.

Audio Example 4-43 Behind the Bridge
CD-1: Track 69

Point the mic at the front of the neck to hear more highs from the guitar, like the sound in Audio Example 4-44. This mic position can produce a good usable sound, but you might have a problem with string and finger noise.

Audio Example 4-44 Over the Neck
CD-1: Track 69

The sound I get from one condenser mic pointed at the front of the neck, between the sound hole and where the neck joins the body of the guitar is very often the most usable. That doesn't mean that I don't use other techniques. Neither does it mean I'm not always trying new approaches on these instruments. In reality, we can do almost anything in almost any way and still get away with it if the sound supports the musical impact. Take these standard techniques and build on them. Push the limits.

When we miked the electric guitar amp, the room began to play an important part in the sound of the instrument. The same is true for miking the acoustic. As we move the mic away from the instrument, the character of the sound changes dramatically. The music you're recording determines the usefulness of room sound.

The acoustic guitar in Audio Example 4-45 was recorded with the mic six inches in front of the instrument, pointed between the sound hole and where the neck joins the body.

Audio Example 4-45
Over the Neck, Near the Sound Hole
CD-1: Track 69

Audio Example 4-46 demonstrates the guitar from Audio Example 4-45 with the mic three feet away from the instrument and pointed at the sound hole.

Audio Example 4-46 Three Feet Away
CD-1: Track 70

Audio Example 4-47 uses the same acoustic guitar as the previous two examples. The mic is still three feet from the guitar, but the guitar is in a smaller room than Audio Example 4-46.

Audio Example 4-47 Smaller Room
CD-1: Track 70

Audio Example 4-48 keeps the same guitar and player as Audio Examples 4-44 to 4-47. This time the guitar is recorded in a bathroom.

Audio Example 4-48 The Bathroom
CD-1: Track 70

The acoustic guitar sounds in Audio Examples 4-44 to 4-48 are all different though theoretically usable in a musical context. Sometimes we get so caught up in wanting more and more reverbs and effects units that we forget what great sounds are right in front of us, in our own living or working space. They're always at hand and at no additional cost. What a deal! In addition, if you add effects to some of these interesting acoustic sounds, you might end up with some unique textures that add individuality to your sound.

Individual acoustic guitars often produce different tonal balance when miked at different spots. In other words, there isn't one microphone placement that works best for every guitar. Experiment with each instrument to find the sounds you like.

Tuning/Instrument Selection

How old are the guitar strings? The age of the strings plays a very important role in the sound of any guitar. It's especially important on acoustic guitars. New strings add clarity and high frequency. Old strings produce a sound that's dull and muffled.

There's one problem with new strings. They squeak more when the guitarist moves around on the neck. This can be a problem when recording. The best players usually have enough technique and finesse to play on brand new strings without much of a problem. For the rest of us, there can be other solutions. The quickest way to get the strings to squeak less is to put something on them that is slippery. Unfortunately, slippery products usually contain some sort of oil. Your local music store has access to commercially manufactured products designed to make guitar strings more slippery. These products can work very well. I even know people who put the thinnest possible coat of vegetable oil on their strings. Use any of these products sparingly. Oil on strings causes them to lose brilliance and clarity. You might end up with no squeaks at the expense of all that great acoustic guitar sound.

Guitar strings come in different gauges, or sizes. Light-gauge strings are thinner than heavy-gauge strings. Light-gauge strings produce a sound that has less bass and more highs. The sound is thinner. Lighter strings also give less volume than heavy strings and don't project as well in a group. These strings might not work well in a live acoustic performance situation, but in the studio, they can give you a very clean, transparent and usable sound. This kind of sound works very well for single-note picking parts and arpeggiated chords.

Medium- and heavy-gauge strings produce more volume and bass frequencies than light-gauge strings; they give the guitar a full sound. The sound of heavier strings is typically even in level, from lows to highs. This kind of sound works very well for rhythm strumming parts.

Picks

Another very important factor in the sound of an acoustic guitar is the pick. Playing with a thin pick gives a sound that has more clear high frequencies. The thin pick slapping as it plucks the strings becomes part of the sound. Playing with a thick pick produces a full sound with more bass and fewer highs, plus we don't get as much of the pick sound.

Audio Examples 4-49 and 4-50 use the same guitar and mic setup. The only change is the guitar pick. Audio Example 4-49 was performed with a very thin pick.

Audio Example 4-49 Thin Pick
CD-1: Track 71

Audio Example 4-50 was performed with a very thick pick.

Audio Example 4-50 Thick Pick
CD-1: Track 71

Dynamic Processing and the Acoustic Guitar

Acoustic guitars have a wide dynamic range. A compressor can help even out the volume level of the different pitch ranges and strings. Some instruments even have individual notes that are

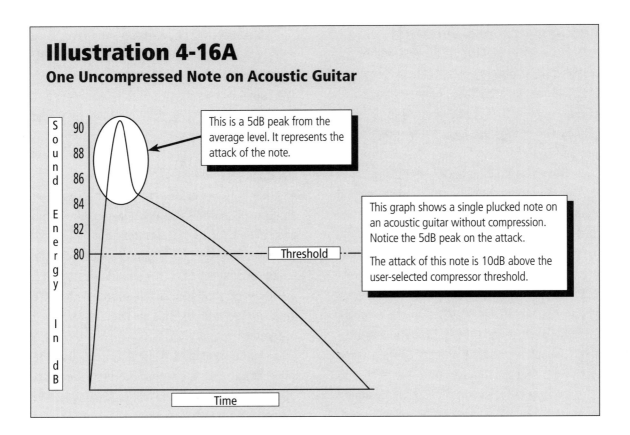

Illustration 4-16A
One Uncompressed Note on Acoustic Guitar

Sound Energy In dB

90
88
86
84
82
80

This is a 5dB peak from the average level. It represents the attack of the note.

Threshold

This graph shows a single plucked note on an acoustic guitar without compression. Notice the 5dB peak on the attack.

The attack of this note is 10dB above the user-selected compressor threshold.

Time

much louder than others. Low notes (on the larger strings) will usually produce a lot more energy and volume than higher notes on the smaller strings. Review Chapter 2 if you aren't familiar with the controls on a compressor.

Try this approach to compressing the acoustic guitar:

- Set the ratio control between 3:1 and 5:1.
- Adjust the attack time. Slower attack times accentuate the sound of the pick. The fastest attack times will de-emphasize the sound of the pick (Illustrations 4-16A to 4-16C).
- Adjust the release time. Setting this control between one and two seconds usually sounds the smoothest.
- Adjust the threshold for a gain reduction of 3 to 7dB on the loudest part of the track.

Audio Example 4-51 demonstrates the acoustic guitar without compression.

Audio Example 4-51 No Compression
CD-1: Track 72

Audio Example 4-52 uses the same acoustic guitar as Audio Example 4-51. This time the signal is compressed with a gain reduction of up to 7dB.

Audio Example 4-52 Compressed
CD-1: Track 72

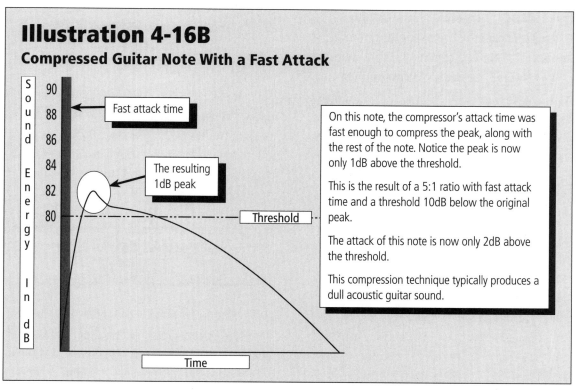

Illustration 4-16B
Compressed Guitar Note With a Fast Attack

Fast attack time

The resulting 1dB peak

Threshold

Time

On this note, the compressor's attack time was fast enough to compress the peak, along with the rest of the note. Notice the peak is now only 1dB above the threshold.

This is the result of a 5:1 ratio with fast attack time and a threshold 10dB below the original peak.

The attack of this note is now only 2dB above the threshold.

This compression technique typically produces a dull acoustic guitar sound.

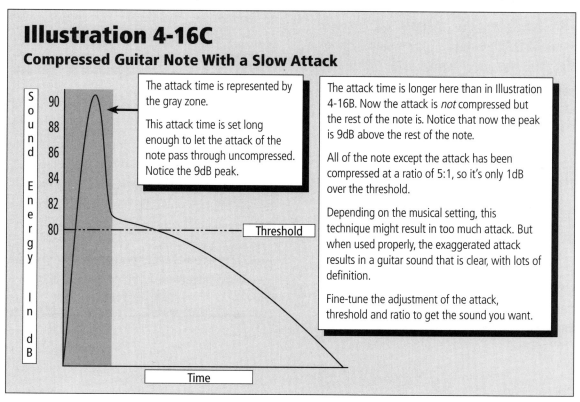

Illustration 4-16C
Compressed Guitar Note With a Slow Attack

The attack time is represented by the gray zone.

This attack time is set long enough to let the attack of the note pass through uncompressed. Notice the 9dB peak.

Threshold

Time

The attack time is longer here than in Illustration 4-16B. Now the attack is *not* compressed but the rest of the note is. Notice that now the peak is 9dB above the rest of the note.

All of the note except the attack has been compressed at a ratio of 5:1, so it's only 1dB over the threshold.

Depending on the musical setting, this technique might result in too much attack. But when used properly, the exaggerated attack results in a guitar sound that is clear, with lots of definition.

Fine-tune the adjustment of the attack, threshold and ratio to get the sound you want.

Equalizing the Acoustic Guitar

We use equalization on acoustic guitar to shape the sound for the space in the mix that we want the guitar to fill. From our audio examples, you can tell that much of the sound can be shaped through mic placement, string selection and pick selection. If we have a well-maintained guitar with the correct mic placed precisely where it should be and a great player playing the appropriate strings with the perfect pick, using impeccable technique to play wonderful parts that have phenomenal artistic expression, we might not need to use much EQ, if any.

Let's look at some common solutions to equalization problems you might encounter when recording acoustic guitars.

The most common equalization of the acoustic guitar involves cutting the low frequencies, below 150Hz, down. Lows can be very predominate and boomy on an acoustic guitar. These low frequencies can clash with the bass guitar, bass drum, piano or any full-range instrument. In Audio Example 4-53, I'll turn the frequencies below 150Hz down. This can make the guitar sound a little thin when the guitar is by itself, but this sound generally works best in the mix.

Audio Example 4-53 Cut 150Hz
CD-1: Track 73

Another common EQ for acoustic guitar involves adding a high-frequency shimmer at about 10 to 12kHz. On the guitar in Audio Example 4-54, I'll boost 12kHz.

Audio Example 4-54 Boost 12kHz
CD-1: Track 73

If the guitar is sounding muddy, we can usually clean the sound up by turning the lower mids down (between 200 and 500Hz). Listen to the change in the guitar sound in Audio Example 4-55 as I turn down the curve centered on 300Hz.

Audio Example 4-55 Cut 300Hz
CD-1: Track 73

When you need more edge or definition from the sound, boost a frequency between 3 and 5kHz. Audio Example 4-56 demonstrates the sound of boosting the acoustic guitar at 4kHz.

Audio Example 4-56 Boost 4kHz
CD-1: Track 73

Adjust a frequency between 1.5 and 2.5kHz to emphasize or de-emphasize the sound of the pick hitting the strings. The actual frequency you select depends on the type of strings, gauge of strings, the physical makeup of the guitar and the pick. In Audio Example 4-57, I boost then cut 2kHz.

Audio Example 4-57 Boost and Cut 2kHz
CD-1: Track 73

Reverb

The choice of reverberation when recording acoustic guitar is dependent on the musical style and arrangement of the song. In folk, country or blues, the acoustic guitar might use little or no reverb. Any reverberation used in these styles is typically very natural sounding. Hall and chamber settings on digital reverbs can smooth out the sound without being intrusive or obvious. Decay times of one to two seconds work very well. These reverberation settings can help the part blend into the mix without dominating the sound of a song.

On the folk style part in Audio Example 4-58, I start with no reverberation, then I add a small amount of chamber reverb with a 1.5 second decay time.

Audio Example 4-58 Chamber Reverb
CD-1: Track 74

Pop and commercial rock musical styles are more likely to use chorus type effects and unnatural sounding reverb. Even in these styles, the acoustic guitar is often treated as a natural instrument. If chorus effects or delays are used, they're typically intended to simulate the effect of double tracking.

Ballads are more likely to use more effect on the acoustic guitar. The rich texture of the reverberated guitar can be heard and appreciated in the open texture of a pop ballad.

If a delay is used, adjust the delay time in relation to the tempo of the song. See Illustration 2-15 in Chapter 2 for a chart of delay times relative to tempo.

In the proper context, any of the chorus, flanger or phase shifter effects can sound great on acoustic guitar. The guitar in Audio Example 4-59 has a stereo flanger and slapback delay set to the same speed as the eighth note. This is a very usable sound, although it doesn't reflect the purist's approach to the acoustic guitar.

Audio Example 4-59 Flange With Delay
CD-1: Track 75

Double Tracking the Acoustic Guitar

One way to get a really full sound from the acoustic is to do a live double track. If the player can duplicate the part, record the duplicate guitar part onto another track. If you play the original track in the headphones, a good guitarist should be able to duplicate the part with a fair degree of accuracy. Pan these two tracks apart during playback. This creates a chorus-delay-flange-phase shifting effect that happens naturally as the two parts work together.

Audio Examples 4-60 and 4-61 demonstrate this double tracking technique. Listen to Audio Example 4-60 for the original track.

Audio Example 4-60 Acoustic Guitar
CD-1: Track 76

Audio Example 4-61 shows how adding the double tracked acoustic adds fullness and depth, especially when the two parts are panned away from each other in the stereo spectrum.

Audio Example 4-61 Adding the Double Track
CD-1: Track 76

Distortion

Distortion is the backbone of the rock guitar sound but is rarely used on acoustic guitar even in the rock style. That's not to say that you shouldn't experiment with distortion on acoustic. You might be the pioneer of some new commercial sound phenomenon.

Synthesized and Sampled Guitar Sounds

These sounds are typically digital recordings of real guitars. After hearing the Audio Examples in this course, you should be familiar with the primary guitar sounds. You've learned some good, reliable techniques for recording them. The same techniques apply to recording synth and sampled guitar sounds. From my experience, all the techniques we've covered in this lesson can apply to recording synth or sampled guitar sounds. If I'm recording a sample of a simple guitar, I approach it as if it's coming from a guitar. If I'm recording a sample of a stereo chorused, echoed, reverberated guitar, then obviously much of the work is already done. I still might try a few different delays or reverb sounds along with what's already incorporated in the sample. Avoid combining effects if the combinations cause the clarity of the sound to disappear, but don't be afraid to use your tools. If you've found a really great sound that enhances the music, use it.

Even the mic techniques we've seen work well on real guitars can be applied to the keyboard guitar sounds. Although we usually run keyboards direct into the mixer, that doesn't mean we can't plug the keyboard into an am-plifier. If we mike the speaker cabinet, we can take advantage of the acoustical interaction of room ambience.

This chapter gives all you keyboard sound designers an edge when it comes to building a great guitar sound. Being familiar with the finer details of the different types of guitar sounds will add to the authenticity of your keyboard work.

Keyboardists can get frustrated because their latest set of great new guitar sounds doesn't really sound like guitar when they're in the context of a song. Much of the problem lies in the musical interpretation rather than in the sound. A guitar is limited in the way that it's laid out physically and harmonically. There are usually only a few ways to play most chords. The order and range of the notes in the chords are dictated by the layout of the guitar neck. If you really want to play guitar parts on the keyboard that sound like guitar, learn the limitations of the instrument and build your simulated guitar parts within those limitations. Besides the physical and harmonic idiosyncrasies of the guitar, you should familiarize yourself with the stylistic nuances that are characteristic of the style for which you're preparing the guitar part. I've found that any instrument has its own set of identifying licks. If you're not playing your synth like a screaming rock guitar, it'll never sound like a screaming rock guitar, no matter how good the sample is.

Keyboard workstations have reverb, chorus and distortion effect built in. These can all work well on guitar type sounds, and they're usually very easy to get to. Try different combinations within the workstation, then go out of the workstation and try the techniques covered in this lesson.

Conclusion

We've gone through some of the basic concepts of recording guitars, and we're starting to put the information in Chapters 1, 2 and 3 to use in ways that apply specifically to guitar. Listen to the Audio Examples enough times to become familiar with the sounds of each type of guitar. Try each of the techniques and concepts outlined in this chapter using your setup. Think of different ways to combine direct sounds with miked sounds. Practice!

Recording is always subject to listener appeal. If people like the sounds you've created, then you've done something right. If they consistently don't like the sounds you've created, it could be time to reevaluate your approach. The techniques I offer in this course are field tested and reliable. They offer solutions to recording situations that you might encounter. The results have been proven to be effective. Work from these ideas and build on them.

In Chapter 5 we'll study different concepts of miking the drum set and common percussion instruments. The percussion family has some of the most unique and interesting sounding instruments, and there are very special considerations to keep in mind when recording them.

5 Acoustic Drums and Percussion

The Percussion Family

The percussion family contains some of the most interesting sounding instruments. Many of these instruments require special consideration and care when they're being recorded. In this chapter, we'll cover these special considerations, plus we'll look at some common ways to process the different sounds. Typically when I refer to drums, I'm talking about a drum set which is also called the kit, or the set. The drum set usually includes a bass drum (also called the kick), a snare drum, tom toms and cymbals.

Percussion usually indicates the instruments like tambourine, triangle, cowbell, congas, bongos or shakers. In reality, the percussion family definitely includes the drum set, and the drum set can contain any member of the percussion family. The terms are used loosely, but in a session, the drum track includes the kit, and the percussion tracks contain any percussion instruments other than the kit.

Most people haven't listened enough with analytical ears to decide what they like and dislike about certain drum sounds. They have nothing on which to base their opinions. When considering drum sounds, there are some common characteristics that exist in drum sounds that most of us would call good. The term good is obviously subject to individual opinion. A good drum sound must also be appropriate for the musical style of the song that it's in. Good drum sounds will almost always have:

- Clean highs that blend with the mix
- Solid lows that blend with the mix
- Enough mids to feel punch
- Not so many mids that the sound is muddy
- Natural sound that possesses a warm tone
- Dimension, often sounding larger than life
- Believably appropriate reverberation
- Balance and blend in the mix

With all of these qualifications in mind, this list of characteristics is worth considering when evaluating and shaping your drum and percussion sounds. Start building your own list of what you think is consistent about good drum sounds.

The most important thing you can do at this point is listen to a lot of different styles of music that have been recorded in a lot of different studios by a lot of different top-notch professionals. Subject yourself to a large quantity of music. Try to be very analytical about the sounds that you're hearing. It's one thing to let the music passively cross your ears, it's another to actually hear what's going on texturally, musically and sonically. Refer to Illustration 5-1 for some guided listening assignments.

Illustration 5-1
Assignment: Listening Exercise

Listen to at least 10 different songs and specifically focus in on the drums. Make a list of all the drums you can hear on each tune. These might include bass drum (also called the kick drum), snare drum, toms, cymbals, shaker, tambourine, triangle or any of a seemingly never-ending list of percussion instruments. Once you've made a list of what you're hearing in the recording, focus on each instrument and write down things that you like or don't like about the different sounds. If you're hearing a kick drum, you might like the way it seems to hit you in the chest every time it's played, or you might like the way the attack of the kick seems to go right through you. These kind of observations can be very valuable as you practice recording the different instruments. One of the consistent problems people have when they're new to recording is that they haven't developed an opinion of what they think a good sound is. When you listen to music in this way, you'll often hear traits of the sounds that you hadn't noticed before. This exercise is well worth going through with each instrument. It will help you increase your understanding of how each instrument functions musically.

Find and study examples of rock, country, R&B, jazz, pop, blues and heavy metal songs. Each of these styles has a little different approach to drums. We can learn quite a bit about our options for shaping drum sounds by recognizing these differences.

For each style, make a list of descriptive adjectives for the drum and percussion sounds. Use words like thin, punchy, tinny, beefy and so on. Also, make a list of how the drum sounds are treated in the mix. Use phrases like close-sounding, very heavy reverb, long thin reverb or dry.

continued…

Theories of Drum Miking

We're going to focus on the drum set first. There are a lot of different ways to mike a drum set. I'll outline some of the miking techniques that are commonly used throughout the recording industry. If you listen to the audio examples and practice these techniques yourself, you'll learn what to expect from these different methods, and you'll develop your own opinions about their comparative advantages and disadvantages.

Anytime you're recording drums, it's best to keep the drums and the drummer in a separate room from the recording equipment, so the engineer can hear what the drums sound like as they're going to tape without acoustic interference from the live drums. This scenario is ideal for most recording situations, but in a home studio it's not always possible or practical simply because of the lack of square footage.

If your recording equipment is in the same

Illustration 5-1

...continued

One common arranging trick used to keep a listener's interest in a song involves varying the percussion instruments on each musical section. Often, producers will record all of the percussion instruments throughout a song, waiting until mixdown to decide which percussion part belongs in each musical section. As an exercise in your understanding of the impact of variation in percussion parts, select your ten favorite recordings then, for each recording, chart the order of the verses, choruses, bridge, solos and any other musical sections (like the diagram below). Under each section, list the percussion instruments you can hear along with their panning position. Depending on the specific music you're analyzing, you'll probably notice that one or two percussion instruments are added on the chorus, and possibly the bridge.

Verse	Pan	Chorus	Pan	Verse	Pan
Conga		Conga		Conga	
Shaker 1		Shaker 1		Shaker 1	
Shaker 2		Shaker 2		Shaker 2	
		Triangle			
		Tambourine			

Chorus	Pan	Bridge	Pan	Chorus	Pan
Conga		Claves		Conga	
Shaker 1		Vibraslap		Shaker 1	
Shaker 2		Cowbell		Shaker 2	
Triangle				Triangle	
Tambourine				Tambourine	
				Claves	
				Cowbell	

room with the drums when you're recording , it takes a little more time and much more trial and error, but you can still get good sounds. You'll need to record 20 to 30 seconds of the track, then rewind and evaluate the sounds you're getting. Make any adjustments you need to, then repeat this process until you're satisfied with the sound. Once you're satisfied that you're record-

ing a workable sound, start laying down the real thing.

Most of the drum sounds you hear on albums are achieved through the use of several microphones recorded separately to several tracks that are blended and balanced during the mixdown. This is ideal. Practically speaking, most people don't have a pile of microphones to use at home, let alone 8 to 12 available tracks on the multitrack for drums. Most people have one or two microphones, and these microphones weren't purchased with drums or percussion in mind, but as your setup and skills build you'll want to build your arsenal of task-specific microphones.

You should have a good condenser mic for over the drum set and for cymbals. Condensers are the mic of choice for percussion, and they do the best job of capturing the true sound of each instrument. The fact that condenser microphones respond to transients more accurately than the other types of microphones makes them an obvious choice for percussion instruments, like tambourine, shaker, cymbals, triangle, claves or guiro.

The mic of choice for close-miking toms, snare and kick is a moving-coil mic, like a Shure SM57, Sennheiser 421 or Electro-Voice RE20. Though they don't have the transient response of condenser microphones, moving-coil microphones work great for close-miking drums because they can withstand intense amounts of volume before distorting. Also, most moving-coil microphones have a built-in sensitivity in the upper frequency range, which provides an EQ that accentuates the attack of the drum.

If you have access to ribbon microphones, try them on the drums or overheads. They can sound great. They don't have the same excellent transient response as a condenser microphone and they typically don't produce the aggressive EQ edge of the moving-coil, but they can provide some excellent sounds. Be careful! Ribbons are fragile, and if used in a close mic configuration, they'll usually break when hit by a misdirected drum stick.

Most reasonably priced condenser and moving-coil microphones can give you good results. I don't recommend buying the least expensive mic, but you don't have to use a $3000 mic to achieve acceptable results either. Believe me, as you record more you'll start to have favorite microphones for each task. With all things in perspective, there are plenty of microphones available that can act as excellent tools for your recordings.

Recording a Drum Set With One Microphone

As we build from the one mic approach to the multiple mic approach, we'll consider techniques that can help optimize each approach. There is definitely something to be learned from each approach and each of these audio examples, so please be diligent in your pursuit of excellent drum sounds.

Mic placement is the main concern when using one mic to record the drums. Where you place the mic in relation to the drums is the primary determining factor of balance between the drums and intimacy of the drum sounds. In Chapter 4, we found that including the acoustic sound of the room that the guitars were in made a big difference in the sound of the guitar track. The same is true of the drum set and individual percussion instruments. The amount of room sound that you include in the drum track can totally change the effect of the drum part. The sound of the room that the drum set is in plays a very important role in the sound of the drum track, especially if you use a distant miking technique.

The advantage of a small recording setup is portability. If you're using a few microphones

Illustration 5-2
One Mic in Front

This setup uses a condenser microphone with a cardioid pickup pattern positioned in front of the set, pointed at the set, approximately 6' above the floor.

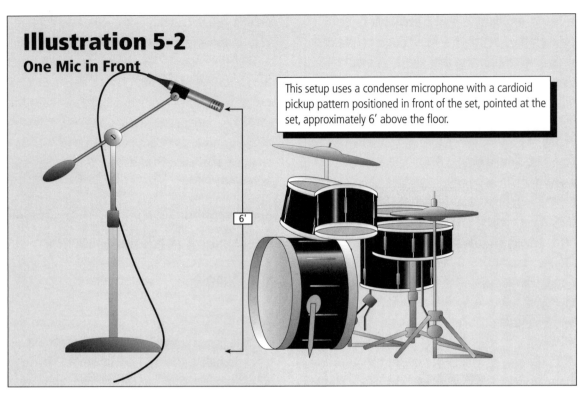

6'

Illustration 5-3
One Mic Over Drummer's Head

This setup uses a condenser microphone with a cardioid pickup pattern behind the kit, directly over the drummer's head, pointed at the set, about 6' above the floor.

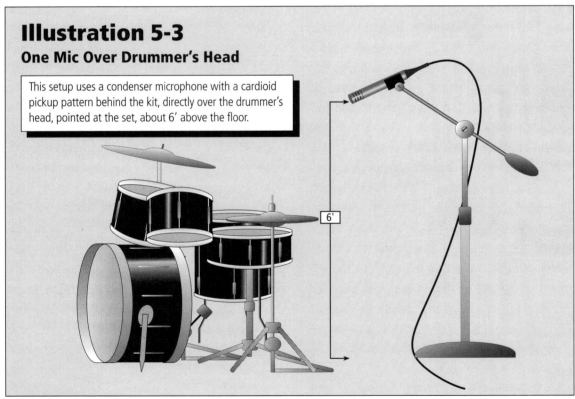

6'

and have a small 4- or 8-track, try moving the recorder and the drums into a warehouse, concert hall or gymnasium. Recording in these larger spaces can give your drum sounds punch, life and character that simply can't be electronically duplicated.

Listen to these examples of a complete drum set recorded with one microphone. Audio Examples 5-1 to 5-5 all use the same drum set in the same studio.

In Audio Example 5-1, the drum set was recorded with one mic directly in front of the kit, pointed at the set and about six feet from the floor (Illustration 5-2).

Audio Example 5-1 Mic in Front
CD-2: Track 1

In Audio Example 5-2 the mic is behind the kit, just above the drummer's head and pointed at the kit (Illustration 5-3).

Audio Example 5-2 Mic Over Drummer's Head
CD-2: Track 2

In Audio Example 5-3, the mic is about four feet above the set and is pointed down at the drums. When a mic is placed over the drums and points down at the set, it's called an overhead (Illustration 5-4).

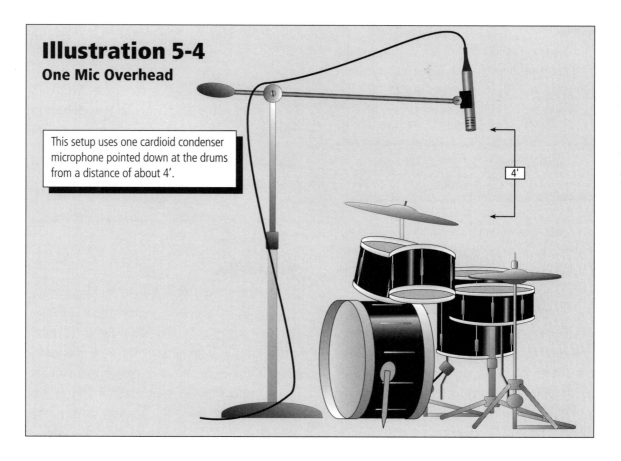

Illustration 5-4
One Mic Overhead

This setup uses one cardioid condenser microphone pointed down at the drums from a distance of about 4'.

4'

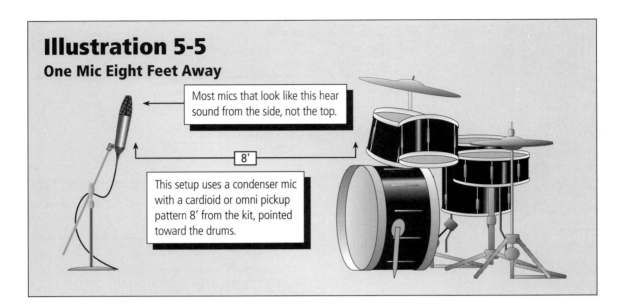

Illustration 5-5
One Mic Eight Feet Away

Most mics that look like this hear sound from the side, not the top.

8'

This setup uses a condenser mic with a cardioid or omni pickup pattern 8' from the kit, pointed toward the drums.

Audio Example 5-3 Overhead
CD-2: Track 3

Finally, in Audio Example 5-4, we hear the drum set from one mic, positioned about eight feet away and pointed toward the kit (Illustration 5-5).

Audio Example 5-4 Eight Feet Away
CD-2: Track 4

Each one of these mic positions has a different sound. The difference lies in the amount of acoustic room sound we include as we move the mic closer to and farther from the set.

The disadvantage to using only one mic is lack of control over the individual drum sounds. If we want to EQ the kick separately or put reverb just on the snare drum, we're really out of luck. If we've used just one or two microphones to pick up the entire kit, any effects that are added to the drums are added to all the drums

at once. In commercial popular music, we almost always want separate control over the level, EQ and effects on the different drums.

Adding reverb to one mic that's picked up the entire kit will tend to produce a distant sound. The drum set can lose punch and definition. Audio Example 5-5 demonstrates the sound of one mic on the drum set with the addition of plate reverb with a two-second decay time.

Audio Example 5-5 Plate on the Set
CD-2: Track 5

Be Mobile!

If you have a drum set or a drummer friend who's willing to be a gracious participant, set the drums up and start recording. Record several passes of the same groove. On each new pass, move the mic. Try any placement you can dream up: put the mic under the snare, put the mic in a different room, place the mic very close to the kit or hang the mic around the drummer's neck.

For real fun, move the drums and the mic to a different space, like a garage, a warehouse, a concert hall, the local high school gymnasium, outside or virtually any space that's available and legal.

In each acoustical environment, move the mic to several different spots to record. Keep a written log of which spaces you recorded in, where the mics were placed and how you liked the sound of each environment. Record a verbal reference on your tapes to help document and duplicate your results. Both the written log and the verbal reference and the written log should contain the tape number, take number, location of the recording, mic placement, type of mics, type of drums and the date.

Study your recordings and rate the sound of each. There will probably be a few spaces that sound far better than the others. That's the nature of acoustics. World class recording studios all have great equipment, but one of the biggest considerations involved in choosing a facility for a major project is the acoustic sound of its recording rooms.

Recording a Kit With Two Mics

Let's expand on our single microphone approach to recording drums. You need to build on the knowledge you've gained while using just one mic on the kit. As you add more microphones, your goal is to gain more control over the sounds and have flexibility when equalizing and putting effects on the individual drums.

With two microphones on the set there are

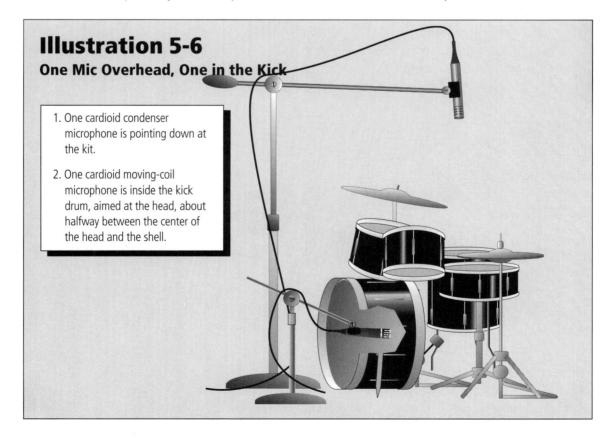

Illustration 5-6
One Mic Overhead, One in the Kick

1. One cardioid condenser microphone is pointing down at the kit.

2. One cardioid moving-coil microphone is inside the kick drum, aimed at the head, about halfway between the center of the head and the shell.

two primary options: you can use both mics together in a stereo configuration or you can use one mic for overall pickup while using the other for a specific instrument.

In Audio Example 5-6, I've set one mic directly over the kit with the second mic in the kick drum. When you use one of the microphones for the overall kit sound you can place the second mic on the kick drum (or possibly the snare) to get individual control, punch and definition in the mix. Choosing to close-mike the kick or the snare is purely a musical decision that's dependent on the drum part and the desired effect in the arrangement. This mic setup is more flexible than the single mic technique, but we're still limited to a monaural sound since the kick or snare would almost always be positioned in the center of the mix with the rest of the set (Illustration 5-6).

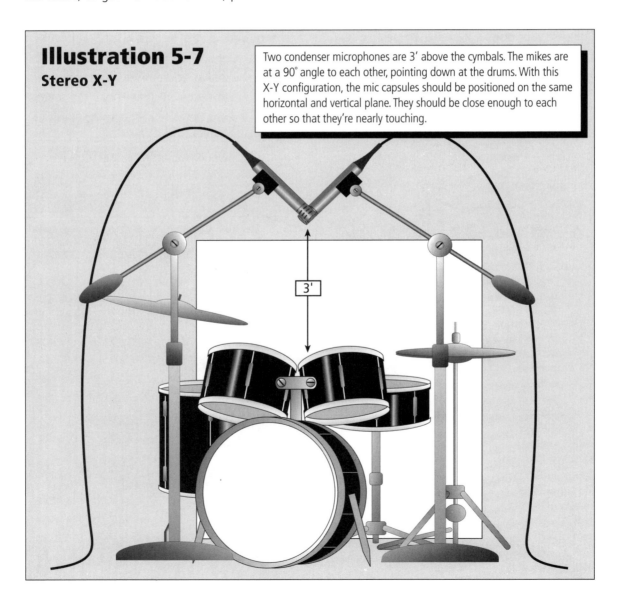

Illustration 5-7
Stereo X-Y

Two condenser microphones are 3' above the cymbals. The mikes are at a 90° angle to each other, pointing down at the drums. With this X-Y configuration, the mic capsules should be positioned on the same horizontal and vertical plane. They should be close enough to each other so that they're nearly touching.

3'

Illustration 5-8
X-Y Mic Technique

The traditional X-Y technique uses two cardioid condenser microphones positioned together to form a 90° angle. The mics should be overlapping and nearly touching.

This is called a coincident mic technique because the capsules are very close to each other and they share the same horizontal and vertical plane.

Coincident stereo mic techniques like the X-Y configuration exhibit the least amount of adverse phase interaction when combined in a mono mix. Since the mic capsules are as close together as they can possibly be without touching, they hear the sound source nearly simultaneously; they receive the sound waves in the same phase.

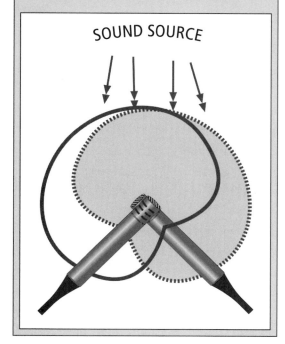

SOUND SOURCE

Audio Example 5-6
One Mic Over Kit, One in the Kick
CD-2: Track 6

Audio Example 5-7 uses the two condenser microphones with cardioid polar patterns as a stereo pair. The two mics are placed in a traditional X-Y configuration, directly above the drum set, at a distance of approximately three feet above the cymbals, pointing down at the drums. With this configuration, we can get a sound that has a stereo spread. The drums on the left side of the kit will be on the left side of the mix. The drums on the right side of the kit will be on the right side of the mix. If all drums aren't panned center, the mix can be opened up for positioning of the lead vocal and other key solo instruments. As we get into the mixing process, we'll see that positioning supportive instruments *away* from the center of the mix helps us hear the solo parts that are typically positioned in the center of the mix (Illustration 5-7).

Audio Example 5-7 Stereo X-Y
CD-2: Track 7

Try the X-Y configuration from different distances and in different rooms (Illustration 5-8). Stereo mic technique is often the best choice for a very natural drum sound, but for contemporary commercial drum sounds, it lacks flexibility. Stereo mic technique doesn't give you separate level, EQ and effects control on individual instruments. Like the single mic approach, if you put reverb on one mic, you've put reverb on the entire kit. Most commercial music is recorded with close microphones on the individual

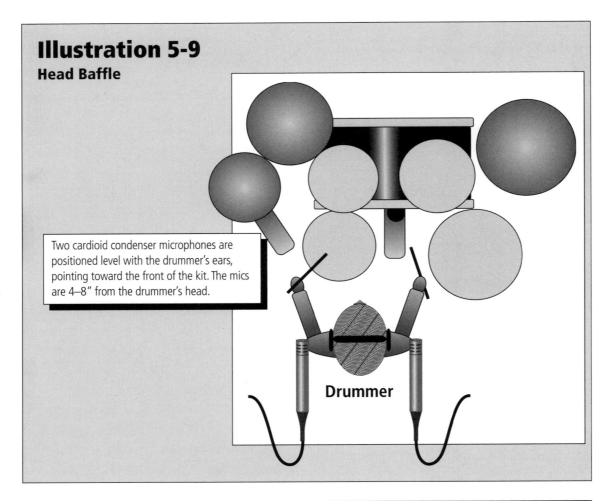

Illustration 5-9
Head Baffle

Two cardioid condenser microphones are positioned level with the drummer's ears, pointing toward the front of the kit. The mics are 4–8" from the drummer's head.

Drummer

drums combined with a stereo pair of mics used in an X-Y or some other stereo configuration.

Another good two-mic technique involves placing one mic on each side of the drummer's head, level with their ears pointing forward toward the drums. Position the microphones with their capsules three to six inches from the drummer's ears to achieve a good stereo image. The drummer's skull will act as a baffle between the two microphones. Audio Example 5-8 demonstrates this technique (Illustration 5-10).

Audio Example 5-8 Head Baffle
CD-2: Track 8

Recording a Kit With Three Mics

If you add one more mic to your setup, you'll usually use one mic on the kick drum, one mic on the snare drum and one mic over the drums. Optionally, you might use one kick mic along with a stereo pair that's positioned over, behind or in front of the kit. Both these approaches have advantages and disadvantages.

If you use one mic on the kick, one mic on the snare and one overhead mic, separate control of the kick and snare is possible. With three microphones, this technique will yield the most commercial and punchy sound. The kick and snare are the two main contributors to the definition of style. Being able to fine tune their level, EQ and effects is an advantage. The drum set in Audio Example 5-9 was miked with one mic inside the kick, one mic two inches above the snare and one mic about two feet above the cymbals. This configuration produces the most commer- cially viable results so far, but it doesn't provide a stereo image of the set. The kick, snare and overhead are almost always positioned together in the center. (Illustration 5-10).

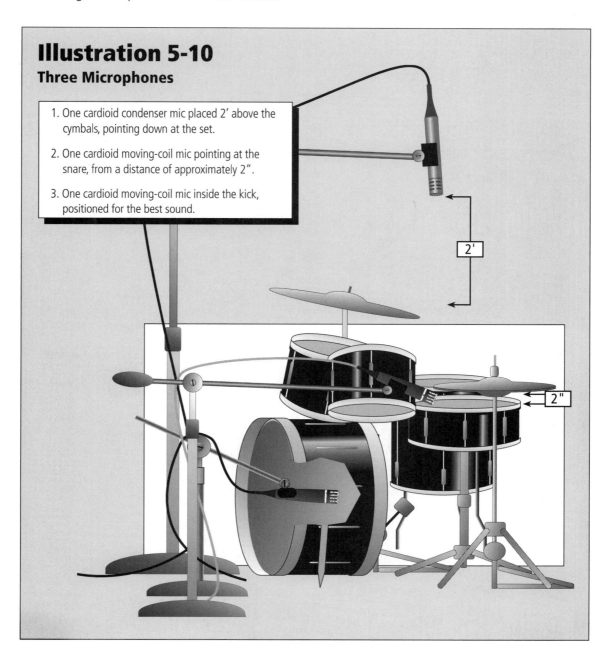

Illustration 5-10
Three Microphones

1. One cardioid condenser mic placed 2' above the cymbals, pointing down at the set.

2. One cardioid moving-coil mic pointing at the snare, from a distance of approximately 2".

3. One cardioid moving-coil mic inside the kick, positioned for the best sound.

2'

2"

Audio Example 5-9 Three Microphones
CD-2: Track 9

If we use a kick and two overheads, we can get a stereo image of the kit, but we lose individual control of the snare. Another option is to put the single mic on the snare instead of the kick, combining that mic with the two overheads. This can be a usable option, but we sacrifice control of the kick. Audio Example 5-10 demonstrates the sound of a drum set with two

microphones overhead, in an X-Y configuration, combined with one mic inside the kick.

Audio Example 5-10
X-Y Overhead, One in the Kick
CD-2: Track 10

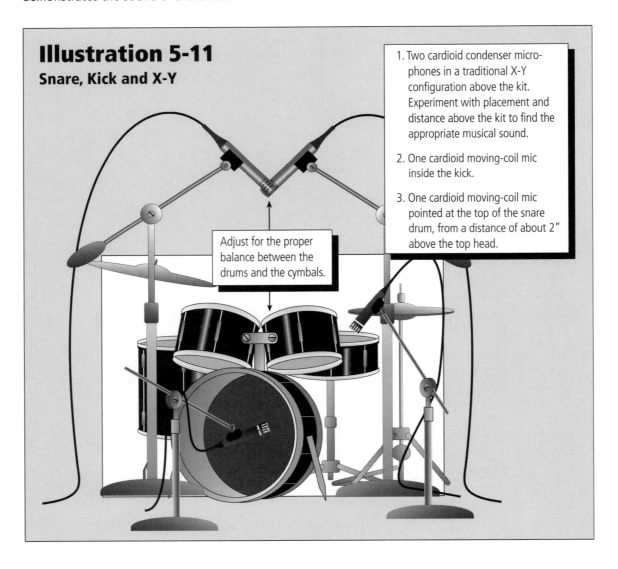

Illustration 5-11
Snare, Kick and X-Y

Adjust for the proper balance between the drums and the cymbals.

1. Two cardioid condenser microphones in a traditional X-Y configuration above the kit. Experiment with placement and distance above the kit to find the appropriate musical sound.

2. One cardioid moving-coil mic inside the kick.

3. One cardioid moving-coil mic pointed at the top of the snare drum, from a distance of about 2" above the top head.

Recording a Kit With Four Mics

With four microphones on the set, you begin to have good control over the kick and snare sounds, plus you can get a stereo image. Some very acceptable drum sounds can be achieved using a setup with one kick mic, one snare mic, and two overheads. You'll need to experiment with placement of the microphones (especially the overheads), but solid and unique kick and snare drum sounds are possible with this mic technique. The individual microphones plus the overheads used in a stereo configuration can provide an excellent stereo image. The set in Audio Example 5-11 was miked with one kick mic, one snare mic and two overheads in an X-Y configuration (Illustration 5-11).

Audio Example 5-11 Snare, Kick and X-Y
CD-2: Track 11

As we add microphones to our setup, we can either print each mic to a separate track on the multitrack, or we can do a sub-mix on the mixer, printing the entire kit to one or two tracks. It's ideal to keep as much flexibility as possible for the mixdown, but, if you're using a 4- or 8-track multitrack you'll probably only be able to justify allocating one or two tracks for the drums. Try recording the individual drum microphones on four to six tracks of an 8-track. Then bounce those tracks down to either a mono track or, in stereo, bounce them to two tracks.

As you consider different approaches to drum miking, it's important to note that no one method is always the perfect choice. Part of the fun of recording is in the creative choices we can make musically and technically.

Close-mike Technique

The most common approach to getting good, punchy, drum sounds that have unique character is to use the close-mic technique. Each drum will typically have its own mic. Each of these microphones plus two overheads will be printed to separate tracks of the multitrack. These tracks will either stay separate until the mixdown, or they might be combined with the assignment buses and bounced to stereo tracks, making room for more instruments or voices.

If tracks are limited, the microphones can be combined through the mixer to one or two tracks of the multitrack on the initial recording. Simply separately record the kick drum, snare drum, two separate tom microphones and two separate overheads to tracks one through six of the 8-track multitrack. Next, assign playback of those tracks to tracks seven and eight of the multitrack with the channel assign bus. With this setup you can re-equalize each track to obtain the optimum sound quality, add effects to individual drums and blend the drum mix for each musical section. If we want to put a lot of gated reverb on the toms but not on the kick or snare, we can do it using the close mic approach. We have flexibility that isn't possible using one or two microphones. If you're bouncing multiple tracks down to a stereo pair, use the pan controls to set up a stereo mix of the entire kit.

It's possible to use up a lot of tracks once you begin close-miking drums. Most projects using 24 tracks or more can justify allotting 8 to 16 tracks just for the drum set. This isn't an option for most people in their home studios,

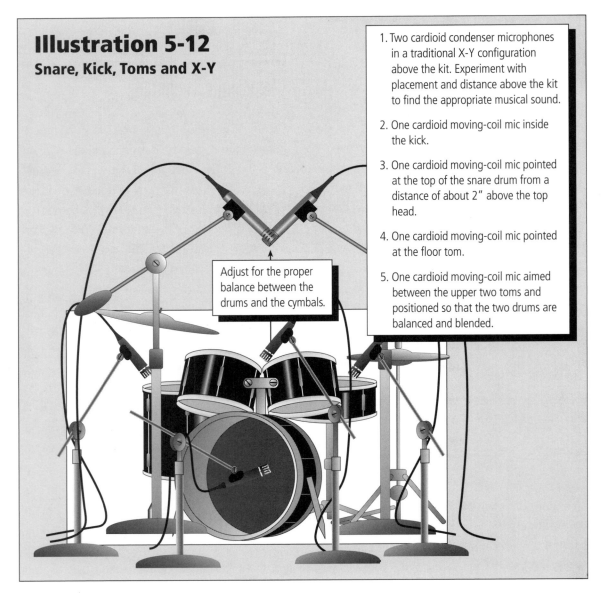

Illustration 5-12
Snare, Kick, Toms and X-Y

1. Two cardioid condenser microphones in a traditional X-Y configuration above the kit. Experiment with placement and distance above the kit to find the appropriate musical sound.

2. One cardioid moving-coil mic inside the kick.

3. One cardioid moving-coil mic pointed at the top of the snare drum from a distance of about 2" above the top head.

4. One cardioid moving-coil mic pointed at the floor tom.

5. One cardioid moving-coil mic aimed between the upper two toms and positioned so that the two drums are balanced and blended.

Adjust for the proper balance between the drums and the cymbals.

but be aware that the more isolation you can get, the more precisely you'll be able to shape each sound. There are even plenty of ways to expand on this approach. Try including room ambience microphones, a mic under the snare, individual cymbal microphones or any creative new approach you can dream up.

The drum set in Audio Example 5-12 is set up with one kick mic, one snare mic, one mic on each tom, two microphones overhead in an X-Y pattern and one hi-hat mic (Illustration 5-12).

Audio Example 5-12 Snare, Kick, Toms and X-Y
CD-2: Track 12

Drum Conditioning

Now that we've heard the results of some different miking configurations, let's focus on drum preparation and tuning (for recording) and techniques for close-miking the drums. To get good drums sounds, it's necessary to be familiar with drum tuning and dampening techniques. A bad sounding drum is nearly impossible to get a good recorded sound from. A good sounding drum can make your recording experience much more enjoyable.

If the drum heads are dented and stretched out, cancel the rest of your appointments for the day. You'll be spending a substantial amount of time getting an acceptable drum sound.

If the drums aren't high quality instruments, there's a good chance that the shells aren't smooth and level, and there's a possibility that the drum aren't even perfectly round. If this is the case, the heads won't seat evenly on the drum shell and there'll be a loss of tone, detracting from the drum sound.

Most major manufacturers offer a decent quality instrument that can sound great on tape if tuned properly. Some drums are of very high quality and consistently sound great on a recording, and most of the higher priced sets from the major drum manufacturers can sound incredible. The extra cost for the more expensive kits typically assures you of good solid shells constructed from excellent materials that are perfectly round and have truly flat edges. Those features combined with strong, attractive hardware usually make the extra cost a worthwhile investment.

Often, the difference between a good sounding drum and a bad sounding drum lies simply in tuning. The standard approach to tuning involves:

- Tuning the top head to the tone you want
- Making sure the pitch is the same all the way around the head by tapping at each lug and adjusting the lugs until they all match
- Duplicating the sound of the top head with the bottom head

If the head isn't tuned evenly all the way around, the head won't resonate well. You'll probably hear more extraneous overtones than smooth tone. Audio Example 5-13 provides an example of a poorly tuned tom.

Audio Example 5-13 A Tom Out of Tune
CD-2: Track 13

The drum in Audio Example 5-14 is the same drum you heard in Audio Example 5-13 with even tension all the way around the head and with the bottom head tuned to match the top.

Audio Example 5-14 A Tom in Tune
CD-2: Track 13

You don't need to be a drummer to get the drums sounding good. You do need to be patient and knowledgeable about drum tuning. It's really not that difficult, but it can take some time to get drums tuned well. If you're a drummer, the single most cost-effective routine you can get into before each session is to have new (or fairly new) heads on your drums that are tuned evenly.

Some drummers are very meticulous about tuning, placement and the status of their heads and cymbals. That's great. Some drummers aren't so meticulous. As the engineer, you need to be able to get the drums to sound good anyway.

If you own drums or know a drummer who's willing to practice creating drum sounds with you, approach each drum separately and start practicing. Start from scratch. Loosen the heads, then build the sounds you want. Try tuning high, medium and low. There are different theories on tuning. Some say that the top and bottom heads should match in pitch. Some say the top head should be higher. Some say the bottom head should be higher. All methods can produce good sounds so try different methods. You'll have the best luck if you adjust the drum for even tension all the way around the head. Beyond that, some drummers suggest loosening one lug after you've achieved even tension to decrease ringing. I prefer not to use that technique, but some drummers use it successfully. Be adaptable and practice! Nothing will give you a feel for drum sounds like tuning and retuning a real drum.

As you work with each drum, you'll hear the results of the dampening and tuning techniques. On each drum, check the heads for wear. Too many extreme dents can stretch a drum head, limiting even vibration and decreasing your chances of successful drum recording.

Muffling the Drum

When a drum is tuned well and has a smooth tone, the decay of the drum can last longer than we really want in the mix. If all the toms are ringing all the time, the drum track can become a wall of rumbling heads. To compensate for this, we'll often dampen the heads to decrease the decay. Some drums played by some drummers might sound great with no dampening. Decisions on the direction for the drum sound are purely based on the needs of the music.

To dampen the drum, we need to put something on the head that'll decrease the vibration. There are several materials that are regularly used to muffle the drum sound.

It's common to use duct tape, applied in three- to six-inch lengths to the outer edge of the top and or bottom head (Illustration 5-13).

Another technique involves taping bathroom tissue, cotton or gauze to the head (Illustration 5-14).

On a snare drum, it's common to tape a wallet to the head at the point farthest from the drummer (Illustration 5-15).

Sometimes a one- to three-inch wide strip of cotton or felt material, stretched under the head, will dampen the head just the right amount, but this doesn't leave room for much speedy flexibility if you want less dampening (Illustration 5-16).

Some drummers like to cut an old head so that only the outer one or two inches is left and the hoop is cut off. This circle can be laid on the top of the drum, dampening evenly around the head (Illustration 5-17).

Most drums have a muffler built in. This is usually a small circular felt pad that can be moved up against the head from the inside by turning a knob on the outside. These hardly ever give a good sound and they'll often rattle. Consider removing them (Illustration 5-18).

The one method of dampening that I've found works consistently and sounds great involves using three- to six-inch lengths of self-sticking weather stripping. Stick the weather stripping directly to the head. The sound is

Illustration 5-13
Dampening With Duct Tape

Stick a piece of duct tape to the top and/or bottom head to control ringing. Add as much as needed to get the desired sound. Placing tape near the rim usually works best.

This technique works equally well on the kick, snare or toms.

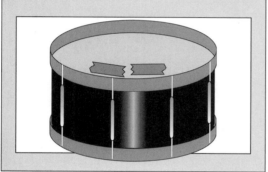

Illustration 5-14
Dampening With Facial Tissue

Use duct tape or masking tape to hold facial tissue, cotton or gauze on the head. Add as much as needed to get the desired sound. Placing tape near the rim usually works best.

This technique works equally well on the kick, snare or toms.

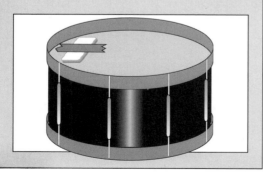

Illustration 5-15
Dampening With a Wallet

1. Lay a billfold on top of the snare drum near the rim. Bring duct tape up over the rim and onto the wallet.

2. It's not necessary for the tape to touch the head. The wallet can move freely for a natural sound and feel.

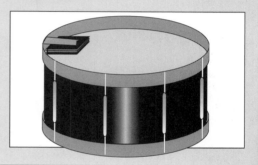

Illustration 5-16
A Cloth Strip Under the Head

1. A 1–3" wide strip of cloth (like a piece of an old sheet) can be sandwiched between the head and the shell about 2–6" from the side of the drum.

2. As you tighten the head, pull the cloth taut with the excess still hanging out from under the head.

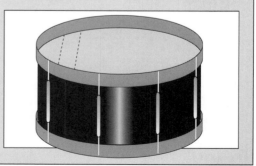

Illustration 5-17
Dampening With a Head Ring

1. Cut a 1–2" wide ring from the outer part of an old drum head.
2. Lay the ring on top of your drum head to evenly dampen the tone. The closer the ring is to the rim, the smaller the amount of dampening. Keep in place with small pieces of duct tape if necessary.

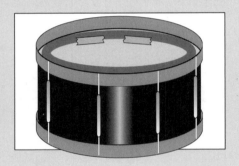

Illustration 5-18
The Internal Muffler

1. A felt pad is moved up against the head from inside the drum.
2. A knob on the outside of the drum controls the positioning of the pad inside. Turn clockwise to move the pad against the head and counter-clockwise to move it away.

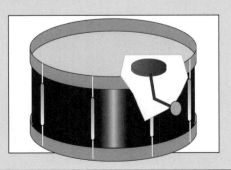

Illustration 5-19
Weather Stripping

1. Use 3–6" pieces of self-adhering weather stripping to dampen the head. Use multiple strips to fine-tune the sound of the drum if necessary.
2. Placing the weather stripping near the rim usually produces the warm est and purest tone.

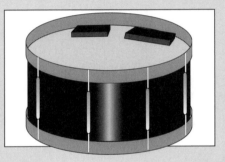

Summary

I've outlined several methods for muffling drums. Each one of these approaches can be successful, but I definitely have my personal favorites. I'm sure you'll develop yours, too.

I've had the best results with the method outlined in Illustration 5-19. The weather stripping provides the fullest tone and offers the greatest flexibility. I've also seen several very fine drummers use the method described in Illustration 5-17. This approach produces an even, warm, smooth sound.

My least favorite drum sound uses the internal muffler shown in Illustration 5-18. I usually remove them from the drum.

warmer and smoother than using duct tape, and just the right amount of dampening can be achieved by moving the weather stripping to different positions on the head and varying the length (Illustration 5-19).

Position the dampening material for the balance between tone and attack that's musically and stylistically appropriate. The drum will retain more tone with a longer resonance when you place dampeners near the rim. Place dampening material toward the center of the drum to decrease the tone most dramatically and to accentuate the attack. Remember, as with everything we do technically, always avoid doing anything or positioning anything in a manner that inhibits musical flow and creativity.

Drum Sticks

The drummer's choice of sticks and their condition can make a big difference in the sound of the drums. Nylon-tipped sticks have a brighter sounding attack than wood-tipped sticks, especially on cymbals. Hickory sticks have a different sound than oak sticks, and they both sound different than graphite or metal sticks. Heavy sticks have a completely different sound than light sticks.

Most experienced studio drummers carry several different types of drum sticks with them, even though they probably have their own overall favorite.

If you want to be prepared when recording drums, it's worth the investment to have some extra sticks available that vary in size and physical composition.

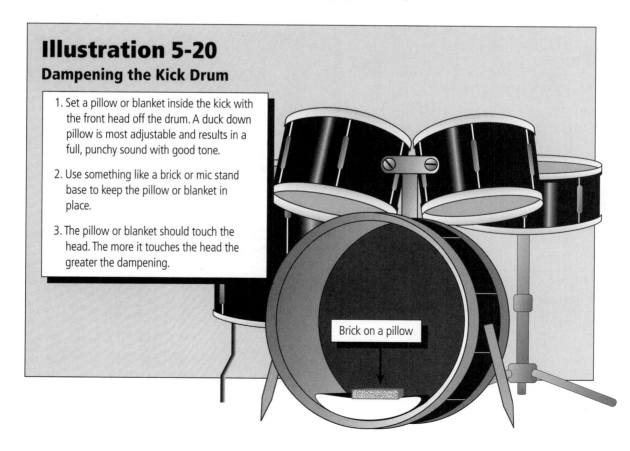

Illustration 5-20
Dampening the Kick Drum

1. Set a pillow or blanket inside the kick with the front head off the drum. A duck down pillow is most adjustable and results in a full, punchy sound with good tone.

2. Use something like a brick or mic stand base to keep the pillow or blanket in place.

3. The pillow or blanket should touch the head. The more it touches the head the greater the dampening.

Brick on a pillow

Kick Drum

The kick drum (bass drum) is very important to the impact of the drum sound. Different styles demand different kick sounds. Some sounds, like jazz and heavy rock kicks, have less dampening and ring longer.

Often in the jazz idiom and some hard rock settings, the kick is left undampened, but the most common kick sound is substantially muffled, with good low-end thump and a clean attack. To achieve this sound, remove the front head and place a blanket or a pillow in the bottom of the drum. The blanket or pillow should be positioned for the desired

amount of dampening—the more contact with the head, the more muffling. The weight of the pillow or blanket affects the sound. I've found that a down pillow works great; I'll usually place a brick or a mic stand base on the pillow to hold it in place (Illustration 5-20).

A moving-coil mic, positioned inside the kick about six inches from the drummer's head and about halfway between the center of the head and the shell, will usually produce a good sound.

Experiment with mic placement to get the best sound you can before you equalize the sound. On any drum, the attack is strongest at the center of the drum, and the tone is strongest toward the shell. Move the mic to the cen-

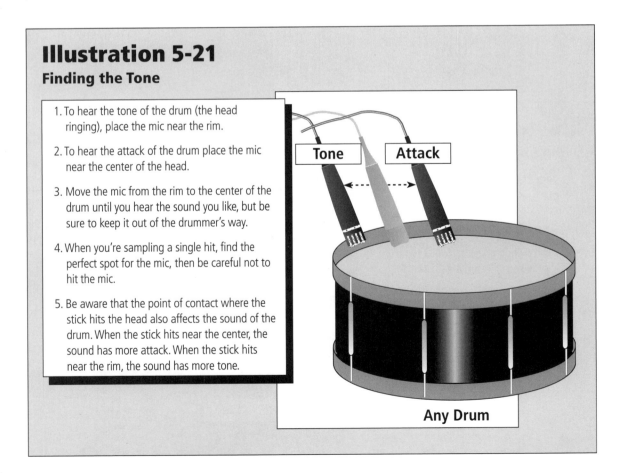

Illustration 5-21
Finding the Tone

1. To hear the tone of the drum (the head ringing), place the mic near the rim.

2. To hear the attack of the drum place the mic near the center of the head.

3. Move the mic from the rim to the center of the drum until you hear the sound you like, but be sure to keep it out of the drummer's way.

4. When you're sampling a single hit, find the perfect spot for the mic, then be careful not to hit the mic.

5. Be aware that the point of contact where the stick hits the head also affects the sound of the drum. When the stick hits near the center, the sound has more attack. When the stick hits near the rim, the sound has more tone.

Tone   Attack

Any Drum

ter of the head if you want more attack. If you need more tone, move the mic toward the shell (Illustration 5-21).

Audio Example 5-15 demonstrates the sound of a kick drum with the mic inside the drum pointing directly at the center of the head where the beater hits, from a distance of six inches. Notice the attack.

Audio Example 5-15 Kick Attack
CD-2: Track 14

Audio Example 5-16 demonstrates the same kick as Audio Example 5-15 with the same mic aimed at the head about two inches in from the shell and about six inches from the head. Notice the tone.

Audio Example 5-16 Kick Tone
CD-2: Track 15

Another factor in the sound of the kick is the distance of the mic from the drum head. Audio Example 5-17 demonstrates the kick with the mic three inches from the head and about halfway between the center of the head and the drum shell.

Audio Example 5-17 Kick Three Inches Away
CD-2: Track 16

The mic in Audio Example 5-18 is about one foot outside of the drum, still pointed about half way between the center and the shell.

Audio Example 5-18 Kick 12 Inches Outside
CD-2: Track 17

As you can tell by these different examples, positioning is critical to the sound of the drum. Not only is the placement of the mic critical, but the tuning of the drum can make all the difference. The tension should be even around the head and there should be appropriate dampening for the sound you need. It's common to hear a very deep sounding kick that has a solid thump in the low end and a good attack. In search of this kind of sound, most drummers tend to loosen the head to get a low sound. This can be a mistake. If the head is tuned too low, the pitch of the drum can be unusable and might not even be audible. To get a warm, punchy thump out of a kick, try tightening the head.

Another very important consideration in the kick sound is the drummer's technique. Drummers that stab at the kick with the beater can choke an otherwise great sound into an unappealing stutter-slap.

Equalizing the Kick Drum

Always find the microphone, mic placement and tuning that sound the best on any drum before beginning the equalization process.

The nature of close-miking a kick drum typically produces a raw sound that's overly abundant in lower midrange frequencies between 200 and 600Hz, and the sound usually needs EQ to be usable.

When I listen to a raw kick sound before it's been equalized, I first listen for the frequencies that are clouding the sound of the kick. That frequency range is almost always somewhere between 200 and 600Hz. Listen to the kick in

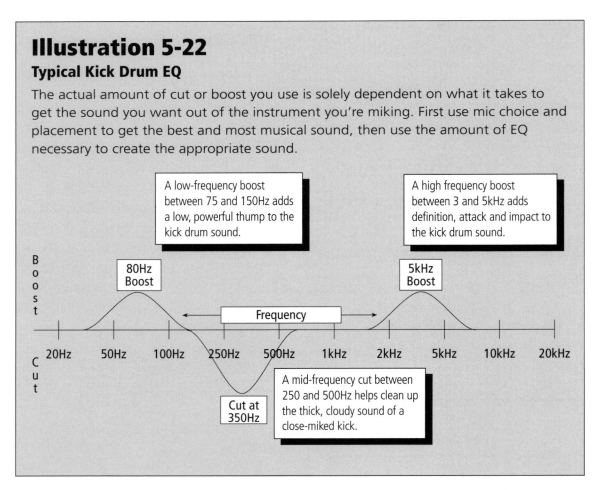

Illustration 5-22
Typical Kick Drum EQ

The actual amount of cut or boost you use is solely dependent on what it takes to get the sound you want out of the instrument you're miking. First use mic choice and placement to get the best and most musical sound, then use the amount of EQ necessary to create the appropriate sound.

A low-frequency boost between 75 and 150Hz adds a low, powerful thump to the kick drum sound.

A high frequency boost between 3 and 5kHz adds definition, attack and impact to the kick drum sound.

80Hz Boost

5kHz Boost

Frequency

20Hz   50Hz   100Hz   250Hz   500Hz   1kHz   2kHz   5kHz   10kHz   20kHz

A mid-frequency cut between 250 and 500Hz helps clean up the thick, cloudy sound of a close-miked kick.

Cut at 350Hz

Audio Example 5-19 as I turn down a one-octave wide bandwidth centered at 300Hz.

Audio Example 5-19 Cut 300Hz
CD-2: Track 18

Once the lower mids are turned down, I'll usually locate a low frequency between 75 and 150Hz to boost. Be conservative in the amount of these bass frequencies you print to tape, especially to the multitrack. If you question how strong the bass frequencies should be, print a little less than you expect to use. You can always boost the lows on mixdown.

Next, I'll typically locate an upper fre-quency to boost that'll emphasize the attack of the beater hitting the head. Boosting a frequency between 3 and 5kHz will usually emphasize this attack. Listen to the kick in Audio Example 5-20. A moving-coil mic is pointed halfway between the center of the drum and the shell, from a distance of six inches. At first, this drum has no EQ. First I'll cut at 300Hz, next I'll boost the low end at about 80Hz, then I'll boost the attack at about 4kHz (Illustration 5-22).

Audio Example 5-20
Cut 300Hz, Boost 80Hz and 4kHz
CD-2: Track 18

Effects on the Kick

For a clean and natural recording, the kick hardly ever has any reverb or delay. There are creative uses for almost any technique, but adding reverb to a kick drum tends to make the mix sound muddy. In some styles, though, it's appropriate to add a substantial amount of gated reverb, or reverb that has a very short decay time, to the kick. The purpose of adding reverb in some R&B and dance styles is to blend the kick with the snare and the toms, which are also heavily effected. Since the decay times are short (below a half second) and the reverb sound is gated, the reverb doesn't get in the way of the rest of the mix. Reverb on the kick in this setting is musically and stylistically correct and can make an arrangement sound very big.

Wait until mixdown to add reverb if you have enough tracks to print the kick to its own track. If you're combining the drums to one or two tracks at the time of the initial recording but have a separate mic for the kick, you might need to print the reverb to the multitrack. This will be the only time in the recording process where you'll have access to the kick separately for send to the reverb. This process can work well, but it takes practice and experience to second-guess what the track will really sound like in the final mix.

As a guideline, the styles that usually use a dry kick sound are country, jazz, blues, vintage rock, some harder rock and metal and most ethnic and international styles. Styles that tend to use more effect on the kick are R&B, funk and some commercial rock.

Recording Levels for Kick Drum

The suggested recording level for a bass drum is 0VU at the loudest part of the track. If the sound is heavy in bass frequencies, I've found no problem printing hot to tape. It's usually safe to record in the range of +1 to +4VU on the loudest parts of the track. If the sound is thin in the low end and has a lot of attack, it's usually necessary to print colder to tape, in the range of -5 to -1VU, to more accurately capture the transient attack.

At first, most students of recording can't figure out just what they like and dislike about the different sounds they're recording. In Audio Example 5-21, I'll play several different kick drums. Each sound is very usable within a particular style. Write down what you notice about each kick. Do you like the sound? How are the lows? Do you like the attack sound? Is it muddy? Is it punchy? Listen very carefully.

Audio Example 5-21 Lots of Kicks
CD-2: Track 19

Snare Drum

Snare drums usually fall into one of two categories: very easy to get a good sound out of or almost impossible to get a good sound out of. Fortunately there are some tricks we can pull out of the hat to help the more difficult drums sound good. It's important for you to know some quick and easy techniques for getting the snare to work. It's amazing how many decent drummers are lost when it comes to drum sounds.

First, make sure the heads are in good shape. A lot of times the top snare head has been stretched and dented so much that the center of the head is actually loose and sagging, even though the rest of the head is tight. This isn't good. Replacing the head will make a huge difference in the sound.

The bottom head is also critical to the snare sound. The most common problem I've seen is a hole in the bottom head. These bottom heads are much thinner than the top heads. Since the drum is continually being put on and taken off the snare stand (which can puncture the head) and usually carried in a case with sticks and drum keys (which can puncture the head) and since drummers tend to set the snare on the floor with the bottom head down (you never know what's on the floor that can puncture the head), sometimes there's a hole in the bottom head. Drummers seem to work on the out of sight, out of mind principle when it comes to the bottom head. When you're trying to get a great sound from a snare, though, it's important that the bottom head is in good shape. If it's not, the head won't resonate evenly, and you'll have problems with annoying overtones.

The heads need to be in good shape. If you're doing much drum recording, it's best to have some extra heads on hand. If you have the appropriate replacement head, you'll save yourself a lot of anguish, plus your sounds will be better and you'll get them faster. This will help your reputation in the community. The next time your local music store has a great deal on heads, pick up a 14-inch top and bottom snare head. Most snare drums are 14-inch drums. The most versatile of the top heads are Remo Ambassador coated, and Ambassador Black Dot. After the session, don't forget to get your heads back from the drummer. Experienced studio drummers carry their own extra heads in case one breaks or if a unique musical sound demands a head change.

Practice tuning your own or a friend's

drums. Tune the top and bottom heads to the same tone, then evaluate the sound of the drum. Tune the bottom head higher than the top head and evaluate the sound of the drum. Finally, tune the top head higher than the bottom head and evaluate the sound of the drum. See what the sound difference is. There has to be enough tension on the head to give the drummer good rebound, and the tension must be even around the head.

With the top head tuned fairly low, the drum sound has a thick texture. This sound can be very usable in some settings. Audio Example 5-22 demonstrates a snare drum tuned low. First you'll hear the drum with the snares off, then with the snares on.

Audio Example 5-22 Snare Tuned Low
CD-2: Track 20

Tuning the snare very high gives a sharp attack and good definition, but the sound can be thin. Audio Example 5-23 demonstrates a snare tuned high. First you'll hear the drum with the snares off, then with the snares on.

Audio Example 5-23 Snare Tuned High
CD-2: Track 20

A medium tuning that's not real high or real low is the most common snare sound. The drum in Audio Example 5-24 is tuned with the top and bottom heads tight but not too tight. First you'll hear the drum with the snares off, then with the snares on.

Illustration 5-23
The Snares

1. Be sure the snare strands are even in tension.
2. If the snares are loose or broken, cut them off.
3. If the snares can't be adjusted for constant tension or if there are too many strands missing, replace the entire set of snares.
4. Applying tape to loose snares can minimize extraneous buzzes, but the tape chokes the sound of the drum.

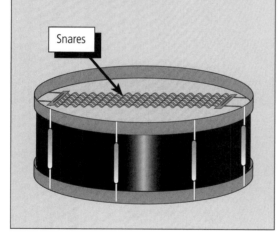

Snares

Audio Example 5-24 Tight Top and Bottom
CD-2: Track 20

On each example, you can hear the drum with the snares off, then on. The snares are the wires that touch the bottom head (Illustration 5-23). If these wires are stretched, broken or uneven in tension, the drum will buzz and rattle when the snare drum is hit and probably when any of the rest of the drums are hit. This isn't good. Check the snares for loose strands and uneven tension. Take the drum off the stand and look at the snares. If one or two strands are loose, I'll usually cut them off. Some drums will have individual adjustments for the snares. If this is the case, adjust the strands for even tension. Sometimes it might help to put a piece of tape on the snares at one end or the other, but I've achieved the best success by adjusting the snares or cutting the strays off.

The snare mechanism also has an adjustment to tighten or loosen all the snares at once. Try tightening the snares if there are too many buzzes, but be careful. If the snares are too tight, the sound of the drum will be choked and undesirable.

A good snare sound is dependent on a lot of factors working perfectly together. If you can handle drum tuning basics, it'll make a big difference in the sound of your live drum recordings, plus you'll have an insight and perspective on drums that'll prove to be a valuable asset.

Once the heads are in shape, tuned and the snares are even in tension, you'll usually need to dampen the head to minimize ring. Dampen the snare in one of the ways described in Illustrations 5-17A to 5-17G. Try each technique for dampening to hear the difference in the sound of each approach. I get the best sounds by using self-adhering weather stripping, applying the amount of weather stripping in the positions that are appropriate for the sound I want. The stripping works very well when placed an inch or two in from the rim. This is a very flexible approach, and the foam weather stripping dampens in a way that sounds natural. Audio Example 5-25 demonstrates a snare with no dampening.

Audio Example 5-25 Snare Without Dampening
CD-2: Track 20

Audio Example 5-26 demonstrates the sound of the snare with weather stripping added to get the sound I wanted.

Audio Example 5-26
Snare With Weather Stripping
CD-2: Track 20

Mic Choice for Snare Drum

Mic choice and placement can vary greatly depending on the purpose of the recording and the desired musical impact. If you're close-miking a set, the snare mic usually points down at the drum and is about two inches from the top head, aimed one or two inches in from the rim. Use a moving-coil mic like a Shure SM57, Sennheiser 421 or an Electro-Voice RE20. Keep the mic out of the drummer's way because a stick hitting the mic can ruin a take or even a microphone. Most mic manufacturers make micro-

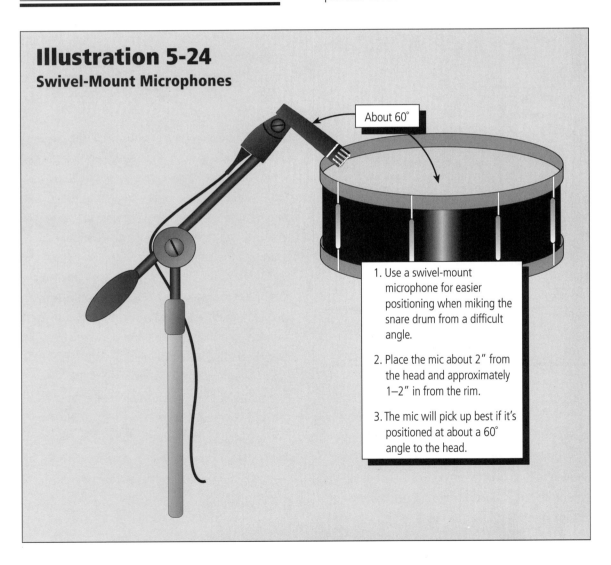

Illustration 5-24
Swivel-Mount Microphones

About 60°

1. Use a swivel-mount microphone for easier positioning when miking the snare drum from a difficult angle.

2. Place the mic about 2" from the head and approximately 1–2" in from the rim.

3. The mic will pick up best if it's positioned at about a 60° angle to the head.

phones that are designed for getting into tight spots like drum sets. Shure makes the SM56, which is the same mic as the SM57 with swivel mount for the upper part of the mic (Illustration 5-24). These adjustable microphones are very handy and can help you get a better drum sound. The ideal is to point the mic at about a 60 degree angle to the drum. If the mic has to be pointing straight across the drum due to space restriction, there will be more leakage of other drums into the snare mic than you really want to deal with. It's best to point the snare drum mic at the snare drum.

If you're sampling and want to capture the full transient and natural sound of the snare, record though a condenser mic from a distance of one or two feet. Condenser microphones can't usually handle the extreme volume of a snare at close range without overdriving their own internal circuitry. Condenser microphones are the mic of choice when recording the snare drum from a distance greater than approximately one foot. They'll give the snare full response and transient clarity. Moving-coil microphones are the mic of choice for close-miking drums. They can typically handle high sound pressure levels and produce a full and aggressive sound in close proximity to the sound source.

The snare in Audio Example 5-27 was miked with a condenser mic pointed at the drum, from a distance of about one foot.

Audio Example 5-27 Snare From One Foot
CD-2: Track 21

This snare in Audio Example 5-28 was miked with a moving-coil mic pointing at the drum, from a distance of about two inches.

Audio Example 5-28 Snare From Two Inches
CD-2: Track 21

Reverb is a very important part of most snare drum sounds. If you have a separate track for the snare, save the addition of reverb until mixdown so you can find just the right sound to blend with the mix in a musical way. If you're combining the drums to a stereo or mono sub-mix as you record, you might want to print the snare reverb with the track or tracks. Experience using this procedure will enable you to second-guess how much reverb you'll eventually need in the mix. If you're unsure about how to use effects sends, returns and how to print reverb to a track, refer to Chapters 1 and 2.

Reverberation on the Snare Drum

Longer reverberation times, in the neighborhood of 1.5 to 3 seconds, are common in ballads of nearly every style and sometimes in commercial pop tunes. A predelay in time with the eighth note or sixteenth note can add an interesting dimension to the sound.

The snare in Audio Example 5-29 has a hall reverb with a reverberation time of about 2.5 seconds.

Audio Example 5-29
Snare Reverb With 2.5 Second Decay Time
CD-2: Track 22

Many R&B, commercial rock songs, uptempo country songs and jazz songs utilize decay times below one second. Gated reverb sounds are very common in R&B, funk and dance grooves.

Audio Example 5-30 demonstrates the snare drum with a gated reverb sound.

Audio Example 5-30 Snare With Gated Reverb
CD-2: Track 23

As we progress through this course, we'll build more options for snare drum effects. The snare drum sound is very definitive of musical style. Modern snare sounds are often quite complex and involved. The snare sound might actually consist of three or four reverberation sounds along with compression and expansion. We don't ever want to overuse signal processing, but we must do what we need to while in search of a sound that supports the musical emotion and feeling dictated by the song.

Equalizing the Snare Drum

Most snare sounds don't need to contain an overabundance of the frequencies below 100Hz. I'll often roll those lows off. The body of the snare is often in the 200 to 300Hz range. To enhance the attack, boost a frequency between 3 and 5kHz. Listen to the snare drum in Audio Example 5-31. The snare sound starts out flat, then I roll off the lows below 100Hz. Next, I boost 250Hz slightly and finally I boost 5kHz.

Audio Example 5-31
Roll Off 100Hz, Boost 250Hz and 5kHz
CD-2: Track 24

As you experiment with your own snare sounds you'll be successful if you keep in mind the three basic frequency ranges outlined in Audio Example 5-31. Though they might shift a

little up or down depending on the actual snare drum you're recording, the characteristic frequency ranges are fairly consistent. We'll build many more snare sounds throughout this course.

Recording Levels for Snare Drum

Suggested recording levels for snare drums vary depending on the sound of the drum. 0VU is normal on the loudest part of the track when recording a full sounding drum. A strong single hit on the snare should typically register about -5 to -3VU. This level leaves little head room for the inevitable fact that drummers play louder as they settle into a song. If a drummer plays an eighth or sixteenth note fill on the snare, the apparent level will increase substantially.

If the sound of the snare is thin in the low end and if there's a lot of transient attack to the sound, the maximum record level should typically be in the range of -7 to -3VU in order to accurately record the transient.

Listen to the examples of different snare sounds in Audio Example 5-32. Take note of what you like and dislike about each. Do you like the attack? Is there much low frequency content? Are there many highs? Is the sound thin? Does the drum sound fat? Is there solid punch to the sound?

Audio Example 5-32 Lots of Snares
CD-2: Track 25

Toms

Recording toms is similar in many ways to recording the kick drum and snare drum. It's im-

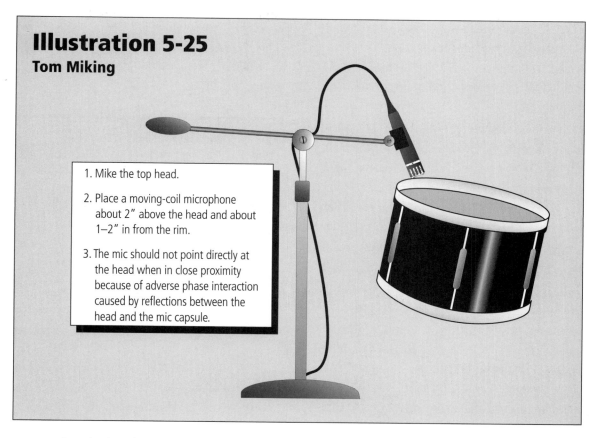

Illustration 5-25
Tom Miking

1. Mike the top head.

2. Place a moving-coil microphone about 2″ above the head and about 1–2″ in from the rim.

3. The mic should not point directly at the head when in close proximity because of adverse phase interaction caused by reflections between the head and the mic capsule.

portant that the heads are in good shape, that they're tuned properly and that the dampening gets the appropriate sound for the track. Tune the top and bottom heads to the same tone and be sure the tension is even around each head.

For dampening toms, I recommend weather stripping instead of duct tape or bathroom tissue. Weather stripping stuck on the drum head provides a warm sound with good tone. The best feature weather stripping offers, aside from the fact that it usually helps you get the best tom sound, is its flexibility. It's easy to remove, reposition and rearrange. You can pull it off easily to shorten a piece, or you can reposition it with exacting precision to tweak the sound and it's as easy to place on the bottom head as it is on the top head.

Some drummers prefer the sound of toms

with the bottom head removed. Some drummers always leave the bottom heads on their toms. The trends seem to shift. These are two different sounds. A properly tuned drum with both the top and bottom head in place has a smooth natural tone that is appealing in most musical textures. With the bottom head off, a tom sounds hollow with less pure tone and has slightly more attack. It's hard to beat the sound of a well tuned tom with both heads on, but be flexible and use the sound that fits the musical context.

For close-miking, use a moving-coil mic like a Shure SM57 or a Sennheiser 421. Point the mic at the drum about two inches in from the rim, at a distance of about two inches above the top head (Illustration 5-25).

If you want more attack in the sound, move the mic toward the center of the drum, but keep it out of the drummer's way. A miked drum sound has more attack when the microphone is positioned near the center of the drum and more tone when the microphone is positioned near the rim.

Sometimes it's very desirable to record drums (except the overhead and hi-hat microphones) at levels exceeding 0VU. A drum that's been recorded hot (in the range of +2 to +5VU) won't usually give a buzzing kind of distortion because, as the analog tape reaches the point where it can't handle more magnetism, it will usually give the drum a compressed rather than distorted sound. This point is called the point of oversaturation. The sound of analog tape approaching the point of oversaturation has become a sound in its own right for recording drums. It's common for kick and toms to be recorded very hot to analog tape specifically for the sound this technique produces. It's also common for kick, snare and toms to be recorded at 0VU (or colder) to ensure that the transient will be accurately recorded. These are musically based decisions that you can make if you're stylistically aware or creatively attuned.

If you're using a digital recorder, don't push the drum levels above the meter's peak. The digital recording process has a pretty hard ceiling. There is no benefit to exceeding the preset maximum recording level for home digital recording. A couple of the mastering engineers I work with push digital levels beyond their intended maximum in an effort to create compact discs that are the loudest on the block. Their equipment is meticulously maintained and they have plenty of headroom in their systems, which are designed to push the limits. They win most of the awards for doing it the best, but when engineering a digital recording, we don't need

to exceed maximum digital recording levels.

Audio Example 5-33 demonstrates a tom, recorded at 0VU using a moving-coil mic from about two inches.

Audio Example 5-33 Tom at 0VU
CD-2: Track 26

The tom in Audio Example 5-34 was recorded at +5VU using a moving-coil mic from about two inches

---

Audio Example 5-34 Tom at +5VU
CD-2: Track 26

If you're sampling, try a condenser mic from a distance of one or two feet. This will usually give the purest, natural sound. The tom in Audio Example 5-35 was recorded with a condenser mic at 0VU from a distance of about one foot.

Audio Example 5-35 Tom at 0VU
CD-2: Track 27

Practice recording each drum at different levels to find the sound you like. Keep a log of what you've recorded and what the recording levels were along with the microphones used for each recording.

Equalizing the Toms

Follow a similar approach to the drums we've covered so far when we EQ the toms. Analyze the lows, highs and mids. There is often a cloudy sound to the lower mids in a close-miked tom, between 250 and 500Hz. I'll often cut a frequency in this range. The bass frequencies below about 100Hz can usually be rolled off, and the attack of a tom can be enhanced by boosting a frequency range between 3 and 5kHz. Listen to the tom in Audio Example 5-36. I start flat, then cut at about 300Hz. Next, I roll off the lows below 100Hz, then boost the attack at about 5kHz.

Audio Example 5-36
Roll Off 100Hz, Cut 300Hz, Boost 5kHz
CD-2: Track 28

Illustration 5-26
Wide Stereo Overheads

For a wide stereo image, use two cardioid condenser microphones over the drum set spaced 1–3' apart. The mics should be at 90° angles to each other and pointing away from each other. If you point the mics toward each other, you'll encounter problems, especially when summing the stereo mix to mono.

Reverberation on the Toms

Choose reverb for the toms that blends with the snare sound. It's normal to use the same reverb on the toms that you use on the snare. If you use another reverb sound, be sure it complements the overall sound of the snare drum. Avoid selecting sounds that indicate completely different acoustical environments unless you're intentionally conforming to a musical judgment.

Listen to the different tom sounds in Audio Example 5-37. Note what you like and dislike about each sound. Is the sound boomy? How do the lows sound? Can you hear the attack? Does the drum sound full? Is the drum thin sounding? Do you hear much tone?

Audio Example 5-37 Lots of Toms
CD-2: Track 29

Overhead Microphones

Once you've positioned the close microphones for the snare, kick and toms, use mics over the drums to capture the cymbals and fill in the overall sound of the drums. It's amazing how much separation we can achieve close-miking the kit. One or two mics over the drums are essential to a blended, natural sound.

Position condenser microphones in a stereo pattern (like the examples of a two-mic setup). A good pattern to use is the standard X-Y configuration, with the microphones pointing down at the set at a 90 degree angle to each other. This will provide the excellent stereo image necessary for a big drum sound and will work well in mono.

Try spreading the X-Y out if the drummer's kit is very large and covers a wide area. Move the microphones away from each other, but be sure they're still pointing away from each other. Also, keep the microphones on the same horizontal plane to minimize adverse phase interactions when listening to the mix in mono (Illustration 5-26).

Overheads on a close-miked kit give definition and position to the cymbals and fill in the overall sound. There isn't much need for the low frequencies since the close microphones give each drum a full, punchy sound. I'll usually roll the lows off below about 150Hz, and I'll often boost a high frequency between 10 and 15kHz, to give extra shimmer to the cymbals.

We want the overheads to accurately capture the transient information. Since the transient level exceeds the average level by as much as 9dB, recording levels on the overheads should read between -7 and -9VU at the peaks to ensure accurately recorded transients.

Pan the overheads hard right and hard left for the most natural sound. The X-Y technique will provide a sound that is evenly spread across the stereo spectrum. The overheads in Audio Example 5-38 are about three feet above the cymbals in an X-Y configuration and are panned hard right and hard left. The lows below 150Hz are rolled off, and the highs are boosted at 12kHz.

Audio Example 5-38 X-Y Panned Hard
CD-2: Track 30

We can add different character to the sound of the drums by moving the overheads closer to or farther from the kit. Positioning the

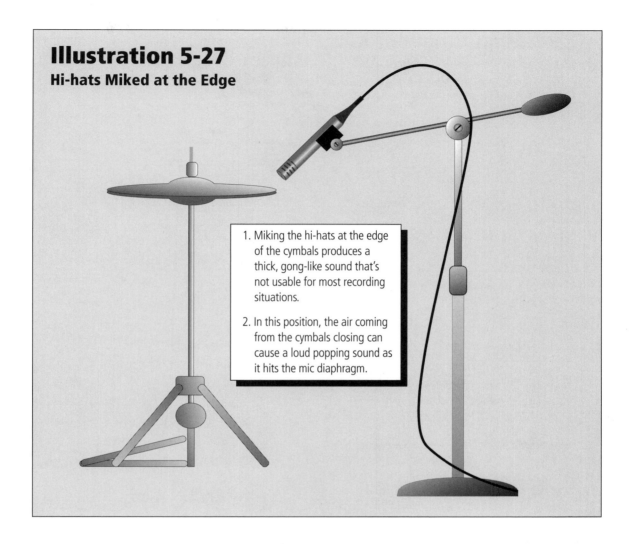

Illustration 5-27
Hi-hats Miked at the Edge

1. Miking the hi-hats at the edge of the cymbals produces a thick, gong-like sound that's not usable for most recording situations.

2. In this position, the air coming from the cymbals closing can cause a loud popping sound as it hits the mic diaphragm.

mic farther away from the set includes more room sound on the track. This can be good or bad depending on the acoustics of the recording environment.

It isn't typically necessary to add reverb to the overheads in a close-miked configuration. The reverb on the snare and toms is usually sufficient to get a smooth, blended sound.

Sometimes it's desirable to put a separate mic on the hi-hat. The choice for or against a hi-hat mic should be based on the style of music and the importance of the hi-hat in the drum part. Most of the time the microphones on the

kick, snare, toms and overheads pick up plenty of hi-hat, but a separate track for the hat adds definition to the hi-hat attack and provides pan control in the mix. Listen to the kit in Audio Example 5-39. After the first few seconds, I'll turn the hi-hat mic on and pan it in the stereo spectrum. Notice that even though the hi-hat track isn't loud in the mix, you can still perceive the position change as I pan the hat between left and right.

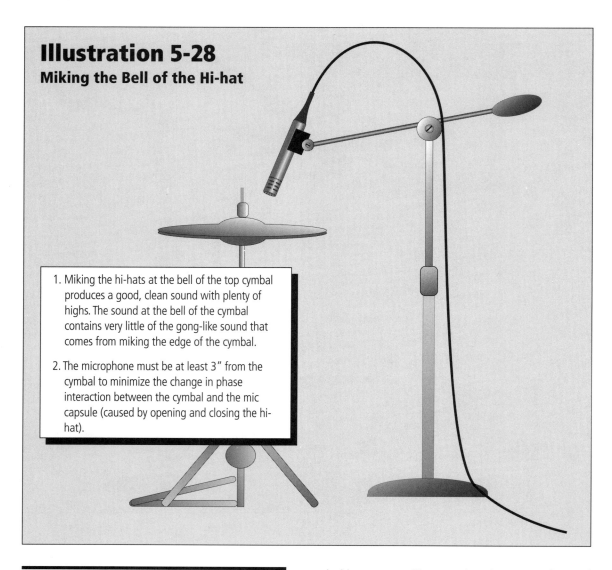

Illustration 5-28
Miking the Bell of the Hi-hat

1. Miking the hi-hats at the bell of the top cymbal produces a good, clean sound with plenty of highs. The sound at the bell of the cymbal contains very little of the gong-like sound that comes from miking the edge of the cymbal.

2. The microphone must be at least 3″ from the cymbal to minimize the change in phase interaction between the cymbal and the mic capsule (caused by opening and closing the hi-hat).

Audio Example 5-39 Panning the Hi-hat
CD-2: Track 31

To get the best transient attack, record the hat track at -7 to -9VU with a cardioid condenser mic. Roll the lows off below about 250Hz. Boost between 300 and 600Hz if you'd like a thick sounding hi-hat. If you'd like a very clean and penetrating hi-hat sound, boost between 6 and 10kHz.

Positioning of the mic is critical. Any cym-bal has a gong-like sound at the outer edge and clear highs at the bell. Audio Example 5-40 demonstrates the sound of a hi-hat miked at the outer edge (Illustration 5-27).

Audio Example 5-40
Hi-hat Miked at the Outer Edge
CD-2: Track 32

Audio Example 5-41 demonstrates the sound of the hi-hat with the mic pointing down at the bell of the top cymbal (Illustration 5-28).

Audio Example 5-41
Hi-hat Miked at the Bell
CD-2: Track 32

If a mic is aimed at a snare drum, it will still hear the rest of the kit as it's played. Everything except the snare drum is leakage into the snare mic. Any sound other than the one you're trying to capture with a microphone is called *leakage*. Leakage is a factor we don't deal with on a drum machine because all instruments are electronically separate and can typically be combined in whatever mix the engineer requires. When recording a live kit, leakage is an important consideration.

Leakage isn't always a bad thing. Often, leakage can help blend and smooth out the sound of the kit. The interaction between microphones and the leakage of acoustic room sound into the drum mics can be good. In fact, given the right acoustical environment, you might *want* a fair amount of leakage between the mics just to add character and personality to the overall drum sound.

Isolating the Drum Tracks

Sometimes we need to isolate the drum tracks, either to equalize them separately, to pan them or to add effects to an individual instrument or group of instruments. To isolate an instrument on a track, use a gate or an expander. Refer to Chapter 2 if you aren't familiar with the use of an expander/gate.

Patch the snare track through a gate. Ad-

just the attack time to its fastest setting and the release time to about half a second. Adjust the range control so that everything below the threshold will be turned off. Finally, adjust the threshold so that the gate only opens when the snare hits. This will isolate the snare. Once the snare drum is isolated, you can process the snare drum sound alone with minimal effect on the rest of the kit. For example, you can add as much reverberation as you want to the snare without leakage adding reverb to the rest of the drums. Listen to the kit in Audio Example 5-42. I'll solo the snare track, then adjust the gate to get rid of the leakage between the snare hits.

Audio Example 5-42 Adjusting The Gate
CD-2: Track 33

Once the gate is adjusted properly, you can put drastic amounts of reverb on the snare by itself. Listen to Audio Example 5-43 as I put a lot of reverb on this gated snare track.

Audio Example 5-43 Reverb on the Gated Snare
CD-2: Track 34

In Audio Example 5-44, listen to the complete kit with a lot of reverb on the gated snare track. After a few seconds, I'll bypass the gate on the snare. Notice the change in the reverb.

Audio Example 5-44 Bypassing the Gate
CD-2: Track 35

Try gating any of the individual drum microphones (kick, toms, snare). Since the overheads are for fill, they don't need to be gated except for special effects. Gating every track can be tricky to set up. You can make the drum set sound unnaturally clean by overusing gates. On the other hand, gates can help make drums sound very punchy and powerful. Experiment and practice!

We've covered the basics of close-miking the drum set. There are many other creative approaches to recording the kit, including different mic selection and placement, uses of acoustics and many processing possibilities. Try different techniques on the drums you record. As this course continues, we'll cover more and more techniques that can be used on drums. We'll do more with signal processing of the drum sounds in the next chapter.

Miscellaneous Percussion

The instruments that fall into our miscellaneous percussion category are all the rest of the percussion instruments other than the drum set, including but not limited to: cowbell, tambourine, claves, cymbals, marimba, xylophone, glockenspiel, shaker, maracas, cabasa, triangle, guiro, wind chimes, congas, bongos and timbales.

The mic of choice for recording percussion instruments is a condenser because of its excellent transient response. You don't need to have the most expensive condenser mic to get great results. There are many microphones available in the low to medium price range that are very good. My strongest recommendation if you're buying a mic is to select a mic made by a major manufacturer. All the major microphone manufacturers make good microphones that are very usable. You can't go wrong if you select a mic

that fits your needs and budget from an established and respected manufacturer. As your experience and budget increase, you'll find you develop certain favorite microphones for very specific tasks. Different mics do sound amazingly different when you listen to them side by side on the same instrument, but that doesn't mean you can't get a very usable sound from a reasonably priced condenser mic.

When recording miscellaneous percussion instruments, the transient is the primary consideration. Almost all these instruments need to be recorded with the loudest part of the track reading about -9 to -7 on the VU meter. Transients continue to arise as an important consideration in many situations, but these percussion instruments have some of the most extreme transient peaks. Any hard wood or metal instrument that's struck with hard wood or metal will have an extreme transient.

Remember, when the VU meter reads -9 while recording these instruments, the tape is really receiving a signal that's at (or above) the suggested recording level for optimum use. In other words, we're not sending a low level to tape when we see -9VU, we're sending the proper level to tape.

If you place a condenser mic too close to a percussion instrument, there's a good chance the transient will overdrive the internal circuitry in the mic. Miking from a distance of one to two feet generally produces the most desirable sound. You'll typically get a natural sound that requires little or no equalization when you mic percussion instruments from distances greater than a foot. You'll know when you're too far from the instrument because the sound will lack intimacy and might get lost in the mix.

It's a good idea to roll off the lows below

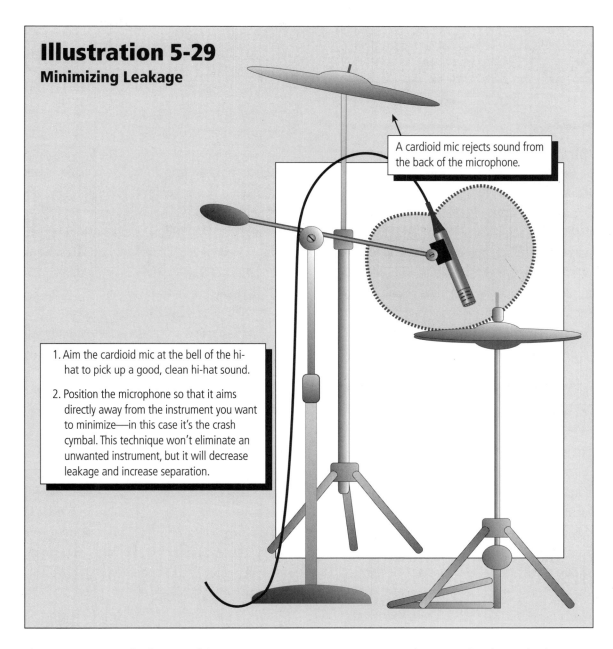

Illustration 5-29
Minimizing Leakage

A cardioid mic rejects sound from the back of the microphone.

1. Aim the cardioid mic at the bell of the hi-hat to pick up a good, clean hi-hat sound.

2. Position the microphone so that it aims directly away from the instrument you want to minimize—in this case it's the crash cymbal. This technique won't eliminate an unwanted instrument, but it will decrease leakage and increase separation.

about 150Hz. Usually the rest of the instruments in the orchestration are covering the low frequencies. Sometimes I'll boost highs between 7 and 15kHz, depending on the instrument and its roll in the mix, but most miscellaneous percussion sounds good when recorded flat through a condenser mic at a distance of one to two feet. If you have several percussion instruments playing at once and you need to boost highs, try to select a different frequency for each instrument.

Listen to the drum and percussion vamp in Audio Example 5-45. I'll solo the different instruments. Notice their tone and placement in the mix.

Audio Example 5-45 Soloing Percussion
CD-2: Track 36

Application of Techniques

It's important to get into the habit of aiming microphones away from sounds you want to exclude from a track. Use the cardioid pickup patterns to your advantage. For example, if you're miking a hi-hat and the mic is pointed at the bell of the top cymbal, that's good. Not only should you point the mic at the bell of the hi-hat, but you should point the back of the mic at a cymbal that's close by. Pointing the back of the hi-hat mic at the crash cymbal helps minimize the amount of crash that is recorded by the hi-hat mic. Use the cardioid pickup pattern to reject the unwanted sound while it captures the intended sound (Illustration 5-29).

It's necessary for the drummer to have a good, well balanced headphone mix. Headphones are the best way for the drummer to monitor the rest of the musicians or tracks. A good drummer is always trying to lock in to a strong rhythmic feel with the rest of the group. The drummer and bass player, especially, need to hear each other well. Be sure both the bass player and the drummer can hear the attack of the kick, snare and hi-hat. Don't make them guess where the beat is. Adjusting the headphone mix can be your most important contribution to the *feel* of a song. Listen to the headphone mix yourself through headphones, so that you can tell exactly what the players are hearing. Respond to their requests for level changes. Spending the time to make the phones an asset

rather than a detriment is time well spent.

Ideally, the drums will be the only sound in the room at the time they're being recorded. This provides ultimate flexibility during mixdown. However, there are times when guitar, bass and drums must be recorded in the same room, usually due to a lack of space or time. When this happens, isolate the instruments as much as you can. Use *baffles* around the drums to shield the drum microphones from other sounds. Baffles are small, freestanding partitions with either two soft, absorptive sides or one soft side and one hard reflective side. They typically measure about four feet square and are four to eight inches thick. They're also called gobos or screens.

Baffles can also be placed around the guitar amp, or blankets can be placed over the amp and the mic. The blanket will shield the guitar mic from unwanted sounds, plus it'll muffle the guitar to help keep it from the drum mics or other microphones in the room.

Though we strive for ultimate separation between tracks and complete control over the sound of each instrument, some great recordings have been achieved with the entire band in one room playing the tracks live. Blues, jazz, some country and some rock styles can benefit from the natural, open sound that a live, one-room recording offers.

Click Track

One feature of a professional sounding recording is a solid rhythmic feel that maintains an even and constant tempo. A sure sign of an amateur band and an amateur recording is a loose rhythmic feel that radically speeds up and slows down.

Most drummers need some assistance to maintain a constant tempo. We call this assistance the click track. A *click track* can simply be a steady metronome pulse, like that from a drum machine or an electronic metronome. It gives the drummer a rhythmic reference to keep the tempo steady.

If a drummer has never played with a click track or a metronome, you might be in trouble if you force him or her to record the track while hearing the click in the phones. Having to actually follow a steady beat can totally ruin the natural rhythmic feel. The drummer will wrestle with the groove, speeding up to catch the click, then slowing down to wait for the click. This is not good. Sometimes you'll need to simply decide on the lesser of the two evils in the interest of getting the song recorded. If you're consistently working with the same drummer, and they have trouble with a click, suggest practicing with a metronome. Drummers can get very good at locking in to a click track while maintaining a natural rhythmic flow, but it takes practice. And wouldn't you know it, about the time they can play solidly with a click, the drummer's time feel is usually solid enough to get by without a click!

A drum machine is a good source for the click because it offers the ability to change the sound. Click sounds with good transients work the best because the transient attack unquestionably defines the placement of the beat.

It's very important that the drummer hear the click well, but the biggest problem with a click track is leakage of the sound of the click from the headphones into the drum microphones. It's difficult to deal with a click leaking into the overheads on a quiet or texturally open part of a song. The click has to be at a certain level for the drummer to hear it, but if it's too loud and is audible on the drum microphones, the drum track might not be usable. The solution lies in finding headphones that enclose the drummers ears well enough to conceal click from the microphones. There are many phones available that will perform well. They usually have solid housings and fluid or air-filled soft plastic pads that completely surround the ears.

Conclusion

Recording drums can be fun, rewarding, frustrating, confusing, exciting, encouraging and discouraging. And all of these feelings can happen within a very short period of time, especially when you're learning. Practice the techniques and principles in this chapter. I've used them all many times and they work. When you're comfortable with this information, try other approaches. Personally, I have the most fun when I'm in search of that great new sound recorded in an unconventional way for a creative piece of music. I also know that there's security and confidence in knowing the basics. Learn the basics!

Credits

The live drum examples on this tape were played by Wade Reeves. Wade is an excellent drummer involved heavily in the Seattle concert rock scene.

The individual examples of different kick drum, snare drum and tom sounds contain some live recordings, and some samples of the actual drum sets of: Dave Weckl (Chick Corea, Diana Ross, George Benson, etc.); Matt Sorum (Greg Wright, The Cult, Guns N' Roses, etc.); Peter

Erskine (Weather Report, Jaco Pastorius, etc.);
Tommy Aldridge (Ozzy Osbourne).

All samples were provided by the Yamaha
RY30 Drum Machine using the Artist Series
Rhythm Sound Cards.

6 Synchronization/Drum Machines

Introduction to Drum Machines

In this chapter, we'll cover drum machines, electronic drums, sampled percussion and synchronization. In Chapter 5, we focused primarily on techniques for recording good clean acoustic drum sounds. Those techniques are very valuable for many recording situations and can be particularly useful in the area of sampling. It's important to note that each technique in this course can be applied to the situation that it's presented in, but they should also be considered for other recording situations. As you learn more and more techniques, apply them to different situations. Practice, experiment and learn.

When we're working with drum machines and presampled sounds, the basic recording of each instrument sound has already been completed for us. Often, all we need to do is get the sounds efficiently to tape, which means that a lot of times we have to shape the sounds in a way that blends with the musical arrangement and fits the musical style. Even though some of the work is already completed in the initial drum samples, we still need to consider several options to get a good musical track from a drum machine:

- Does the drum sound need processing?
- Is there much transient information to contend with?

- Is there already lots of processing and effect in the sound?
- Is it okay to add reverb to a sampled sound that already includes reverb?
- Are the drum and percussion sounds blending in a natural way?
- Are all of the drum sounds coming from one output of the sound module, or are the parts split up to come out of multiple outputs?
- Should I record the drum parts to the multitrack, or should I use time code to drive the drum machine clock?

Basically, once you have the raw sounds from a drum machine, sampler or acoustic drum, there can be a lot more work to do before the overall drum sound is complete and usable. In this chapter we'll look at some techniques that will help your drum machine parts sound more real, plus we'll study some different ways to get the drum parts to the final mixed master.

When I refer to drum machines, I'm also implying sound modules that contain drum sounds. A drum machine is really just a drum sound module with a built-in sequencer that's designed to sequence the drum parts using the sounds within the drum machine. The sequencer in a drum machine isn't usually designed to hold other sequencing information for other parts of the song.

Patching in the Drum Machine

Most outputs from most drum machines or sound modules can plug straight into line in of the mixer. With some mixers, especially professional mixers operating at +4, more gain might be needed to get a strong enough signal to tape. In this case, plugging into a direct box first, then from the direct box into the mic input of the board will give you ample gain. Once you've plugged into the direct box, you have all of the advantages of the balanced low impedance run from the direct box to the mixer (less noise and virtually unlimited cable length).

Within a drum machine there can be many different sounds playing at once. Some drum machines have simple mono or stereo outputs of the overall mix with individual volume and/or pan settings performed within the drum machine. This type of operation can be very convenient for a small live performance situation or for recording with limited tracks and channels, but it's our goal to gain as much control over the individual sounds as we can.

If the sounds are all coming from one or two outputs, even if the drum machine allows for instrument level and pan control, we can't control effects or EQ on each individual instrument. If we add reverb at all, we add it to the entire drum pattern. Adding reverberation to all the drums at once can create a distant or muddy sound. Audio Example 6-1 demonstrates the sound of the mono output of a drum machine with the addition of plate reverb (Illustration 6-1).

Audio Example 6-1 Mono Drums
CD-2: Track 37

Some drum machines and sound modules have multiple outputs and any instrument can be assigned to play out of any output. Most machines with multiple outputs have four to eight outputs. With this many outputs, we can assign individual instruments as well as groups of instruments to different outputs. These outputs can be printed to different tracks on the multitrack or they can be played from MIDI in sync with the taped tracks. Multiple outputs are ideal but can quickly use up a lot of tape tracks and mixer channels.

Most home setups can't afford the number of tracks it takes to print all of the percussion sounds to individual tracks. One solution to this problem is to run the individual outputs of the drum machine into the mixer, using the bus assignments to send all of the instruments to one or two tracks on the multitrack.

So what's the advantage to combining with the bus assignments instead of within the drum machine? Once the instruments are spread out on the mixer, the effects sends and EQ can be used on the separate channels. If we need to put lots of reverb on the snare, put some low end in the kick and add highs to the crash cymbal, we can. Each change will only affect the instruments coming from one output. Typically, in a small setup, the equalization changes *and* the reverb will be printed to the multitrack. If the reverb is to go to the multitrack, bring the returns from the reverb into one or two available channels on the mixer. Once the reverberation returns are plugged into channels, they can be assigned to the same bus outputs as the rest

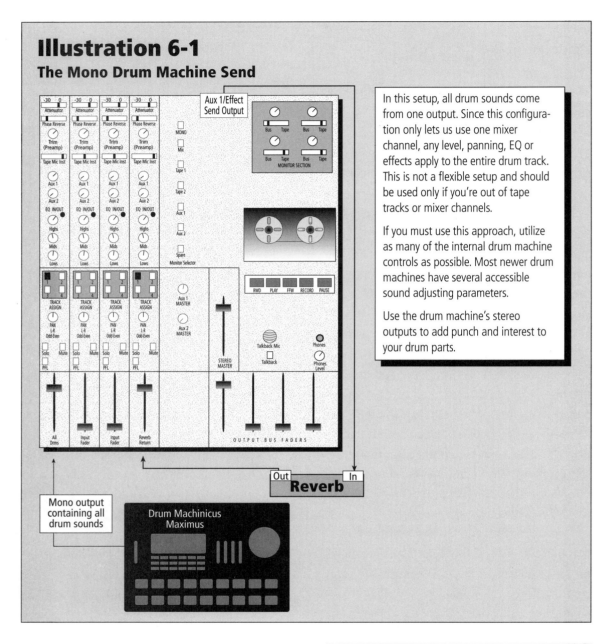

Illustration 6-1
The Mono Drum Machine Send

In this setup, all drum sounds come from one output. Since this configuration only lets us use one mixer channel, any level, panning, EQ or effects apply to the entire drum track. This is not a flexible setup and should be used only if you're out of tape tracks or mixer channels.

If you must use this approach, utilize as many of the internal drum machine controls as possible. Most newer drum machines have several accessible sound adjusting parameters.

Use the drum machine's stereo outputs to add punch and interest to your drum parts.

of the drums (Illustration 6-2). Audio Example 6-2 demonstrates the same drum pattern as the previous example, with the individual outs plugged into the mixer and each sound adjusted for the mix. First you'll hear the mono pattern with reverb on the entire pattern, then you'll hear the pattern with this new setup.

Audio Example 6-2 Outputs Separated
CD-2: Track 38

Illustration 6-2
Sub-mixing Multiple Outputs

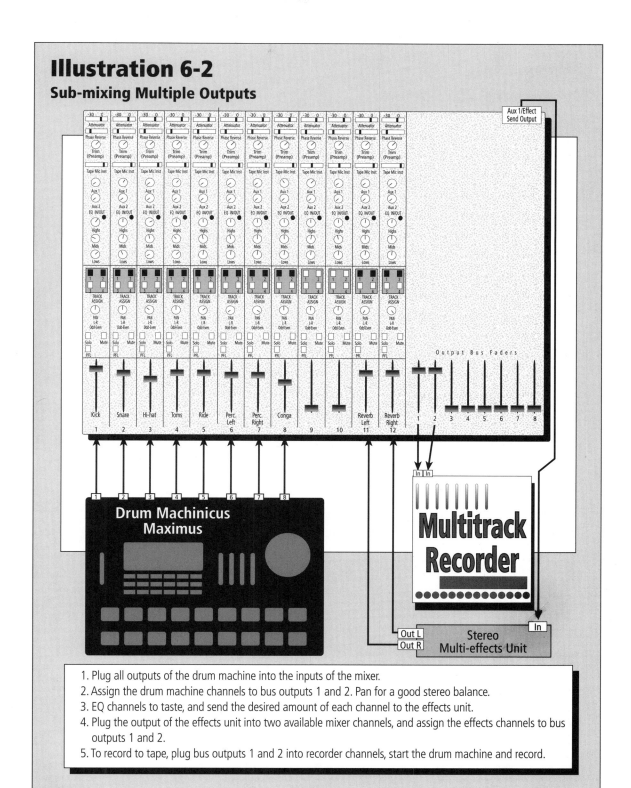

1. Plug all outputs of the drum machine into the inputs of the mixer.
2. Assign the drum machine channels to bus outputs 1 and 2. Pan for a good stereo balance.
3. EQ channels to taste, and send the desired amount of each channel to the effects unit.
4. Plug the output of the effects unit into two available mixer channels, and assign the effects channels to bus outputs 1 and 2.
5. To record to tape, plug bus outputs 1 and 2 into recorder channels, start the drum machine and record.

Illustration 6-3
Sub-mixing Main Mixer

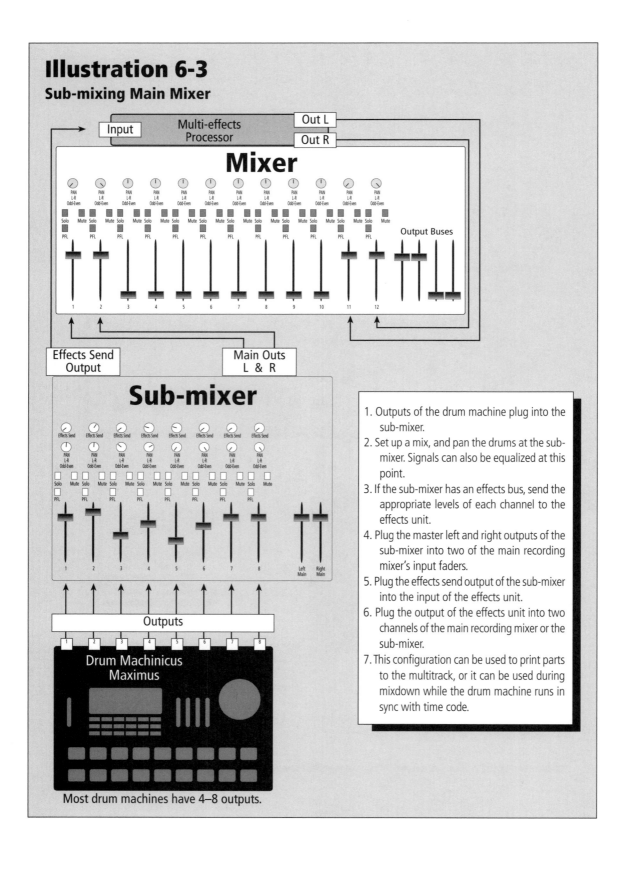

1. Outputs of the drum machine plug into the sub-mixer.
2. Set up a mix, and pan the drums at the sub-mixer. Signals can also be equalized at this point.
3. If the sub-mixer has an effects bus, send the appropriate levels of each channel to the effects unit.
4. Plug the master left and right outputs of the sub-mixer into two of the main recording mixer's input faders.
5. Plug the effects send output of the sub-mixer into the input of the effects unit.
6. Plug the output of the effects unit into two channels of the main recording mixer or the sub-mixer.
7. This configuration can be used to print parts to the multitrack, or it can be used during mixdown while the drum machine runs in sync with time code.

Most drum machines have 4–8 outputs.

Sub-mixing

If your mixer doesn't have enough inputs to accept all your drum machine outputs, try using a sub-mixer or printing some of the key drum parts to tape while running the remaining drum tracks from your sequencer synchronized to time code.

A sub-mixer is a very handy tool for many recording situations; it's simply a small mixer. You might plug the individual outputs of your drum machine into the channels of the sub-mixer, create a mix, then plug the mono or stereo outputs of the sub-mix into your board. This would use only one or two of your recording mixer's channels, instead of up to 8 or 12 (Illustration 6-3).

I've had good results printing some of the tracks to the multitrack, then playing the remaining tracks from the sequencer referenced to time code. This is a very common technique for recordings that use sequencers and drum machines. The actual sequenced parts never need to go onto tape, they just run in sync with the tape tracks, over and over. Each time the tape starts, the sequencer refers to the time code to find the correct measure and beat.

Time Code and Sync Pulse

What is time code? What is sync pulse? What does time code do and how does it work? First off, let's understand that sync pulse and time code are used to synchronize multiple machine-driven mechanisms, or timing clocks, so that all synchronized systems run at the same speed and in a constant relation to one another. Both sync pulse and time code are a series of electronic pulses that are produced by a sequencer, drum machine or time code generator. These pulses are typically recorded onto one track of an audio or video tape recorder. Later, the signal from the tape track is plugged into the sync in jack of the sequencer or machine synchronizer to serve as a tempo guide for future tracks. Sync pulse is the simplest and least flexible of these systems but is still common in lower priced drum machines and sequencers. We'll start with the simple approach and build from there. For now, we'll take a look at synchronizing drum machines or sequencers to an audio tape recorder. However, keep in mind that these principles also pertain to synchronization of audio machines, video machines, film machines and computers.

Synchronizing two sequencers means to make their tempos match perfectly. Sync pulse can accomplish this. Time code can accomplish this with more control and flexibility.

Synchronizing two tape recorders means to make their motors run at the same speed. A relative of sync pulse, called pilot tone, can accomplish this. Time code can accomplish this with more control and flexibility.

Synchronizing a sequencer to a tape recorder means to enable a sequencer to imitate and duplicate a tempo map in relation to parts recorded on tape. Sync pulse can accomplish this. Time code can accomplish this with more control and flexibility.

Sync Pulse

Sync pulse is the simplest synchronizing system. This system uses a specified number of electronic pulses per quarter note to drive the tempo of a sequencer. Most sync pulse is generated at 24 pulses per quarter note, and each pulse is identical. The only factor that establishes synchronization is how fast the pulses are being sent or received.

It's very simple. When a drum machine or sequencer is set to an external clock and a sync pulse is sent into the sync in jack, the tempo of the sequencer follows according to the rate of the sync pulse. Every time 24 pulses go by, the sequencer plays another quarter note's worth of your sequence. The faster the sync pulses, the faster the tempo. When you listen to the sound of sync pulse, you'll notice that the pitch of the sync tone raises and lowers as the tempo speeds up and slows down.

Sync pulse has one major disadvantage: Each pulse is identical. There is no way for this system to indicate to the sequencer which measure of the sequence should be playing. The sequencer always needs to hear the sync pulse from the beginning of the song to be precisely in sync with a previously recorded track.

Almost all sequencers that accept external clock information respond to sync pulse. Most newer equipment will also accept time code.

SMPTE/Time Code

Time Code gives much more control and flexibility than sync pulse. The most common form of time code is SMPTE, pronounced (simp' • tee). The initials S-M-P-T-E stand for the Society of Motion Picture and Television Engineers. This society of professionals developed SMPTE time code as a means of interlocking (synchronizing) audio, video and film transports.

A piece of equipment that produces SMPTE time code is said to *generate* time code. A piece of equipment that accepts and operates from time code is said to *read* time code. The time

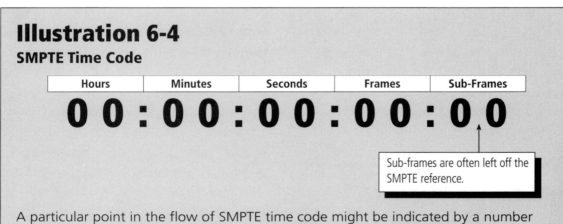

Illustration 6-4
SMPTE Time Code

Hours	Minutes	Seconds	Frames	Sub-Frames
0 0 :	0 0 :	0 0 :	0 0 :	0 0

Sub-frames are often left off the SMPTE reference.

A particular point in the flow of SMPTE time code might be indicated by a number like 01:32:51:12. This number indicates the specific point in the flow of time code at 1 hour, 32 minutes, 51 seconds and 12 frames.

If a sequencer is set to start a song at SMPTE reference 01:32:51:12, then as the sequencer receives the continuous flow of time code, it waits until that exact set of code numbers comes up to play beat one of measure one of the song.

Time code is a 24-hour clock. It runs from 00:00:00:00 to 23:59:59:29 before it starts over again at 00:00:00:00.

code reader and generator are almost always in the same piece of equipment, often with other MIDI functions and features.

Now that we have the formal introduction out of the way, this is how SMPTE works: This code is a continuous flow of binary information—a stream of constantly changing zeros and ones that lasts for 24 hours before starting over. Each single point in time has its own unique binary number. These unique binary numbers are referenced to a 24-hour clock. This gives us a way of pinpointing a particular position in the flow of the code. Each point in the code has a unique address that's described in hours, minutes, seconds, frames and sometimes sub-frames. The term frame comes from the film world, which calls each picture in the film a frame (Illustration 6-4).

SMPTE time code is generated at a constant speed. Tempo isn't changed by the time code speeding up and slowing down; tempo is changed by the sequencer calculating where the song should be in relation to the time code's 24-hour clock. The 24-hour SMPTE clock runs from 00:00:00:00 to 23:59:59:29 before it starts over again at 00:00:00:00.

If a sequence is set to external sync and is set to start at 1 hour, 20 minutes and 10 seconds (01:20:10:00), beat one of measure one of the sequence will play at 01:20:10:00. All tempo settings and changes are controlled within the sequencer, but all changes will be in mathematical relation to time code.

When a sequence is referencing to time code, it's not necessary to start at the beginning of the song to be in sync with previously recorded tracks of the sequence. The sequencer calculates the measure and beat of the sequence in relation to the start time of the song. The tape

can be started at any point of the song, and as soon as it receives time code, the sequencer will find its place and join in, perfectly in sync. This is a great advantage over sync pulse (where the song must start at the beginning each time to be in sync with previously recorded tracks.)

Most SMPTE time code is generated at the rate of 30 frames per second. This is the standard time code rate for audio machine synchronizing and for syncing to black and white video.

Sync to color video uses a different type of frame rate called drop frame. Drop frame time code is generated at 30 frames per second, but one frame is omitted every two minutes, except for minutes 00, 10, 20, 30, 40 and 50. Try not to think too hard about this concept—it will only confuse you! The reason for leaving these frames out is to make SMPTE time match the real time of color video. Color video operates at the speed of 29.97 frames per second, slightly slower than the 30 frames per second of SMPTE. Leaving these selected frames out lets the SMPTE rate stay at 30 frames per second while maintaining real time integrity.

The European standard time code rate, established by the European Broadcast Union (EBU), is 25 frames per second for color *and* black and white video. Film synchronization utilizes 24 frames per second (Illustration 6-5).

MIDI Time Code

MIDI Time Code (MTC) is simply the MIDI equivalent of SMPTE time code. MTC uses real time reference, like SMPTE, of hours, minutes, seconds and frames per second. SMPTE time code, printed to tape, is read by a SMPTE reader and converted to MTC for time code communication within the MIDI domain.

Illustration 6-5
SMPTE Time Code Frame Rates

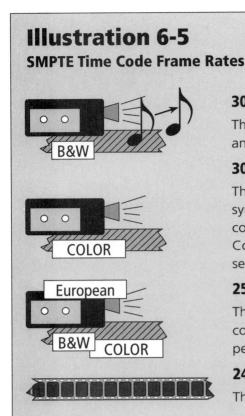

30 Frames per Second

This is the rate for American black and white video and most audio-to-audio synchronization.

30 Frames per Second - Drop Frame

This is the rate for American color video to audio synchronizing. 108 frames per hour are omitted to compensate for the National Television Standards Committee (NTSC) frame rate of 29.97 frames per second.

25 Frames per Second

This is the rate for European black and white and color video synchronizing, established by the European Broadcasting Union (EBU).

24 Frames per Second

This is the standard synchronization rate for film.

Using Time Code

This is how the procedure for using time code works on most systems: There will be a Sync Out jack from your sequencer or drum machine. Sometimes Sync Out is labeled SMPTE Out, Time Code Out, or on some units, the sync pulse comes out of the Tape Out jack. Plug this jack into the line input of your tape recorder or the line input of the mixer, and assign the code to one of the tape tracks.

It's most common to record time code onto an outer track, also called an edge track. Usually the track with the highest number is designated as the time code track. On an 8-track, time code is typically recorded on track eight.

Suggested recording level for recording time code is usually -3VU. Time code doesn't have a very appealing sound, and the hotter the code signal is on tape the higher the chance of it bleeding into the rest of the mix.

Sync pulse come out of the sync jacks while the sequence or drum pattern is playing, so record a reference track of your drums while you record the sync pulse to an edge track. Later you can refine the drum parts as much as you want.

SMPTE time code, unlike sync pulse, can be laid down independently from the sequence. Usually, it's best to record continuous time code on the edge track of the entire reel of tape for the sake of convenience as you record more songs on the reel. Recording time code on tape is called *striping*.

Once the code is recorded on the tape, plug

the output of the code track into the sequencer's Sync In jack. Sync In can also be labeled SMPTE In, Time Code In or on some units, the Tape In jack is used to accept time code.

When time code is successfully plugged into the sequencer, set the sequencer to External Clock. This may also be labeled External Sync, Slave to External Sync, Slave or just External.

If you're using sync pulse, simply play the tape. As soon as the sync pulses begin, the sequencer will start.

If you're using SMPTE, before you play the tape you must set the start point for the sequence in hours, minutes, seconds and frames (02:05:37:02). Once the start point is defined within the sequencer, play the tape. The first beat of the first measure will begin at the start point you selected. From this point on, the sequence should follow along. Again, the advantage to SMPTE is that wherever you begin during the song, the sequencer will calculate the measure and beat, then lock into sync. The disadvantage to sync pulse is that you need to start at the beginning of the sequence every time to stay in sync with parts that are already on tape (Illustration 6-6).

Being literate with time code is very important when it comes to optimizing the recording process. Everything we've seen so far about time code is used very extensively on many recording projects. You're capable of getting much more from your equipment if you're comfortable with synchronizing techniques.

Drum Machine Recording Levels

We must consider the output levels within the drum machine before adjusting recording levels to tape. We need to verify that the level coming from the drum machine outputs is as strong as possible. The mixer inputs and channels will need to be boosted if the drum machine levels are set low. When we boost the mixer channel, the noise level raises in relation to the signal, producing an undesirable signal-to-noise ratio.

Most of the time in a small setup with limited channels, it's necessary to use only the mono or stereo outs from the drum machine. The drum mix is set internally on the drum machine. Be sure the master volume is at maximum and the mix levels in the drum machine are high. It's ideal if the loudest instrument in the drum mix is set at maximum and the remaining instruments are adjusted to blend.

Audio Example 6-3 is an example of a drum machine recorded with the machine outputs low. Notice the amount of noise.

Audio Example 6-3 Outputs Low
CD-2: Track 39

Audio Example 6-4 demonstrates the drum machine from Audio Example 6-3 playing the same pattern with the master output at maximum. Notice how different the noise level is between these two examples.

Audio Example 6-4 Outputs Maximum
CD-2: Track 39

If you're going to be printing individual parts to the multitrack, be sure to adjust the internal levels to maximum before recording. Usually the individual instruments have been adjusted for a mix within a pattern. They might

Illustration 6-6
Synchronizing to SMPTE

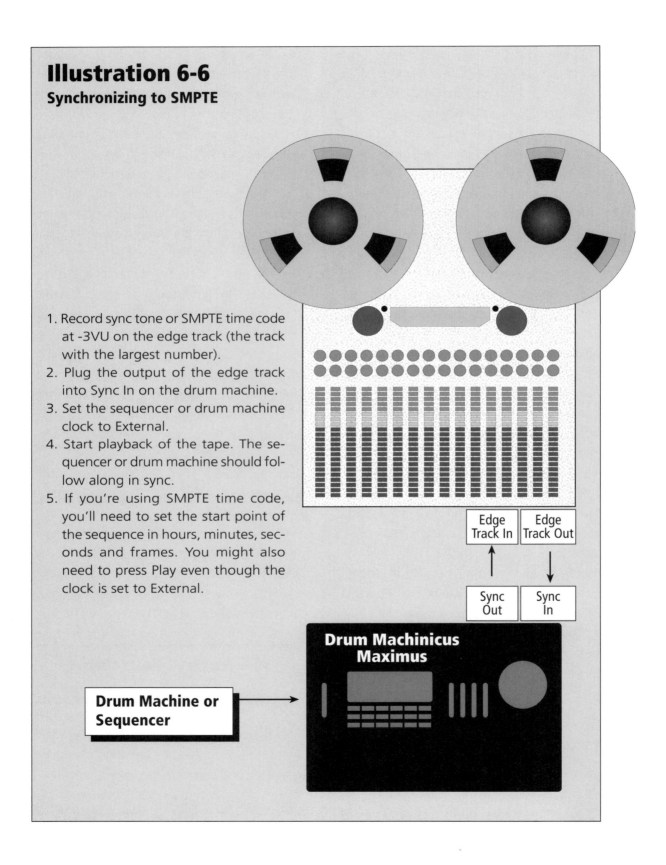

1. Record sync tone or SMPTE time code at -3VU on the edge track (the track with the largest number).
2. Plug the output of the edge track into Sync In on the drum machine.
3. Set the sequencer or drum machine clock to External.
4. Start playback of the tape. The sequencer or drum machine should follow along in sync.
5. If you're using SMPTE time code, you'll need to set the start point of the sequence in hours, minutes, seconds and frames. You might also need to press Play even though the clock is set to External.

Edge Track In

Edge Track Out

Sync Out

Sync In

Drum Machinicus Maximus

Drum Machine or Sequencer

have been panned and their output level might be very low. If this is the case, it'll be nearly impossible to get a strong and noise-free signal on tape until you increase the drum machine or sound module levels.

Adjust the internal output level to maximum for every instrument that you'll be recording to the multitrack, then adjust the master volume for the unit to maximum. Be sure to adjust the input preamp on your mixer so that the overdrive LED doesn't flash when the drums are sounding. If you have no input LED, listen closely for distortion and adjust accordingly. If you hear distortion, turn the input preamp down until you don't hear distortion. If the input preamp is low and you hear no distortion, turn the preamp up until you hear distortion, then back the preamp off. Our goal is to adjust the signal to be as hot as possible at each point, from the beginning of the signal path to the end, with minimal distortion.

Some sequencers allow for easy MIDI control over volume and panning. This equates to automatic level controls throughout the mix. Being able to adjust levels during a song and having those adjustments remembered and duplicated by the sequencer is useful, to say the least. Explaining how to accomplish MIDI automated moves isn't practical right now, but if you're using this feature, it's still important that your levels within the drum machine are as hot as possible .

Programming

Programming drum parts can be difficult and confusing for musicians who aren't drummers. In this chapter, we focus on how to record drum machines rather than how to program drum parts, but there are a couple of concepts we can use to help our drum machine recordings sound more realistic. If you're trying to get the drum machine to sound like a real drummer playing a real drum set, try to imagine a real drummer playing the part. First of all, a drummer only has two hands and two feet. An authentic drum set part can only have so many parts happening at once and still be believable. The part should contain one activity for each hand and foot at any one time.

The main beat typically contains bass drum, snare drum and hi-hat. Hi-hat is typically played with the right hand while sometimes being opened and closed with the left foot. If the right hand plays the ride cymbal, the left foot can be closing the hi-hat, usually on beats two and four. Drum fills usually occupy both hands, so whatever parts were theoretically being played by the hands should stop while the fill is happening. There can be exceptions to these guidelines, depending on the song and the style, but it's helpful to keep these considerations in mind.

Auxiliary percussion parts in live instrument recordings would be played by other musicians, so they can be layered over the drum set part. In Chapter 5 we noticed that as musical sections change, the percussion sounds and parts usually change. Following this guideline will help you produce a percussion track that moves the arrangement from section to section and creates a momentum from the beginning to the end.

Real-time Programming
Drum machines have a feature called *quantize* or *auto correct* that takes an inaccurate rhyth-

mic performance and makes it rhythmically perfect on playback. This can be the one feature that makes the drum parts work if the performer isn't an accurate rhythmic player. This can also be the one feature that makes the drum machine parts feel stiff and computerized.

The thing that makes one drummer's parts different from another is the interpretation of beat placement. Human beings (drummers or not) don't play music in perfect rhythm. If one drummer tends to play the snare drum a little ahead of the beat and another drummer tends to play both the kick and the snare behind the beat, their drum parts will have a different musical effect. Neither is wrong, but one might fit a particular song better than the other. The human feel of a drummer can't be duplicated by perfectly quantized drum parts.

Some sequencers let the user partially quantize the parts. This is called *quantize strength* and can be very useful. Essentially, this feature lets you quantize but only to a certain degree. You can make the parts closer to perfect but still maintain some of the original rhythmic tendencies of the musician. Look for a feature like this on your computer sequencer or drum machine. It'll help your parts sound more realistic.

Another way to put life into your parts is to play them into the drum machine or sequencer without quantizing at all. This can sound great if you have the technical ability to play the parts with proper feel and accuracy. Playing into a sequencer or drum machine, without quantizing, is called *real-time* recording.

In reality, most musicians have a problem playing drum and percussion parts that have enough accuracy to work in real time. Try slowing the tempo down substantially to make it easier to tell where each beat should go. When you speed the tempo back up, the parts will probably sound very good and they'll have a more believable *human* feel.

Listen to Audio Examples 6-5 and 6-6—two versions of the same drum pattern. In Audio Example 6-5, the pattern is quantized to be computer perfect.

Audio Example 6-5 Quantized Pattern
CD-2: Track 40

Audio Example 6-6 demonstrates the pattern again, this time with more of a human feel. This pattern has not been quantized to be computer perfect. Notice the difference in the rhythmic feel.

Audio Example 6-6 Human Feel
CD-2: Track 40

Separating and Organizing Tracks

It's time to consider some of the options and variables when recording specific drum sounds. If your drum machine or sound module has multiple outputs to which you can assign individual instruments or groups of instruments, you'll find much greater freedom in fine-tuning each sound. Earlier in this chapter, we heard the difference in impact of a drum machine that had effects on the overall stereo outputs and one that had been fine-tuned on each of the multiple outputs. There is a difference. As we look at these individual sounds and some of our options for effects and dynamic processing, we'll assume that our drum machine has multiple outputs and that we're able to access each instrument separately.

Once you've made the decision to split the drum parts up and record them on separate tracks of the multitrack, organizing a system of track arrangement is essential. Sometimes you'll need to deviate from your system, but most of the time you'll be able to stick to a format. Following a standard track assignment procedure results in faster and more confident setups.

When laying drum tracks, I always try to follow the same track assignment procedures. This order of track assignment is common throughout the recording industry. Of course, everything is dependent on the total number of tracks and which specific tracks are available when you record the drums. The track assignments we'll cover in this chapter also apply to acoustic drums. We equate the overhead tracks on the acoustic drum set with the cymbal tracks of the drum machine.

24 Tracks

If you have 24 or more tracks available, try this common tack assignment procedure:
- Track 1: Kick drum
- Track 2: Snare drum
- Track 3: High tom
- Track 4: Mid tom
- Track 5: Low tom
- Track 6: Cymbals/left overhead
- Track 7: Cymbals/right overhead
- Track 8: Hi-hat

Even if you need to combine all the drum microphones to one track, this is a good order to memorize. Ideally, you'll be able to use multiple microphones on the kit even if you must combine them. Use this order for plugging the

mics into your mixer. That way you won't always have to wonder which mic was plugged into which input. Once you use this order of assignment a few times, you'll move through the drum set up quickly.

When I do deviate from this procedure, I print the hi-hat on track one and bump everything else up one track. I only do this if I'm using analog tape, and I don't think the hi-hat track will be a major part of the overall drum sound. Track one is on the top edge of an analog tape, and I know from experience that the outer tracks are the first to degrade, because the oxide sometimes wears more on this track than the rest. However, I never worry about this when I'm recording digitally or using new tape on a machine that is well maintained.

This kind of track arrangement can expand or compress quickly depending on the drummer's set. There might be more or less toms, cymbals, kicks, etc. Track assignments can always come from a basic starting point. If you learn this order, you can adapt to any drum miking situation without having to think so hard about it. Approach drum track assignments using this order, starting from track one and moving up in track number:
- Kick drum
- Snare drum
- Toms (high to low)
- Overheads (drummer's left to drummer's right)

Use a track sheet to organize and document the instruments you're recording (Illustration 6-7). It's best to keep track of as many details as you can on the track sheet. Ideally, you'll be able to note:
- The instrument that's on each track
- The date of each performance (this is very im-

Illustration 6-7
Track Sheet: 24-Track Studio

AAAA Studios

Client _____
Producer _____
Engineer _____
Reel Number _____
Speed _____
Tape Stock _____
Date _____

TITLE _____
ARTIST _____
Counter _____
Time _____

1	2	3	4	5	6	7	8
Kick	Snare	High Toms	Mid Toms	Low Toms	Left Over-head	Right Over-head	opt. Hi-Hat
9	10	11	12	13	14	15	16
17	18	19	20	21	22	23	24

Comments: _____

_____

_____

Offset To __:__:__:__/
Offset To __:__:__:__/
Start Time __:__:__:__/

portant when trying to figure out which take was the most recent)
- Microphone choice and placement
- Type of sound module and the patch name
- Time code reference for verses, choruses, bridge, solos, etc. (this is very useful if you have backing vocals that only happen a few times in the entire song)
- The performer's name

16 Tracks

In the 16-track world, if we don't need a lot of other tracks for the rest of the musicians, we can use the same track assignment procedure we used for the 24-track setup. In a straight ahead rock band, where the instrumentation might consist of drums, a couple of guitars and a lead vocalist, we can usually afford to spread the drums out to about eight tracks. In fact, 16-track recording using two-inch analog tape is an accepted standard for a very punchy rock sound.

Most of the time we need to condense the number of drum tracks to make room for the rest of the musical parts (Illustration 6-8). This is a very common track order for drums in the 16-track domain:

- Track 1: Kick drum
- Track 2: Snare drum
- Track 3: Left drums sub-mix (high toms and left overheads [cymbals])
- Track 4: Right drums sub-mix (low toms and right overheads [cymbals])
- Track 5: Hi-hat (optional)

8 Tracks

In the 8-track world, we obviously need to sacrifice the number of tracks we allot for drums. When recording acoustic drums, try to keep at least the kick and snare on separate tracks, combining the rest of the drums to one or two tracks in a sub-mix. The exact number of tracks you can allot depends entirely on the musical requirements (Illustration 6-9).

Sometimes, if you're using an 8-track multitrack, you'll need to print all the drums to one track to make room for background vocals or other key orchestration considerations. It's best

Illustration 6-8
Track Sheet: 16-Track Studio

AAAA Studios

Client _____
Producer _____
Engineer _____
Reel Number _____
Speed _____
Tape Stock _____
Date _____

TITLE _____
ARTIST _____
Counter _____
Time _____

1	2	3	4	5	6	7	8
Kick	Snare	Left Drums	Right Drums	Opt. Hi-Hat			
9	10	11	12	13	14	15	16
							SMPTE

Comments: _____   Offset To   __:__:__:__/
_____   Offset To   __:__:__:__/
_____   Start Time __:__:__:__/

Illustration 6-9
Tack Sheet: 8-Track Studio

AAAA Studios

Client _____

Producer _____

Engineer _____

Reel Number _____

Speed _____

Counter _____

Time _____

Date _____

Tape _____

TITLE _____   Counter/SMPTE _____

ARTIST _____   Song Number _____

1	2	3	4	5	6	7	8
Kick	Sub-mix						SMPTE

TITLE _____   Counter/SMPTE _____

ARTIST _____   Song Number _____

1	2	3	4	5	6	7	8
Left Drums	Right Drums						SMPTE

Comments: _____   Offset To __:__:__:__/

_____   Offset To __:__:__:__/

_____   Start Time __:__:__:__/

for the drum sound to spread the sounds out over as many tracks as you can spare. If you're using a drum machine or sequencer, use one track of the multitrack for time code, so you might never need to print the drums to tape. The drum part can run in sync to the multitrack as your sequencer follows time code.

For a simple arrangement when you're recording acoustic drums or printing drum machine tracks to tape, use this track arrangement if you have the tracks available:

- Track 1: Kick drum
- Track 2: Snare drum
- Track 3: Mono sub-mix of the remaining drums or sub-mix left
- Track 4: Optional sub-mix right

If tracks are running low, try the following approach. At least it gives you control over presence, effects and EQ for one of the key drums:

- Track 1: Kick or snare
- Track 2: Sub-mix of everything except the instrument assigned to track one

4 Tracks

The 4-track domain is limited. If you're recording acoustic drums, your best bet is to use multiple microphones assigned to one track. If you're recording drum machine or sequenced drum parts, use time code and set up so the sequence plays in reference to SMPTE. This way none of the MIDI instruments ever need to touch the multitrack tape. Even though that only leaves three remaining tracks for vocals, solos, guitar and the rest, you've still dramatically improved your 4-track potential (Illustration 6-10).

Kick Drum

Sounds that come from a drum machine are often digital recordings of acoustic drums, just as they would be heard from a microphone pointed at the drum. Sometimes the sounds have been compressed, effected and combined with natural ambience. In either case, there can be excellent uses for these sounds, and there are plenty of adjustments we can make to fine-tune the sound for the song.

Listen to Audio Example 6-7. In this ex-

Illustration 6-10
Track Sheet: 4-Track Studio

Client	
Producer	
Engineer	
Reel Number	
Speed	

AAAA Studios

Counter	
Time	
Date	
Tape	

TITLE _____ Counter/SMPTE _____
ARTIST _____ Song Number _____

1	2	3	4
			SMPTE

TITLE _____ Counter/SMPTE _____
ARTIST _____ Song Number _____

1	2	3	4
D r u m s			SMPTE

Comments: _____ Offset To __:__:__:__/
_____ Offset To __:__:__:__/
_____ Start Time __:__:__:__/

ample, you hear sampled kick drums from a few popular drum machines, samplers and sound modules. Notice how natural and unaffected some of them are and how processed and effected others are.

Audio Example 6-7 Kick Drums
CD-2: Track 41

All of these sounds are very good and very usable in many musical settings. Let's start with a very simple kick sound and build to a very complex sound. For instructional purposes, we'll keep building on the sound as we go. For your own music, the most appropriate sound might be the most simple and pure sound or the most complex and involved sound. Let the music guide you to the sounds you need.

Most of the very complicated and interesting kick drum sounds that come from a drum machine start as a simple kick like the one in Audio Example 6-8. This is the sound of one moving-coil mic inside a kick drum with the front head off and a pillow in the bottom of the drum touching the head. It's like the sound of the live kick drum in Chapter 5.

Audio Example 6-8 Simple Kick
CD-2: Track 42

Any processing we perform on the drum machine kick can almost always be done to the live kick.

Tuning the Kick

Test the tuning of the drum first. Often, lowering or raising the pitch of the drum instantly produces the sound your music needs with no effort. I like the sound of the kick in Audio Example 6-9 when it's tuned lower. (I'm assuming that you're familiar enough with your drum machine or sound module controls to change the basic parameters, like level, tuning and panning.)

Audio Example 6-9 Tuning the Kick
CD-2: Track 42

Equalizing the Kick

The same equalization considerations need to be evaluated on drum machine sounds as on live drums—lows, mids and highs. On kick drum, I usually like a good solid low end and a well-defined attack. Remember, in order to hear the lows and highs better, first find the mid-frequencies that are clouding the sound and cut them. These mids are typically between about 250 and 500Hz. A sweepable or parametric EQ is ideal for shaping drum sounds. Being able to sweep the cut or boost can enable you to find just the right EQ curve. I'll cut the mids on the kick in Audio Example 6-10.

Audio Example 6-10 Cut Mids
CD-2: Track 43

The sampled kick can be reinforced in the low frequencies at about 80 to 150Hz, and the attack can be accentuated between 3 and 5kHz. The exact frequencies you select are usually determined by other instruments in the mix. If the bass is boosted at 150Hz, then you'd be better off boosting the kick at a low frequency other than 150Hz. Listen to Audio Example 6-11 as I enhance the lows and highs on the kick. This is the same drum we just cut the mids on in Audio Example 6-10.

Audio Example 6-11 Enhance Lows
CD-2: Track 44

To keep track of the progress we're making with this basic kick drum, Audio Example 6-12 demonstrates the kick drum before EQ and after EQ. First you hear the kick we started with, then the kick as we've shaped the sound to this point.

Audio Example 6-12 Before and After
CD-2: Track 45

Most of the time, this clean, punchy kick sound will work best in the mix. It's ideal to print a good raw sound like this to the multitrack and add reverb or effects later in the mix. If you save the rest of the processing for mixdown, you can fine-tune the sound specifically for the music as it stands in the particular mix you've created.

Recording Levels for the Kick Drum

Recording the kick drum at 0VU (on the loudest part of the track) works best most of the time. Low-frequency energy dominates recording levels, so if you increase the lows, the overall level increases dramatically. When you're dealing with transients on drum sounds, you need to identify whether the sound has a lot of low-frequency content and/or lots of attack. Sounds predominant in low frequencies can typically be recorded hotter, in the range of 0 to +2VU, because the

low-frequency energy controls the level. Sounds with very little or no low-frequency content that have a definite percussive transient should typically be recorded at lower levels in the range of -5 to -3VU. The ideal level depends on the individual sound, its transient and the amount of low frequency. If you're not familiar with the concept of transients, refer to Chapters 1 and 2.

Once the kick is recorded on its own track, there are still a few details to look after. On the acoustic drums in Chapter 5, we dealt with leakage between the drum mics when the kick drum mic also picked up the rest of the kit. To compensate for leakage, we used a gate. We don't really have leakage using a drum machine, but drum machines have a tendency to crosstalk between output channels, so it's a good idea to use gates on tracks playing back from tape. In other words, even though you've sent the kick alone out an individual output, the rest of the drum sounds might be heard faintly in the background.

The other (and more important) reason for using gates on recorded drum machine tracks is noise. You've boosted tape noise if you've added any high end to the track after it's been recorded. The drum tracks are often very dominant in the mix, making any noise from them constant and consistently noticeable. Audio Example 6-13 demonstrates a noisy kick track playing back from the multitrack.

Audio Example 6-13 Noisy Kick
CD-2: Track 46

See Illustration 6-11 for a diagram of the patching process for a gate in this context.

To adjust a gate on drums, set the attack

time to its fastest setting. Start with the release time at about half a second. Set the range control so that all sound below the threshold is turned completely down. Finally, adjust the threshold so the gate turns on any time the kick hits and turns completely off between hits (Illustrations 6-12 and 6-13).

Listen to the kick in Audio Example 6-14. I start without the gate, then I include the gate in the signal path. Notice the difference in the amount of noise between the kicks.

Audio Example 6-14 Gate the Kick
CD-2: Track 46

In the majority of styles, reverb is inappropriate for the kick drum—especially reverb with decay times over about a half second long. Since the kick typically has ample low end and is usually playing throughout a song, adding a lot of reverb to the kick produces a constant wash of reverberation that can reduce clarity and make the mix sound muddy and distant. In the drum pattern in Audio Example 6-15, I start with no

Illustration 6-11
Patching in the Gate

1. Patch the tape track into the input of the gate. It's almost always preferable to get the signal for the gate directly from the source. In this case, the source is the multitrack. Avoid using sends for the gate that are post fader or post EQ.
2. Plug the output of the gate into the line input of an available mixer channel.

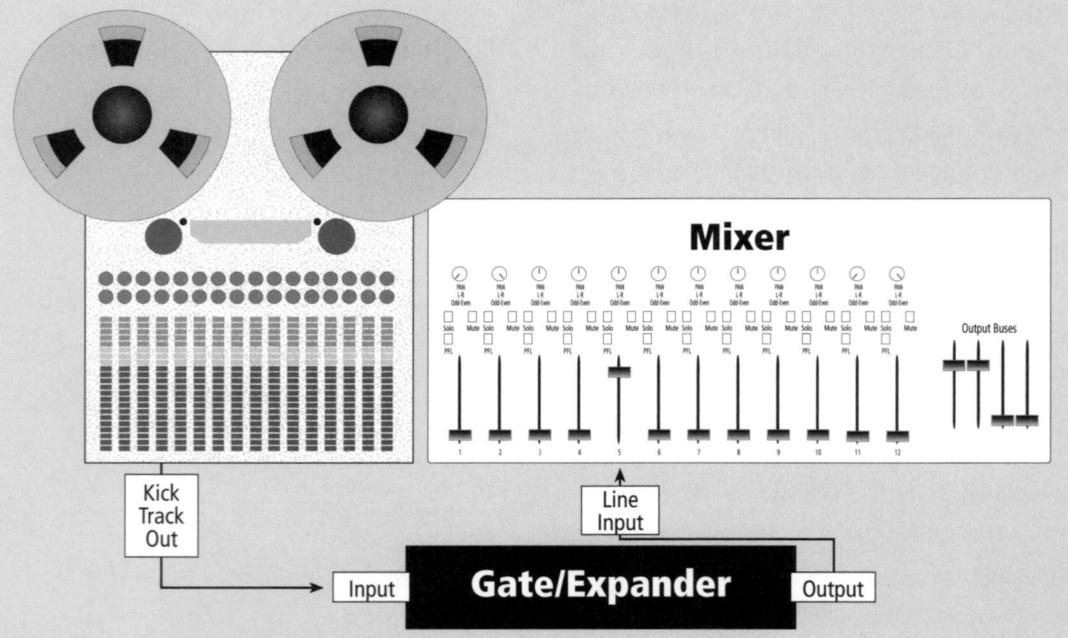

Mixer

Output Buses

Kick Track Out

Line Input

Input **Gate/Expander** Output

Illustration 6-12
Gating Drum Machine Parts on Playback From the Multitrack

1. Set the attack to its fastest setting.
2. Set the release time between .25 and 1 second (depending on the sound source and musical requirements).
3. Set the range control for maximum reduction of signal below the threshold.
4. Adjust the threshold so the instrument sounds normal and the gate turns the track off whenever there's no sound.
5. If your processor has a Gate/Expander button, select the smoothest sounding position. The Expander setting usually works best on long, smooth sounds like crash cymbals or drums with lots of ring.

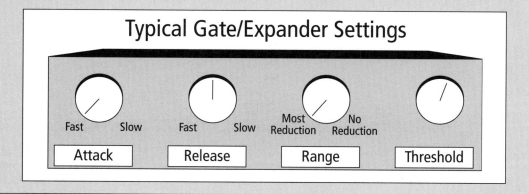

Typical Gate/Expander Settings

| Attack | Release | Range | Threshold |
| Fast — Slow | Fast — Slow | Most Reduction — No Reduction | |

reverb on the kick, then I add it. Notice the change in the clarity and the distinguishability of the drum sound.

Audio Example 6-15 Kick Reverb
CD-2: Track 47

In some styles, reverb is common on the kick. Short decay times and gated reverb sounds are most common. These reverb sounds often become very important to the musical impact of the kick. Print the reverb to the multitrack with the kick if tracks and effects are limited. Reverb is often part of the sampled sounds in a drum machine or sound module. The sampled kick drum sounds in Audio Example 6-16 include short or gated reverb.

Audio Example 6-16 Short Reverb
CD-2: Track 48

On the kick in Audio Example 6-17, the drum starts out dry, then I add gated reverb.

Audio Example 6-17 Gated Reverb
CD-2: Track 49

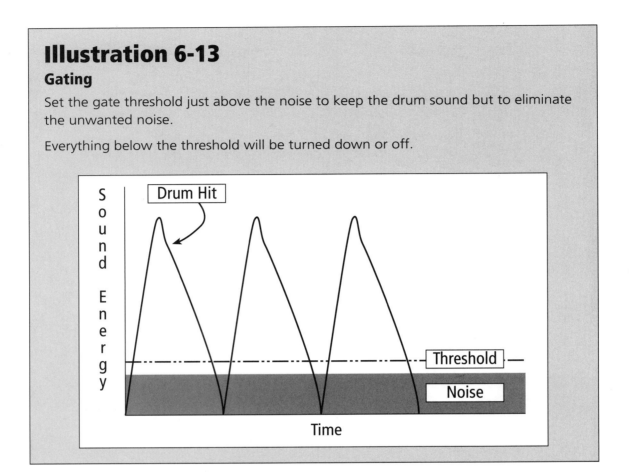

Illustration 6-13
Gating

Set the gate threshold just above the noise to keep the drum sound but to eliminate the unwanted noise.

Everything below the threshold will be turned down or off.

The kick in Audio Example 6-18 starts dry, then I add plate reverb with a decay time of .5 seconds.

Audio Example 6-18 Plate Reverb
CD-2: Track 49

As you can tell from the previous three Audio Examples, the addition of these reverb sounds can increase the interest of the kick. It's most common to hear reverb on the kick in R&B, rap and sometimes pop songs. Country, jazz, fusion and vintage rock songs almost always use dry kick drum sounds. Sometimes on heavier rock recordings that simulate an arena concert sound,

a little hall reverb on the kick can help blend it with the mix. In each case, use reverberation sparingly on the kick drum or you'll lose edge, clarity and intensity.

Panning the Kick

The kick track is almost always panned to the center position. Since it has lots of low end, the kick can be a dominant force in the level of a mix. If the kick is panned to one side, the mix level will be very heavy on the kick side and weak on the other side. This isn't good since we want to create a mix that's even in level from left to right.

Low frequencies are omnidirectional, which means it's difficult to tell where they're coming from. Therefore, panning instruments with primarily low frequencies gives little if any benefit to the sound of the mix. Sometimes, depending on the sounds of the instruments, a mix will work well if the bass guitar and kick drum are panned slightly apart, but there's usually not much benefit to that, especially in the context of a full range mix.

Decisions about shaping the kick sound, or any sound for that matter, always involve musical considerations. If the kick is appropriate for the song, then you've done your job. On the other hand, the most interesting sounding kick in the wrong musical surroundings isn't doing anybody any good. Let's strive to search for sounds based on musical considerations rather than simply sticking a neat sound in an inappropriate musical setting.

Snare Drum

The range of different snare drum sounds that are available in drum machines and sound modules is vast. The snare drum is an instrument that comes in several sizes, from a small piccolo snare to a very large marching snare drum. Each size can be tuned in a wide range from very high to very low. Snares are the wires that touch the bottom head of the drum. The snares can be tight or loose, made from different materials with greater or fewer numbers of them. Also, different heads can have different sounds, and different types of wood and hardware designs can change the sound. In other words, there's no one definitive snare drum sound, and there are plenty of options to chose from. Spend time researching the sounds available to you. Find a snare sound that fits the musical context and

fits with the sound of the other drums.

Listen to the sampled snare drum sounds in Audio Example 6-19 to hear some of the options available.

Audio Example 6-19 Snare Drums
CD-2: Track 50

Some of the sampled sounds from drum machines sound as natural as they would from one mic close-miking the drum. Some of the sounds have a complex blend of dry, processed and acoustic sound. Let's start with the simple snare and build our own sound that's more complex. Audio Example 6-20 demonstrates our reference snare for the next six audio examples.

Audio Example 6-20 Simple Snare
CD-2: Track 51

Any processing we do to a drum machine snare can be applied to a live acoustic snare drum.

Since there are so many different types of snare drum sounds, there's no single equalization technique that works all the time. Often, the sound of the drum machine output works great with no EQ. Frequently, changes are made in the EQ to make the track fit with other instruments in the mix. Sometimes you'll need to cut the lows and boost the highs. Other times you'll need to boost the mids and cut the highs. It's not even uncommon to boost the lows and cut the highs. Listen to your music to decide what's necessary for the song. The more mixes you've completed using these mixing techniques, the better your judgment will become.

When recording to the multitrack, the primary objective is to get a sound to tape that's clean and gives you the option of final sound shaping in the mix. When you're shaping a sound in the final mix, your main consideration is the blend, balance and musical impact to the listener. Use all these concepts and theories together in your specific situation to help enhance the emotion and feeling of your song.

The next five Audio Examples demonstrate some specific frequencies that adjust different aspects of most snare drum sounds.

8–10kHz is the very high buzz of the snares plus the sound of the stick hitting the drum. In Audio Example 6-21, I boost then cut 8kHz.

Audio Example 6-21 8kHz
CD-2: Track 51

3–5kHz is the aggressive and penetrating edge sound. This frequency range includes the sound of the snares rattling in response to the snare drum being hit. In Audio Example 6-22, I boost then cut 4kHz.

Audio Example 6-22 4kHz
CD-2: Track 51

1.5–2.5kHz is a papery sound. This isn't usually a good range to boost on the snare. In Audio Example 6-23, I boost then cut 2kHz.

Audio Example 6-23 2kHz
CD-2: Track 51

200–500Hz is often the body of the snare sound. Boosting here can thicken the sound of the snare drum. Cutting here can clean up the sound. This range is boosted or cut depending totally on the other instruments in the song and the desired effect. In Audio Example 6-24, I boost then cut 250Hz.

Audio Example 6-24 250Hz
CD-2: Track 51

Below 100Hz is generally a range of frequencies that isn't useful on most snare drums in most mixes. Boosting these frequencies can cause a conflict with the bass guitar, kick drum or other low-frequency instruments. In Audio Example 6-25, I roll the lows off below 100Hz.

Audio Example 6-25 100Hz
CD-2: Track 51

Recording Levels for the Snare Drum

These are guidelines for setting levels, but the further you get into recording, the more you'll see that the engineer needs to hear the sound and then make informed choices for adjustments.

Normal recording levels for snare drum can vary depending on the sound. If the sound has plenty of low end and is very natural sounding, adjust the level for 0VU at the loudest part of the track. This usually means about -3 to -5VU on a single hit to allow for level accumulating on an eighth- or sixteenth-note snare fill.

Different snare sounds provide different reading on a VU meter. We come back to the fact that if the sound is thin with lots of transient attack, you need to record at lower levels to accurately record the transient and avoid oversaturating the tape. Depending on the sound, the levels might need to be as cold as -9VU. Adjusting the levels between -7 and -3VU at the loudest part of the track usually works well on thin snare drum sounds.

Tuning the Snare

Tuning the drum lower or higher (within the drum machine) can make the difference between a drum that works great in a song and one that doesn't. In Chapter 5, when we tuned the acoustic drum higher and lower, the sound obviously changed. In that case, we had the same drum being tuned higher and lower. When we tune the sample higher and lower, we're really hearing a sound change that is closer to changing the pitch *and* the size of the drum. As the sample is tuned higher, the drum sounds smaller and higher. As we tune the sample lower, the drum sounds larger and lower. If you want a huge, low, beefy snare drum sound, start with a drum sound that's naturally low and full. If you tune that sound down, it will sound much more realistic than if you tune a high thin sound way down.

Gating the Snare

As we discovered with the kick drum track, it can be helpful to gate the snare track on playback from the multitrack. The gate will eliminate any channel crosstalk from the drum machine or multitrack and, more importantly, it'll eliminate tape noise between the snare hits (Illustration 6-11).

On the snare track in Audio Example 6-26, I boost the high frequencies to accentu-ate the snare sound but turning the highs up also turns the tape noise up. Listen as the snare plays. After a few seconds, I insert the gate. Notice the change in noise level between hits.

Audio Example 6-26 Gate the Snare
CD-2: Track 52

Compressing the Snare Sound

A common technique on snare drum that's also very popular on toms and kick is compression. Compression has two primary effects on drum tracks. First, since the compressor is an automatic level control, it evens out the volume of each hit. This can be a very good thing on a commercial rock tune, where the snare part is a simple backbeat on two and four. The compressor keeps the level even so that a weak hit doesn't detract from the groove.

The second benefit of compression is its ability, with proper use, to accentuate the attack of the snare drum. If the compressor controls are adjusted correctly, we can exaggerate the attack of the snare, giving the snare a very aggressive and penetrating edge. This technique involves setting the attack time of the compressor slow enough so that the attack isn't compressed but the remaining portion of the sound is (Illustrations 6-14 and 6-15).

This is how to set the compressor to exaggerate the attack of any drum:

1. Set the ratio between 3:1 and 10:1.
2. Set the release time at about .5 seconds. This will need to be adjusted according to the length of the snare sound. Just be sure the LEDs showing gain reduction have all gone off before the next major hit of the drum. This

Illustration 6-14
Exaggerating the Snare Transient
This graph shows the sound energy of a snare drum without compression. (Threshold and attack time are only indicated as references.)

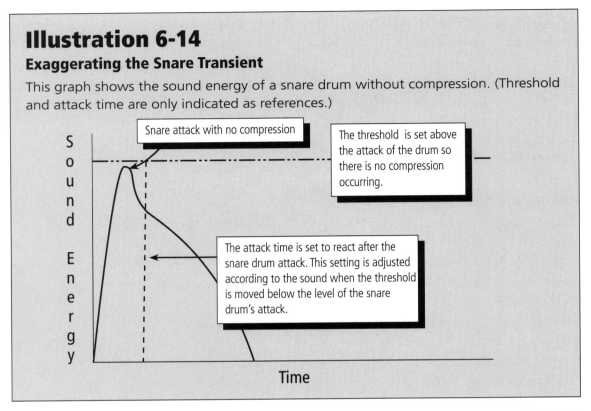

Snare attack with no compression

The threshold is set above the attack of the drum so there is no compression occurring.

The attack time is set to react after the snare drum attack. This setting is adjusted according to the sound when the threshold is moved below the level of the snare drum's attack.

Illustration 6-15
The Result of Compression

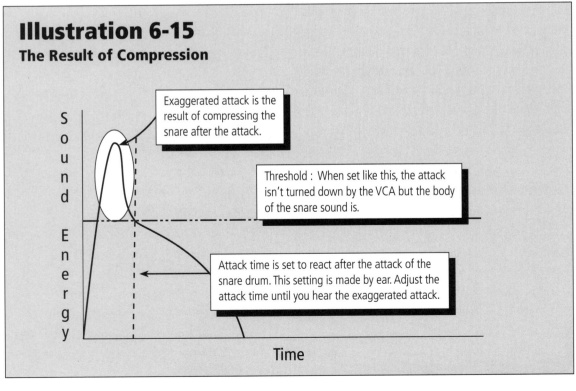

Exaggerated attack is the result of compressing the snare after the attack.

Threshold : When set like this, the attack isn't turned down by the VCA but the body of the snare sound is.

Attack time is set to react after the attack of the snare drum. This setting is made by ear. Adjust the attack time until you hear the exaggerated attack.

doesn't apply to fills, but if the snare is hitting on 2 and 4, the LEDs should be out before each hit.

3. At this point, set the attack time to its fastest setting.

4. Adjust the threshold for 3 to 9dB of gain reduction.

5. Finally, readjust the attack time. As you slow

the attack time of the compressor, it doesn't react in time to compress the transient, but it can react in time to compress the rest of the drum sound.

Compression isn't musically effective on some jazz styles where the snare may be doing little jabs and fills within the beat that are mostly for the feel. These jabs and fills aren't really

Illustration 6-16
Gating and Compressing the Snare

1. Patch the output of the snare track into the gate.

2. Adjust the gate to get rid of the noise between the snare hits.

3. Adjust the compressor to compress the body of the snare but not the attack.

4. Patch the output of the compressor into a line input of the recording mixer.

Note: From the purist's standpoint, inserting a gate and a compressor in the signal path is degrading to the signal because each unit introduces another VCA to the path. Though that is true, we must weigh the options to achieve the sound and musical effect that's appropriate for the song.

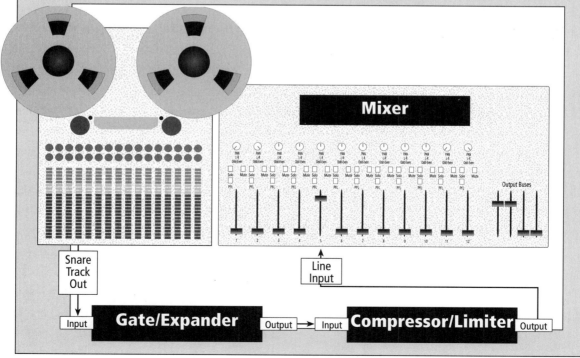

meant to be heard predominantly in the mix, so the compressor might ruin the feel of a jazz drum track rather than solidifying or enhancing the feel.

Listen to the snare drum in Audio Example 6-27. It has no compression.

Audio Example 6-27 No Compression
CD-2: Track 53

Audio Example 6-28 is the same snare drum from Audio Example 6-27 with a compressor in the signal path adjusted to emphasize the attack.

Audio Example 6-28 Compressed Snare
CD-2: Track 53

Compressing drum sounds has a practical disadvantage. Since the compressor is turning down the loudest hits, the entire track can be turned up, which also turns up the noise (and leakage from the other drums if you're recording acoustic drums) in relation to the snare hits. This gives us another reason to gate the track on playback.

If you gate the tape track before you compress the tape track, the gate turns down the tape noise, so as the compressor turns back up, there's no more tape noise to turn up. Always place the gate before the compressor in the signal path when gating and compressing a tape track (Illustration 6-16).

Listen to the snare in Audio Example 6-29. The gate and compressor have been bypassed.

Audio Example 6-29 Normal Snare
CD-2: Track 54

In Audio Example 6-30, I insert the compressor. Listen for the change in the sound and the change in the amount of audible noise between the snare hits.

Audio Example 6-30 Compressed Snare
CD-2: Track 54

Finally, I insert the gate in Audio Example 6-31. Notice the attack stays and the noise is gone.

Audio Example 6-31 Gate the Compressed Snare
CD-2: Track 54

Reverberation on the Snare

The reverb on the snare track often sets the sound for the entire arrangement. The fact that the snare is nearly always playing, combined with the fact that the snare is usually a predominant instrument in the mix, makes the selection of its reverb and effects particularly important.

We'll build from the simple dry snare drum sound. Keep in mind that drum machines include sounds that might already include many of the techniques we're covering. Evaluate the sound from the unit, then apply these techniques as they seem appropriate.

It's common to use more than one reverb on a snare drum. Many interesting commercial drum sounds are accomplished using two or three or even more reverb sounds simulta-

Illustration 6-17

Aux Buses for Reverb

It's ideal to use multiple aux buses for multiple reverb sends. This lets you send any amount of each channel to the reverb.

1. Turn the snare track up in Aux 1, 2 and 3.
2. Patch the outputs of Aux 1, 2 and 3 into reverberation devices 1, 2 and 3.
3. Patch the outputs of reverberation devices 1, 2 and 3 into line inputs or dedicated effects returns.
4. Blend the reverb sounds by adjusting the aux sends.

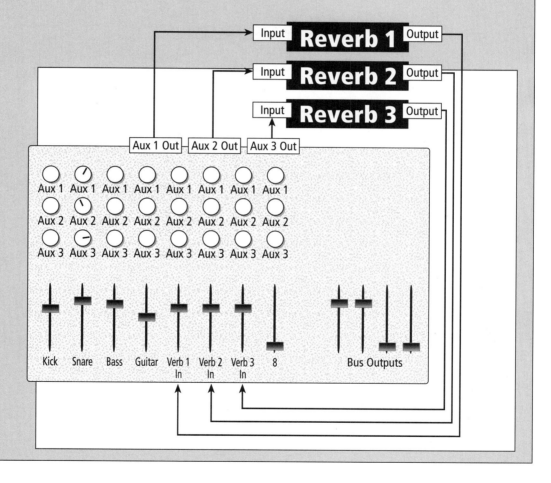

neously. The use of multiple reverb sounds can help you create a very interesting and multifaceted snare sound. Sometimes these techniques can get out of hand and blur the image instead of enhancing it, but with a little practice and moderation, this approach can facilitate some great sounds.

If we use three reverberation devices on

the snare, we're usually just trying to emphasize what would happen in many acoustical environments. We're exaggerating the interesting sounds. (See Illustrations 6-17, 6-18 and 6-19 for suggestions on patching multiple reverberation devices.)

First, I'll usually add a tight ambience reverb sound. This sound can be a plate or bright hall type sound with a short decay time, below about a half second. Some reverberation units

Illustration 6-18
Splitting the Aux Out

If your mixer doesn't have three aux sends, try splitting the output of one aux send three ways.

1. Turn up the snare in the aux bus.
2. Use a 2- or 3-way Y-connection from aux out.
3. Plug into each reverberation device from the aux out split.
4. Plug the output of the effects into the line input or dedicated effects returns.
5. Blend the reverb sounds with the return level adjustments.

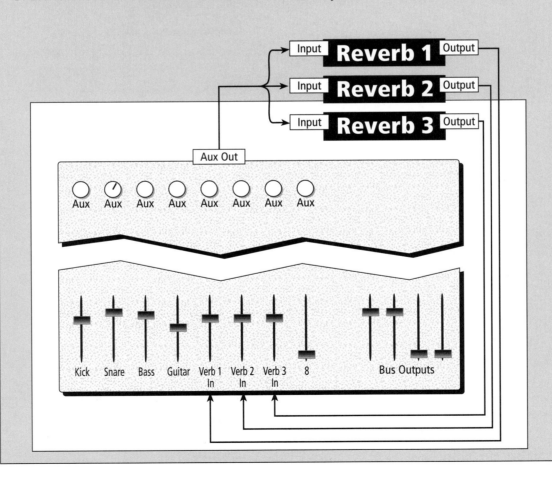

Illustration 6-19
Avoid Daisy Chaining!

Daisy chaining means patching from the output of one effect into the input of another effect, then from the output of that effect into the input of yet another effect and so on. Avoid daisy chaining reverberation devices! The sound achieved by these devices lacks intelligibility and focus. It's only useful as a special effect.

Input	**Reverb 1**	Output
Input	**Reverb 2**	Output
Input	**Reverb 3**	Output

Aux 1 Out

Aux 1 Aux 1 Aux 1 Aux 1 Aux 1 Aux 1 Aux 1 Aux 1
Aux 2 Aux 2 Aux 2 Aux 2 Aux 2 Aux 2 Aux 2 Aux 2
Aux 3 Aux 3 Aux 3 Aux 3 Aux 3 Aux 3 Aux 3 Aux 3

Kick   Snare   Bass   Guitar   Verb 1 In   Bus Outputs

even have programs specifically for early reflections or small-room ambience. This type of sound helps define the ambience of the immediate recording space. Even in a large recording room or concert hall, an element of the immediate space that the drum is in can be heard in the overall snare drum sound. That's what we're trying to simulate with this reverb sound. Listen as I add the tight ambience to this snare in Audio Example 6-32.

Audio Example 6-32 Ambience
CD-2: Track 55

If we were just combining two reverberation devices, the next sound would be a larger hall or chamber sound with a decay time between 2 and 3.5 seconds. This is the reverb that adds the real size and depth to the sound. In a real acoustic setting, the other reverberation devices are important but act as support to the larger ambience. When we're shaping the sound and have separate control of these different ambient simulations, we can shape the sound to emphasize the ambience that blends with the rest of the mix. This is often the same sound used for the main reverb on the vocals and instruments. I add a larger reverb to the tight ambience on the snare sound in Audio Example 6-33.

Audio Example 6-33 Add Large Reverb
CD-2: Track 56

If I'm using three reverb sounds, I'll usually add the tight ambience first, then I'll add a medium length reverb with a decay time of about one second. Plates and chambers usually work well for this application. Think of this reverb as simulating the sound of the instrument within an immediate larger space, like the stage area of a large concert hall. In Audio Example 6-34, you'll hear the dry sound first, then I add a chamber sound with a one second decay time. Finally, I add the tight ambience. Notice how each reverb adds its own depth to the snare sound.

Audio Example 6-34 Two Reverbs
CD-2: Track 57

In Audio Example 6-35, you first hear the dry snare, then the addition of a tight ambience sound, followed by a chamber reverberation sound with a one second decay time. To complete the snare sound, I add hall reverb with a decay time of 2.5 seconds.

Audio Example 6-35 Three Reverbs
CD-2: Track 58

There's a lot of room for experimentation when you start adding these reverb sounds. Setting the predelays to increasingly longer settings on the second and third reverberation devices can produce an overall reverb sound that seamlessly blends from the tight ambience to the large hall sound. These sounds are difficult or impossible to create with one simple reverb sound.

I realize that not everybody has three reverberation devices available for the snare drum, but you could print one or two reverberation devices to the multitrack, then add another on the mixdown. Or you could start with a sampled sound that already includes one or two reverb sounds and work from there. If you're thoroughly aware of your options and implement them when tasteful and appropriate, you'll create some interesting and creatively stimulating sounds that'll make a big difference in the impact of your music.

Delay effects are not common on snare drum. A repeating echo is sometimes an interesting special effect. A chorus on the reverb or flange on the snare sound is sometimes fun, but these are exceptions and only work well in certain instances.

Panning the Snare

The snare drum is almost always panned to the center position. Since the snare usually plays constantly throughout a song, it needs to be placed in the center of the stereo spectrum to hold the focal point. If the snare is panned to one side, the mix will feel lopsided, and the snare will probably distract the listener rather than drawing them in. If you pan the snare and the kick apart in the mix, with one left and the other right, your mix will ping-pong back and forth throughout the song (this is not usually a good thing).

The kick drum and snare drum are two of the most crucial style-defining instruments, so it's important that these tracks are interesting and appropriate. Spending the time to get these sounds together is a worthwhile investment in the development of your song. Try any or all of these techniques on the kick or the snare, but always try to maintain the punch and presence of the dry sound while enhancing the ambience, quieting the noise or emphasizing the attack.

Toms

The sound-shaping techniques that we've used on kick drum and snare drum are also appropriate for use when recording toms. Always select sounds for toms that blend with and complement the sounds you've created for the kick and snare.

In addition to finding the appropriate effects for the toms that blend with the kick and snare, it's important to use basic sounds that blend well. Drum machines typically contain several different tom sounds that are very usable but the trick is to find sounds that blend with the rest of the drum sounds. If the snare and kick sounds are very aggressive with lots of attack and solid punch, the toms should be likewise. If the snare and kick are very natural and warm, the toms should match that feeling. Using the same reverb sound on the toms as the snare or kick will help.

Some drum machine toms are clean and pure just like the sound from one mic placed correctly and recorded at proper levels. Some drum machine toms include room ambience and multiple effects. Listen to the wide variety of sampled tom sounds in Audio Example 6-36.

Audio Example 6-36 Toms
CD-2: Track 59

Recording Levels for Toms

The normal recording level for sampled toms is 0VU. These levels can be pushed a bit higher when recording to the analog multitrack. In Chapter 5, we saw that it was sometimes alright to record toms as hot as +3 or +4VU to take advantage of the natural tape compression that occurs when analog tape approaches the point of oversaturation. This technique can work well on sampled toms, too.

When we talk about recording hot levels above 0VU, we're talking about recording to analog tape. Whenever recording to any digital format, whether a sampler, DAT, reel-to-reel digital or hard disk-based digital recorder, the primary concern is to avoid recording at levels above 0 on the meter. For our purposes, there is no benefit to recording abnormally hot on a digital recorder.

Tuning Drum Machine Toms

Many tom fills require drums that blend well and make a smooth transition from high to low. It can be difficult to find several different tom samples that blend together. Since most drum machines let you assign the individual drums to whichever pad you choose and tune whichever instrument is assigned to any one pad, try assigning the same tom sound to four or five different pads. Then tune the different tom pads from high to low. This procedure usually produces a sound that's smooth and even around the toms. The tom fill in Audio Example 6-37 uses the same sample tuned differently from high to low.

Audio Example 6-37 Tuned Tom
CD-2: Track 60

Equalizing the Toms

Most sampled toms sound pretty good straight out of the drum machine. This only makes sense when you consider that most of the samples in a good drum machine use very good drums that have been recorded in a very good studio. Even though the raw sound is usually great, we still might need to fine-tune the EQ to match the rest of the set.

Since there are so many types of tom sounds, there are no definite rules for equalizing drum machine toms. You need to evaluate the sound from the unit in the three main frequency ranges that we considered in Chapter 5: lows, mids and highs. Listen for the frequency range that's hiding the part of the sound you'd like to hear and cut it. Next, listen for frequencies to enhance and boost them.

Consider the following frequency ranges when evaluating a tom sound. Learning the sound of boosting and cutting these frequencies will speed up your EQ process in both acoustic and drum machine sounds. Fullness is between 100 and 500Hz. Boost or cut between 250 and 500Hz to increase or decrease the full sound of a higher pitched tom. Boost or cut between 100 and 250Hz to increase or decrease the fullness of a low pitched tom sound.

Notice the sound of the tom in Audio Example 6-38 as I change the EQ. First you hear the drum with no EQ. Next, I boost a curve centered on 250Hz, sweep down to 100Hz and up to 500Hz. Finally, I cut at 250Hz, then sweep the cut from 100 to 500Hz.

Audio Example 6-38 100 to 500Hz
CD-2: Track 61

The sound of the stick hitting the tom is usually between 7 and 9kHz. Listen to Audio Example 6-39 as I boost and cut between 7 and 9kHz.

Audio Example 6-39 7 to 9kHz
CD-2: Track 62

The more aggressive attack is usually between 3 and 5kHz. Audio Example 6-40 demonstrates a boost and cut between 3 and 5kHz.

Audio Example 6-40 3 to 5kHz
CD-2: Track 62

Again, different tom samples might require boosting or cutting any of these frequencies or none of these frequencies. Some toms might work well with no changes at all. Some toms might need radical changes to blend with the other drums. Your job is to listen, evaluate and make logical and informed choices.

The compression and gating techniques that we heard on the snare drum can be very effective on toms, too. Gates and expanders often come configured with four gates in one single unit. One or two of these multiple gates can be very useful. Even more useful are units that have multiple gates and compressors in one rack-mountable frame.

I've found gates to be very effective noise reducing tools. Our goal when gating tracks is to eliminate all unwanted noise from each track in order to attain a close and punchy sound, like the drum sound in Audio Example 6-41.

Audio Example 6-41 Clean Drums
CD-2: Track 63

The reverb you select for the toms needs to blend with the other drum sounds. Usually, using the same reverb on the toms that you've used on the snare works best.

Reverberation on Toms

The old rule of thumb was that there should be only one kind of reverb on any one mix. Anything else wouldn't be natural and pure; it wouldn't be like a live recording in a concert hall. That's a theory we can build from. The drum set should really sound like it's all coming from the same space for a natural sounding mix. Choosing the same main reverb for the main drums can accomplish this.

Current audio trends dictate that it's appropriate to use more than one reverb on a mix. The approach you take in designing the sound of the mix can be based on decisions to enhance the musical impact of the song. In other words, the sky's the limit. Some songs sound wonderful with a very natural approach using hardly any EQ or effects. Some songs are incredible with the creative use of many of the tools at hand, including multiple reverberation devices, dynamic processors and special unconventional techniques. Always be sure you use musical considerations when making technical decisions.

Panning the Toms

Panning the toms requires a decision about the concept of the final mix. If you're trying to create a final product that sounds like a live band with a live drummer, you'll need to pan accordingly. Imagine the drummer's position on stage, and place all of the drums within that space. Since the drums are usually center stage, the toms are usually panned very close around the center when using this approach.

Panning from high to low between about 10 and 2 o'clock can still give the impression of the drums being center stage while clearing out the middle of the stereo image for lead instruments.

Since it's usually so easy to pan the toms in a drum machine, it can be tempting to pan the toms hard left and right, but that tends to be distracting if overdone. Be sure that any panning is supporting the musical power and impact of the song.

Listen to the drum balance through a good set of headphones. Some pan settings sound good on monitor speakers but are very distracting in headphones.

Cymbals

Cymbals from a drum machine often have the same transient as live cymbals. Record these cymbals between -7 and -9VU to accurately record the transient attack.

There are many different crash cymbals, ride cymbals and hi-hats in different drum machines, and they can usually all be tuned to different pitches for different sounds. Select the cymbal sound that is closest to the desired pitch and tonal character. Use minimal pitch change and equalization whenever possible.

Evaluate the three main frequency ranges (lows, mids and highs), and adjust for the sound you want. Try to imagine the sound you want, then achieve that sound.

The clear highs that sizzle over a mix are between 7 and 12kHz. Listen to the cymbal in Audio Example 6-42 as I boost and sweep between 7 and 12kHz.

Audio Example 6-42 7 to 12kHz
CD-2: Track 64

The drum machine/sound module you're using might or might not contain very high frequencies. Check your owner's manual to find the frequency range of your unit. It'll only add noise if you boost frequencies above the highest frequency produced by your drum machine.

If you're in the process of buying a drum machine, look for a unit that uses full range 16- or 20-bit samples. High quality, full range drum machines or sound modules will provide very clean and powerful sounds that give good clarity and transparency. The drums will also sound better throughout a wider tuning range when using 16- or 20-bit samples.

The penetrating edge in a cymbal comes from around 4kHz. I boost and sweep between 3 and 5kHz in Audio Example 6-43.

Audio Example 6-43 3 to 5kHz
CD-2: Track 65

The frequencies between 1.5 and 2.5kHz aren't usually very pleasant on most cymbals. I boost and cut the frequencies between 1.5 and 2.5kHz in Audio Example 6-44.

Audio Example 6-44 1.5 to 2.5kHz
CD-2: Track 66

The full gong-like sound comes from between 200 and 600Hz. Audio Example 6-45 demonstrates a boost and cut between 200 and 600Hz.

Audio Example 6-45 200 to 600Hz
CD-2: Track 67

The cymbal frequencies below about 80Hz aren't very useful within a mix. Cutting below 80Hz typically has little or no effect on the sound of the cymbal in the song, and cutting this frequency range can help clear out the low end for other instruments that are musically covering the low end. On the cymbal in Audio Example 6-46, I cut below 80Hz.

Audio Example 6-46 Cut Below 80Hz
CD-2: Track 68

Gating the drum machine's crash cymbal track after it's printed to tape is usually a good choice. Since the crash only happens occasionally, eliminating the tape noise between hits can help clean up the mix. Gating is only necessary if you're printing the crash to tape. If the sounds are coming from the sequenced drum machine part, noise is a minimal consideration.

Reverb on Cymbals

Reverb isn't usually necessary on cymbals and, in fact, can be distracting on the hi-hat. The hi-hat is usually constant and contains high frequency transients. If the hi-hat is reverberated, you can end up with a constant reverb sizzle that fills all the holes in the musical texture, eliminating audio transparency.

Listen to the pattern with reverb on the hi-hat in Audio Example 6-47. I turn the reverb on and off as the pattern plays. Notice the change in clarity and transparency as the reverb comes and goes.

Audio Example 6-47 Reverb on Hi-hat
CD-2: Track 69

Reverb can be very advantageous on crash cymbals. One of the worst sounds in most drum machines is the crash cymbal sound. The samples are usually short, and the end of the sound is often unnaturally abrupt. These short crashes can be made to ring as long as you want with the addition of plate reverb. The highs in the plate reverb sound can sound just like the natural decay of a crash cymbal. I'll often print the plate to the multitrack with the crash. Listen to the crash in Audio Example 6-48. You hear the crash first without the plate. When I add plate reverb, the decay sounds more natural.

Audio Example 6-48 Crash With Plate
CD-2: Track 70

One technique that works very well, although it requires a combination of acoustic drums and drum machine, is to record acoustic cymbals along with the drum machine kick, snare and tom. You can get the solid, punchy feel of the sampled drums along with the natural sound and feel of real cymbals. Miking the cymbals with two condenser mikes overhead in an X-Y configuration will provide a good stereo image to combine with the drum machine.

In Audio Example 6-49, I programmed the hi-hat and crash parts in the drum machine and recorded real cymbals on the multitrack. I start with the programmed cymbals, then switch to the acoustic cymbals. Notice the change in the rhythmic feel.

Audio Example 6-49
Real Cymbals With Sequence
CD-2: Track 71

Percussion

Whenever recording miscellaneous percussion instruments, like triangle, tambourine, claves, shakers and bells, keep one consideration in mind: the transient. This is true whether the instrument is being recorded acoustically or from a digital sample.

The sounds with the least amount of low end and sharp attacks should be recorded with the most conservative levels. For example, a triangle should be recorded at about -9VU since its sound has predominantly high frequencies and the metal triangle beater against the metal triangle produces an extreme transient. On the other hand, congas can usually be recorded at 0VU since the conga sound contains low frequencies and hands against the conga heads don't usually produce extremely sharp transients. Bongos have fewer low frequencies and, if played by an animal player with heavily callused hands, can produce a stronger transient. Levels around -3VU usually work well for bongos.

Tambourine is another instrument that produces an extreme transient. Let's listen to what happens when these instruments are recorded too hot to analog tape. We expect that the transient will oversaturate the tape. This typically sounds a little like the instrument is combined with a splat sound. Besides oversaturating the tape, we expect that the strong level will cause the sound to bleed onto the adjacent tracks. In other words, it's possible that we'll be able to hear the tambourine on the tracks adjacent to the tambourine track, even when the tambourine track is off.

Listen to the tambourine track in Audio Example 6-50. This demonstrates the sound of the tambourine recorded directly to DAT as a reference.

Audio Example 6-50 Tambourine
CD-2: Track 72

Audio Example 6-51 demonstrates the reference tambourine, this time recorded from the drum machine to the multitrack at 0VU. Notice the loss of clarity and attack.

Audio Example 6-51 Oversaturated Tambourine
CD-2: Track 72

Audio Example 6-52 reveals the sound from the adjacent tracks. Notice that, even though I've turned the tambourine track off, you can still hear the tambourine. What you're hearing is the excess magnetism that has actually been recorded on the tracks next to the tambourine track. However, this is only a problem when recording to analog tape.

Audio Example 6-52 Result of Oversaturation
CD-2: Track 72

If you've recorded the tambourine next to the lead vocal track or another important track and the tambourine has oversaturated the tape, it becomes a permanent part of the lead vocal track. If you decide to axe the tambourine part, the only way you'll get rid of the tambourine sound on the lead vocal track is to rerecord the lead vocal. For this reason, always be careful when recording instruments with extreme transients next to important parts.

The tambourine in Audio Example 6-53 was recorded at -9VU to the analog multitrack. Notice how much more clarity this tambourine recording has than when the same tambourine was recorded at 0VU.

Audio Example 6-53
Properly Recorded Tambourine
CD-2: Track 72

In Chapter 5, we noticed that it's common for different percussion instruments to enter a song on a musical section change. Often, two auxiliary percussion instruments will play at once. It's common to pan two percussion instruments apart so that if both instruments are playing consistent parts, they'll balance against each other in the mix.

If there's only one auxiliary percussion part and it's panned to one side without another in-

Illustration 6-20
Reverb Panned Away From the Instrument

1. Pan the clave track left and the cowbell track right. Aux 1 is the send to the left channel of the reverb. Aux 2 is the send to the right channel of the reverb.
2. Patch the stereo outputs of the reverberation device into the line inputs of two mixer channels. Pan the channels hard left and hard right corresponding to the left and right sends.
3. The clave is panned left, so send it from Aux 2 to the right channel of the reverb.
4. The cowbell is panned right, so send from Aux 1 to the left channel of the reverb.
5. Enjoy cool stereo sounds!

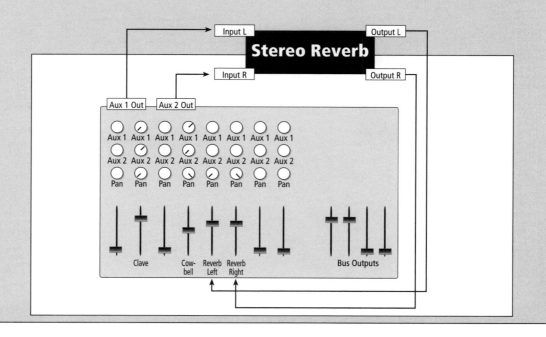

Illustration 6-21
Room Sound

1. Set up a mix of the drums in an aux bus.
2. Patch the output of the aux bus into a power amplifier that's connected to speakers. This technique is easiest if the amp and speakers are in a room other than the one with your recording gear. Large rooms usually work best.
3. Set up one or two mics in the room with the speakers. Plug the mics into your mixer. If you use two microphones, try an X-Y configuration or experiment with different mic placement to fine-tune the sound.
4. Blend the sound of the direct electronic drums (or previously recorded acoustic drums) with the sound of the drums in a room.

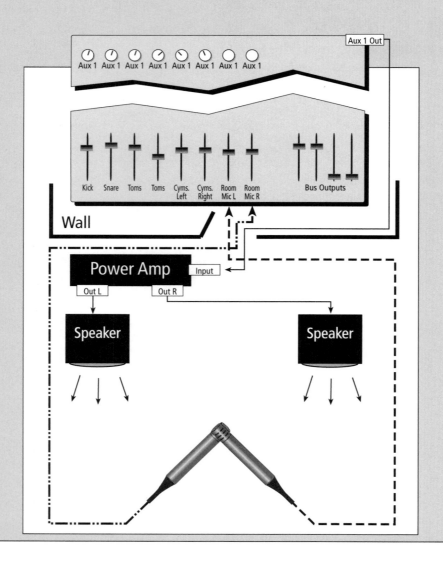

strument to balance against, the mix will sound lopsided. On the drum pattern in Audio Example 6-54, I have the claves panned to one side and the triangle to the other. This sounds even and balanced.

Audio Example 6-54 Balanced Percussion
CD-2: Track 73

Audio Example 6-55 demonstrates the same drum pattern as Audio Example 6-54, but I've taken the clave part out, leaving the triangle panned to one side. This sounds unbalanced. In a mix this would be distracting.

Audio Example 6-55 Distracting Triangle
CD-2: Track 74

Your choice regarding whether or not to include reverb in the percussion sounds depends on the activity of the parts. A simple part that plays occasionally can benefit from a nice, warm, smooth reverb sound or an interesting tight ambience. A part that plays constantly is usually best if not reverberated. As with the hi-hat track, the constant activity always keeps the reverb sizzling in the background. This is distracting and can produce a mix that sounds muddy and hazy.

Try this technique if you have separate sends to your reverb for the left and right channel: Pan a percussion part to one side and send the reverb on the other side. For example, pan the claves right, but select the reverb send for the left side. This produces a very spacious effect as the reverb opens up on the opposite side from the instrument, plus you get the close feel of having the dry instrument on one side of the mix. Listen to the clave track in Audio Example 6-56, panned right with the reverb left.

Audio Example 6-56 Reverb Panned Away
CD-2: Track 75

Audio Example 6-57 demonstrates the cowbell panned left with its reverb panned right (Illustration 6-20).

Audio Example 6-57 Reverb Panned Away
CD-2: Track 75

Using small ambience reverberation often adds an interesting edge to a percussion track. Listen to the conga track in Audio Example 6-58. After a few seconds, I add a tight room sound with a short decay time.

Audio Example 6-58 Small-Room Reverb
CD-2: Track 76

More Stuff

One of the disadvantages to drum machine recording is the lack of acoustic interaction. Active sounds combining in an acoustical environment produces a blend that can't be duplicated electronically.

In Chapter 4 we heard the difference between a guitar sound running direct into the mixer and a miked guitar amp combined with the room sound. The differences in sound and emotional impact were dramatic. The same theory pertains to the drum machine, but you *can* include the room sound on your drum machine parts! Plug the output of an aux bus into a power amplifier that's connected to speakers in a room. A guitar amp will work for this technique, but high quality reference monitors work best. It's ideal if the speakers are in a room other than the room with your mixer. If you have multiple drum tracks, using an aux bus as the send to the speakers lets you send a separate mix of the drums and percussion to the speakers. This is convenient and flexible since sometimes it sounds the best if the room sound is only applied to certain instruments.

Now place a mic or two in the room away from the speakers. Connect the mics to the mixer inputs. You can either print the room sound to the multitrack, or you can use the room as a natural ambience chamber during mixdown. In Audio Example 6-59, you hear the dry drum pattern first, then you hear just the room sound, and finally I blend the room sound with the dry sound (Illustration 6-21).

Audio Example 6-59 Add Acoustic Ambience
CD-2: Track 77

Conclusion

We've covered a lot of material about recording drums and drum machines. All the processing and effects that I've suggested in this lesson can work great on drum machines *or* acoustic drums. Practice these techniques. I've referred to print-

ing drum machine tracks to tape, and I've referred to simply running the drum track on the mix with your sequencer chasing SMPTE from the multitrack. The number of available tracks and the feel of the music are the indicators that you should use to determine the best approach for your music using your recording tools. Sometimes I prefer the sound of just printing synth and drum machine parts to tape. Other times I want to wait for mixdown to really fine-tune some of the sounds, so I'd rather run them from the sequencer.

Don't be afraid to try these procedures, even when under fire in the middle of a session with other musicians around. Mistakes made in pressure situations make a deep impression and are rarely repeated. Casual mistakes made on your own time don't usually sink in quite as deeply.

If a procedure is new, think it through systematically. Take each small step, one at a time, in order. You'll be amazed at what you can pull off if you give it your best shot and are patiently diligent.

Glossary

+4dBm: A line level signal strength that's typically associated with balanced, professional tape recorders, mixers and outboard equipment. +4 equipment works well only with other +4 equipment. A level matching interface is required to facilitate the use of +4dBm equipment with -10dBV equipment.

-10dBV: A line level signal strength that's typically associated with semipro and home tape recorders, mixers and outboard equipment. -10 equipment works well only with other -10 equipment. A level matching interface is required to facilitate the use of -10dBV equipment with +4dBm equipment.

1/4" phone connector: The type of connector found on a regular guitar cable.

60-cycle hum: An actual waveform that's induced into recording equipment from the 60-cycle AC current that runs the equipment. Inducement of 60-cycle hum is usually the result of improper grounding or shielding.

active direct box: A transformer designed to match high impedance to low impedance. This type of direct box contains amplifying circuitry to restore clarity in the high end and punch in the low end that's been lost in the impedance transformation process.

adjacent track: A track that is directly next to a specified track on a multitrack tape recorder. The track numbered one higher or one less than a specified track. For example, tracks four and six are adjacent to track five.

afuché: An African percussion instrument that has as its body a cylinder or large hollow gourd. The surface of this cylinder usually has a rough texture. A handle protrudes from one end of the cylinder or gourd. Several strings of metal, plastic or organic beads are strung around the cylinder or gourd. The instrument can be played by either shaking or rotating. Often, the right hand holds the handle and twists to the beat of the song while the left hand holds the beads against the surface of the cylinder. The Americanized version of this instrument has a highly textured metal surface with 20 to 40 strands of chrome-plated metal beads. The African version is made from natural, organic materials. Also called a **cabasa**.

amplitude: The amount of energy in a sound wave.

amps: In relation to volts, amps are the actual strength behind the voltage. Amp stands for amperes or amperage. A voltage with very low amperage can't harm the user. Voltage with very high amperage can kill the user.

arpeggiated chord: A chord whose individual notes are played separately. The individual notes are often played in time with the rhythmic structure of the song and are commonly played in order from the lowest to the highest then back to the lowest.

assign switches: Controls that route signals to different locations.

attack time: The amount of time it takes for sound to reach its peak amount of energy or volume. Regarding dynamic processors, this refers to the amount of time it takes the VCA to begin turning the signal down then back up.

attenuator: Used at the mic input to reduce the amount of signal from the mic or direct box as it enters the mixer circuitry. Attenuators are carefully designed to cause minimal change in sound quality while reducing the signal strength to an acceptable level for a specific point in the signal path. Also called a **pad**.

auto correct: This process, used by a drum machine or sequencer, compensates for a rhythmically imperfect performance by moving each note to the closest user-defined note value (quarter note, eighth note, sixteenth note, etc.). Certain sequencers have varying degrees of auto correct, giving the user the option of making the performance closer to perfect without being mathematically computer perfect. Also called **quantize**.

auxiliary input: A line level input on a mixer or amplifier. Auxiliary inputs are typically used for cassette inputs, CD inputs, reverb inputs or other miscellaneous audio equipment.

auxiliary output: A mixer output that's used to send signals to a piece of outboard gear or headphones.

balanced: An equipment scheme that uses three wires to make a connection. Two of these are hot leads (they both carry the signal), and one is connected to the shield, or housing, of the connector. Balanced lines can be very long (up to about 1000 feet), and because of a clever phase arrangement, they induce the least noise into the system by canceling noise that is picked up along the signal path.

bandwidth: The width, in octaves or fractions of an octave, of the affected range of frequencies altered with an equalizer. If we say a specific frequency is boosted or cut, we are actually referring to a range of consecutive frequencies with the center point at the specified frequency. From a flat EQ (no cut or boost), the affect of the EQ change on the frequency spectrum is a continually increasing boost or cut to the center point of a bell curve then back to flat. That curve can be a very wide bell shape or a very narrow peak. The size of the curve is the bandwidth.

bass drum: Typically the largest drum in the drum set. It sits on the floor on its side and is played with a foot pedal. The bass drum provides the foundation for most drum set grooves or beats. Also called the **kick** or **kick drum**.

board: A complex series of combining circuits that let you send multiple signals to multiple destinations or combine multiple signals to individual destinations. It can also be connected to several tape recorders and can accept and distribute signals from mics, instruments, signal processors and tape recorders. Also called a **mixer**, **console** and **desk**.

boomy: An abundance of low frequencies. A boomy sound is resonant and often out of control at a particular low frequency, usually below about 200Hz.

boost: To increase the level.

bouncing tracks: Bouncing or rerecording two or more tracks of the multitrack to a single available track of the multitrack. This is accomplished through the track assignment bus. A separate mono or stereo mix of a group of recorded tracks is typically set up, then that mix is routed to one or two additional tracks on the multitrack and recorded. This operation is typically performed to open up tracks for more musical parts but is also commonly performed to aid in the mixing process. For example, a compilation track of background vocals might be bounced to one track or a stereo pair of tracks to allow attention to vocal blend that might not be possible without computer-assisted mixing. Also called **ping-ponging** and **combining tracks**.

bus: Any place where signals are combined. A bus is normally used to get signals to the multitrack, headphones, effects or mixdown recorder.

bus assign switches: Controls that let you send signals to the buses.

cabasa: See **afuché**.

channel insert: A patch point on each individual channel that lets you patch in any outboard signal processor. A channel insert lets the user access only one channel at a time.

claves: Two rosewood sticks (about 7-inches long and about 1.5 inches in diameter) that are struck together to produce a high and penetrating sound. Claves are typically used in Latin rhythms, though they are also common in commercial pop music.

click track: The tempo reference for a song. The sound that comes from the audio output of an electronic metronome or the click output of a drum machine. It can be recorded onto tape while the band is playing the initial parts. The drummer follows the tempo of the click. When a drum machine is used as a source for the click, any instrument can be used as a click sound by simply programming it to play all quarter notes, then adjusting the tempo to the song. Instruments with good transients work best for this purpose. Some drummers prefer using a complete drum pattern, programmed into the drum machine, as a click.

cold: Recorded with insufficient level to tape. Any weak signal.

combining tracks: See **bouncing tracks**.

compressor: This is an automatic level control that uses a VCA (voltage controlled amplifier) to turn a signal down. This VCA only turns the signal down when it exceeds a user-selected threshold. It then turns the signal back up again when the signal is no longer above the threshold. Compressors use a ratio setting between 1:1 and 10:1. See **ratio**.

console: See **board**.

control room: The separate room where the engineer and recording equipment are, as opposed to the studio where the band plays.

control room monitors: The speakers in the control room.

crash cymbal: One of the cymbals in the kit used for accents. The crash cymbal is often hit at the beginning of a new musical section to indicate a musical change. The crash is also used to accent rhythmic punches with the rest of the rhythm section. A drum set can contain as few as one crash or as many as the drummer wants or can afford. It's not uncommon to see a set with three or four crash cymbals. Most crash cymbals are between 14 and 18 inches in diameter.

cue mix: Headphone mix.

cue send: Usually an auxiliary bus that's connected to headphones. It can also be used for any other aux bus functions. Also called **headphone bus**.

cut: To decrease the level.

daisy chain: Patching from the output of one piece of equipment to the input of another piece of equipment, often through two or more units. This can be common with individual effects (especially guitar effects) patching from the output of the compressor to the input of the distortion, then from the output of the distortion to the input of the chorus, then from the output of the chorus to the input of the delay, etc. Daisy chaining is also common when using MIDI keyboards and sound modules, patching from MIDI Thru of keyboard 1 to MIDI In of keyboard 2, then from MIDI Thru of keyboard 2 to MIDI In of keyboard 3, then from MIDI Thru of keyboard 3 to MIDI In of keyboard 4, etc.

DAT: Digital audio tape recorder. A fully digital recorder that uses a rotating head and transport very similar to a VHS video cassette recorder. This offers full bandwidth with great specifications and typically three different digital sample rates: 32kHz, 44.1kHz and 48kHz.

dB: Pronounced (dee • bee). dB expresses a ratio between two powers and can be tagged to many different types of power that we encounter in recording. Most often we think of dB in reference to volume, which is vaguely accurate when we consider dB SPL (sound pressure level/energy at our ears) at a specified frequency range and volume range (perceived loudness).

definition: The clarity of the attack or the understandability of the sound.

delay: An outboard unit used to create time-dependent effects. These can include slapback, multiple hits, chorusing, flanging, etc.

desk: See **board**.

DI: Direct injection. A unit that matches impedance levels, enabling a high-impedance instrument, or mic, to be successfully plugged into a low-impedance input and vice versa. Also called a **direct box**.

diffusion: Controls the space between the reflections of reverb. Low diffusion can be equated with a grainy picture. On a low diffusion setting, individual repeats can be heard within the reverb. High diffusion can be equated with a fine-grain photograph. High diffusion reverberation produces a smooth wash of reverb where none of the individual delays can be heard.

direct box: See **DI**.

direct sound: A sound recorded without a microphone. On an electric guitar, the direct sound is the sound that comes from the pickups. On a synthesizer, the direct sound is the sound that comes from the instrument output. Acoustically, the direct sound is the nonreflected sound— the sound that travels straight from the instrument to the listener or microphone without first bouncing off surrounding surfaces.

distortion: The usually unwanted sound that occurs when a piece of equipment is driven with a level that's too strong. Any alteration of the source waveform is considered to be a distortion. Some forms of distortion are desirable, like distortion effects on a guitar.

doubled electronically: A slightly delayed (less than 50ms) signal combined with the original signal to achieve the effect of double tracking (duplicating a performance live). Also called **electronic double**.

dry: With no effect.

dynamic range: The distance, in dB, from the softest sound to the loudest sound. An orchestra that played its loudest note at 115dB and its softest note at 20dB would have a dynamic range of 95dB (115dB - 20dB = a dynamic range of 95dB). Dynamic range also refers to the operating parameters for a piece of audio equipment while maintaining a specified degree of signal integrity.

dynamic range processors: Equipment that changes the dynamic range of a signal. In other words, equipment that can change the distance from the loudest sound to the softest sound in a particular audio signal.

edge: A musical term used to define the biting quality of a sound.

edge track: The tracks on a multitrack tape recorder that are on the top and bottom of the record and playback heads. These tracks are printed on the outer edges of the oxide-coated surface of the tape. The edge tracks are the tracks with the highest and lowest numerical reference (i.e., on an 8-track recorder, tracks 1 and 8 are considered the edge tracks).

effects bus: An auxiliary bus that's normally used as a send bus to an effect. This bus can also perform any other normal bus functions.

effects send: The output of an effects bus.

electronic double: See **doubled electronically**.

EQ: Equalization; tone control; adjusting the balance of high frequencies, mid frequencies and low frequencies.

fader: A level control that slides smoothly from the bottom of its throw (full off) to the top of its throw (full on).

fader throw: The distance from the full off position of a fader to the full on position.

far-field reference monitor: A speaker designed to work with the acoustics of a room to produce an accurate representation of the sound of a mix.

feedback: This control feeds the delayed signal from a digital delay back into the input, therefore delaying the delay, the delay of the delay, etc. This creates regenerating echoes. Feedback is also called regeneration or repeat.

feel: The rhythmic emotion in a song. Certain rhythmic interpretations give certain emotional tendencies. An aggressive feel typically contains several parts that are slightly ahead of the beat. A laid-back feel contains many parts that are slightly behind the beat.

final mix: The end product from a recording session or group of sessions. The final mix contains the desired balance in level and panning of all instruments along with precise amounts of processing and effects. This mix is stored on a reel-to-reel tape, DAT, DCC, hard disk, stereo Hi-fi VHS or possibly on cassette.

flat: Using no equalization.

frequency: The number of times a sound wave completes its cycle in one second. The higher the frequency of a sound, the higher its pitch.

full range instrument: An instrument that contains almost all audible frequencies in a fairly even balance from lows to highs.

full range mix: A mix that contains a fairly even balance of all audible frequencies.

gain: The total level coming into a unit.

ground lifted: To isolate the third pin of the AC power cord from its intended grounding point in the wall receptacle.

guiro: This percussion instrument is usually one to two feet in length and three to four inches in diameter. It's cylindrical and hollow, and the front end comes to a blunt point while the back end gently tapers. There are fairly deep grooves around the cylinder, and the instrument is played by scraping a small wooden stick back and forth, lengthwise, across the grooves. A guiro can be made of wood or metal

hard pan: Stereo positioning in a mix that is either all the way left or all the way right.

head: This is the part of the snare drum, tom tom or bass drum that's hit. On modern drums, the head is made of durable plastic and is mounted on a hoop that fits over the end of the drum shell. Originally, drums used animal skin (typically calf skin) stretched over the drum shell. Many drummers, especially orchestral purists, prefer animal skin heads for drums. Skin heads respond to changes in humidity by loosening or tightening and are hard to keep in tune but have a unique

sound character. Plastic heads don't respond to changes in humidity and are therefore easier to keep in tune.

headphone bus: See **cue send**.

hertz: Refers to the frequency of a sound wave. Abbreviated Hz.

hi-hat: Two cymbals mounted on a stand with the top cymbal upside-down (bell down) and the bottom cymbal right-side-up (bell up). The bottom cymbal rests on a pad, and the top cymbal is mounted on a clamp attached to a rod that moves up and down when the hi-hat pedal is depressed and released.

high end: High frequencies, usually above 3kHz.

high impedance: A wiring system with greater resistance to the flow of current in the range of 10 to 20k ohms. Most guitars and synthesizers use a high-impedance wiring scheme. A line matching transformer (impedance transformer) is required to enable the use of high-impedance instruments with a low-impedance recording console. Abbreviated hi Z.

highpass filter: A filter that lets the high frequencies pass through uneffected but cuts the low frequencies, typically below about 80Hz.

hot: Recorded with ample level to tape. Any strong signal.

hot wire/hot lead: The wire that carries the signal.

impedance: Resistance to the flow of current, measured in ohms. Often indicated simply by the letter Z. Hi Z or lo Z indicates high impedance or low impedance.

kick: See **bass drum**.

kick drum: See **bass drum**.

kilohertz: One thousand hertz. 32 kilohertz = 32,000Hz. Abbreviated kHz.

kit: Another term for the drum set. The kit usually contains a bass drum, snare drum, toms and cymbals. The kit can also contain any other percussion instruments that the drummer wants to include, depending on player preference and stylistic demands.

leakage: Sound that's picked up by a microphone other than the sound it's meant to pick up. A mic on the snare is meant to pick up the sound of the snare being hit, but it also picks up the sound of the rest of the kit being played. Any sound other than the snare drum is leakage into the snare mic.

LED: Light-emitting diode. A small red light generally used as a peak level indicator, on/off indicator or solo indicator. Some multipurpose LEDs change in color from green to yellow to red in response to variations in signal strength.

limiter: This is an automatic level control that uses a voltage controlled amplifier (VCA) to turn a signal down. This VCA only turns the signal down when it exceeds a user-selected threshold. It then turns the signal back up again once the signal is no longer above the threshold. Limiters use a ratio setting between 10:1 and ∞:1. See **ratio**.

line level: The operating level of the mixer's signal path after the mic preamp has boosted the mic level signal. Tape recorder ins and outs, outboard equipment and instrument outputs are all examples of line level signals.

live double: Simultaneous performance of the same musical part, either by two performers as a duet or by one musician, to separate tracks on a multitrack recorder. A live double is different from an electronic double in that, with a live double, the musical part is actually performed two separate times rather than duplicated electronically.

low end: Low frequencies, usually below about 250Hz.

low impedance: A wiring system with less resistance to the flow of current, in the range of 150 to 1000 ohms. Recording mixers are almost always low impedance. Low-impedance equipment is not compatible with high-impedance equipment without the use of a line matching transformer (impedance transformer). Abbreviated lo Z.

lowpass filter: A filter that lets the low frequencies pass through uneffected while cutting the highs typically above about 8kHz.

lug: The long screw that goes through the holes of the rim on a drum. The lugs screw into hardware that's mounted on the shell of the drum. Lugs are used to increase or decrease the tension on the drum head. Drum tuning is accomplished by tightening or loosening the lugs.

mic level: The signal strength that comes from a microphone. This must be amplified to line level for mixing board circuitry.

microphone: A device that changes variations in air pressure (sound waves) into variations in voltage.

microphone preamp: An amplifying circuit that boosts mic level to line level.

microsecond: A millionth of a second.

miking the amp: Pointing a microphone at the speaker in the cabinet that contains the amplifier and speaker. The amplifier makes no sound; it only boosts the signal to a level that can drive the speaker. The speaker moves air. That movement of air is what we perceive as sound.

millisecond: A thousandth of a second. Abbreviated ms.

mixer: See **board**.

modulation: A variation in pitch caused by constantly changing the delay time. The low-frequency oscillator (LFO) is the circuit that continually slows down and speeds up the delay. As the delay speeds up and slows down, the pitch of the signal rises and lowers, either very slightly or drastically, depending on the depth of the modulation.

mono: The one speaker/one channel listening system. With two speakers, the identical signal is fed to both speakers.

MTC: MIDI Time Code. This is the MIDI equivalent to SMPTE time code, where all tempos are referenced to a continuous binary code. This code is generated at a constant rate, and each unique point in the flow of MIDI Time Code indicates a point in time referenced in hours, minutes, seconds and frames per second (00:00:00:00). See **time code**.

muddy: Usually a musical sound that's overabundant in lower mid frequencies between about 200Hz and 1kHz. These frequencies, when boosted, can detract from high-frequency clarity and low-frequency punch.

multi-effects processor: An effects processor containing several effects that can be combined, stacked and used independently. These units often contain reverbs, delays, dynamic range processors, equalization, chorus effects and sometimes sampling.

multitrack: A tape recorder with more than two tracks. Different material can be stored on each track, and one or more tracks can be listened to on playback while one or more tracks are being simultaneously recorded on.

near-field reference monitor: A speaker designed to be listened to with the listener's head at one point of a three-foot equilateral triangle and the speakers at the other two points.

normal: In a patch bay, this term refers to wiring schemes in which, without external patching, the signal normally goes to a specific location. Two points on the patch bay are normally connected together inside the patch bay. For example, an aux send can be normally wired to the input of a reverb inside the patch bay. This normal can be broken if a connector is plugged into this point of the patch bay, but in the meantime, the aux send is connected to the reverb without the addition of an external patch cable.

notch filter: A filter tuned to remove or reduce in level a very narrow frequency band.

oscillator: Unit that produces specific sine waves at various frequencies used for setting levels and calibrating electronic equipment. The most common frequencies (also called tones) produced are 100Hz, 1000Hz and 10kHz.

outboard: A piece of equipment that isn't within the mixer, such as delays, compressors, reverbs, etc.

output: Where the signal comes out of a piece of equipment.

overdrive: To produce a signal that has too much signal strength for the receiving input. This causes a buzzing distortion that's unacceptable in a vast majority of recording scenarios. Guitarists often overdrive their amplification circuitry to increase sustain and to enhance the aggressive edge of commercial pop and rock music.

overheads: Mics placed over the drum set and aimed down at the set. Condenser mics typically work best for this application.

overtones: On drums, overtones are any tones or pitches heard other than the primary tone or pitch. Overtones are always part of the sound of any instrument, but often the tuning of a drum can be so far off that the overtones are more audible than the fundamental pitch and tone. Problems with unwanted overtones can be reduced by proper tuning and dampening. In general, overtones are a fact of physics. Along with the fundamental frequency (the frequency that determines the note name), each instrument's individual sound contains a unique blend of simultaneously occurring overtones. Overtones are mathematically calculated as whole number multiples of the fundamental frequency. If the fundamental frequency is 200Hz, the overtone series is 1x200, 2x200, 3x200, 4x200, 5x200, etc. (200Hz, 400Hz, 600Hz, 800Hz, 1000Hz, etc.). The balance and blend of the overtones in relation to the fundamental frequency determines the sonic character and unique personality of each instrument, voice or noise maker.

pad: See **attenuator**.

pan: To move a signal left or right in the stereo panorama.

parametric EQ: An equalizer (tone control) that can sweep a range of frequencies to boost or cut and also vary the bandwidth of the selected frequency range.

pass: One attempt to record a track. Each time the tape is rolling in an effort to record or monitor is called a pass.

passive: Components that do not amplify a signal. Passive devices typically cause a decrease in total signal level output due to their non-amplifying nature. A passive direct box simply matches impedances without the use of active amplification circuitry to compensate for a loss of signal. A passive filter offers a cut at a specific range of frequencies but has no amplification circuitry to enable a boost of frequencies.

patch cord: A cable used to connect pieces of equipment together, usually at the patch bay.

patch bay: A junction panel with jacks on the front and corresponding jacks on the back. All available equipment outputs and inputs are plugged into the back of the panel, and the corresponding points in front are labeled. This lets us patch any output to any input on the front of the patch bay using short patch cords.

peak LED: Light-emitting diode that responds quickly and accurately meters fast attacks of percussive instruments (transients) and other momentary overloads of electronic circuits.

peak meter: A series of lights or LEDs that accurately reads peak signal strength (transients).

PFL: Pre fader listen. This soloing feature lets us hear individual signals or groups of signals immediately before they get to the channel fader.

phantom power: DC voltage that's supplied to the mic, active direct box or other device requiring power to operate from the console through the mic cable. This eliminates the need for battery power in these units. Phantom power can also be provided by an external phantom power supply if the mixer isn't equipped internally to provide this power source. Phantom power is preferred over battery power because it provides a constant voltage at a constant amperage over long periods of time. Batteries are in a constant state of drainage so they only support optimum performance for a brief time period before they begin to lose power.

phase: The relation between two sources in time. Two identical electronic signals are in phase if the corresponding crest of each waveform reaches the same physical position at the same point in time. When two identical waveforms are in phase, the result is a doubling of amplitude (energy). If two identical waveforms are completely out of phase, the result is complete cancelation. Phase is indicated in degrees. One complete cycle is indicated by 360 degrees and includes the crest and trough of the waveform.

phasing: This term is commonly associated with the overheads on a drum set. If the overheads are too close to the crash cymbals when the cymbals are struck, the movement of the cymbals changes the phase interaction between the mic and the surface of the cymbal. As the distance changes from the mic to the cymbal, different frequencies sum and cancel between the mic and the cymbal. This is often referred to as phasing. The term phasing is also applied to any audio situation where there is a continually varying phase relationship, whether the cause originates electronically or acoustically.

ping-ponging: See **bouncing tracks.**

power surges: Fast increases in the 120V current from the electrical outlets that your equipment is plugged into. These can be very damaging, especially to computer- and microprocessor-controlled gear.

predelay: A time delay that happens after the original sound source and before the reverberation is heard.

preamp: An amplifying circuit that either boosts mic level to line level or maintains line level strength at various points in the signal path.

prime number: Any number that can only be divided evenly by one and itself. 1, 3, 5, 7, 11, 13, 17, 19 and 23 are examples of prime numbers.

print: To record something to tape.

quantize: See **auto correct.**

ratio: On a compressor/limiter, this is the control that determines how far the VCA will turn the signal down once it exceeds the threshold. This is expressed in the form of a ratio. This ratio is a comparison between how far the signal exceeds the threshold at the input and how far the signal exceeds the threshold at the output. With a ratio of 2:1, if the signal exceeds the threshold at the input by 10dB, the signal would only exceed the threshold by 5dB at the output.

recording purist: Typically, one who shuns signal processing and effects as being unnatural and degrading. One who prefers very natural and pure sounds recorded using the most fundamentally solid techniques and principles.

release time: Acoustically, the amount of time it takes for a sound and its reflections to become completely inaudible once production of the sound has ceased. In regard to dynamic processors, release time refers to the amount of time it takes for the voltage controlled amplifier to return the signal to its unity state (back to where it would have been if the VCA weren't in the signal path) once the audio input has ceased or dropped below the user-set threshold.

return: The point of the mixer where the output of an effect is patched into the mix bus.

reverberation time: Reverberation time, decay time, reverb time and decay time all refer to the same thing. The traditional definition of reverberation time is the time it takes for the sound to decrease to one-millionth of its original sound pressure level.

ride cymbal: Usually the largest cymbal in the drum set, used for keeping time rather than accenting punches or indicating section changes. Most ride cymbals are between 18 and 22 inches in diameter.

rim: The part of the drum that fits over the hoop of the head. This ring has holes around it that lugs go through. Lugs attach to hardware on the shell, and tightening the lugs pulls the rim down against the hoop on the head.

RMS: An abbreviation for root-mean-square. A power measurement that provides an indication of an amplifier's continuous power output capabilities at a specified distortion level, bandwidth and impedance load. RMS is a key specification when comparing power amplifiers because it indicates usable power at specific parameters. Always compare RMS to RMS when reviewing power amplifiers for an accurate comparison. Peak power (usually a very impressive number) is often touted by manufacturers but is of little value as a comparison since distortion and bandwidth at peak power ratings are typically far out of the acceptable and usable range.

roll off: To roll off a frequency means to turn the frequency down. A bass roll-off switch on a microphone turns the low frequencies down before the signal leaves the microphone. Most bass roll-offs affect frequencies below 150Hz. While normal EQ change will boost or cut a curve that has a center point at the EQ frequency, the term roll-off indicates that all frequencies above or below a specified frequency are turned down at a rate specified in dB per octave.

schematic diagram: A block diagram of all of the electronic circuits in a particular piece of gear.

semiparametric EQ: An equalizer (tone control) that can sweep a range of frequencies to boost or cut but has no control over the bandwidth.

send: The output of a bus that's typically used to send a separate mix of instruments and tracks to an effects input or other audio device.

sequence: A piece of music stored in a microprocessor-based MIDI recorder. The binary representation of notes and the interpretation of notes as they're performed on a MIDI keyboard or any other MIDI controller. To sequence is to input MIDI data into a MIDI recorder. MIDI data is not the actual musical waveform. It is binary numerical data that is emitted from the MIDI Out jack of a MIDI keyboard or other controller in response to notes played, key velocity, aftertouch, duration and controller use.

sequencer: A MIDI recorder. A sequencer accepts MIDI data from any MIDI controller and stores that data for future playback. A sequencer doesn't record the actual musical waveform but records binary numerical data that corresponds to each note or other transmittable action on a MIDI keyboard or controller. If middle C is pressed on a MIDI keyboard, a binary number is transmitted from the MIDI Output jack. This binary number is recorded by a sequencer, then later the same number is transmitted by the sequencer back into the MIDI keyboard through the MIDI Input jack. When the MIDI keyboard sees the number for middle C, it produces whatever sound is selected to play middle C.

set: The assortment of drums used by the drummer in a rock, pop, country or jazz band. Usually contains a bass drum, snare drum, toms and cymbals. The set can also contain other percussion instruments, depending on player preference and stylistic demands.

shell: The cylindrical structure of a drum. Usually constructed from laminated wood but also occasionally constructed from metal and plastic. The precision of construction and quality of material are critical to the sound of a drum.

shelving EQ: The type of equalization that cuts or boosts all frequencies above or below a specific frequency at a rate referenced in dB per octave.

shield: The braided wire around the hot lead or leads of a cable. Its purpose is to diffuse extraneous radio interference and electrostatic noise.

signal path: The distinct route that a signal follows from its point of origin to its destination.

signal-to-noise ratio: Technically, this is calculated by using a VTVM (vacuum tube volt meter) and a specific routine for comparison between signal and noise. For the sake of simplicity, think of the signal-to-noise ratio as being the distance, in dB, from a specific signal to the constant level of noise, like that created by tape hiss, amplifier noise, noise from outboard gear or inherent noise in the mixer. This constant noise is called the noise floor. If tape noise on a specific recorder registers a constant 35dB and the peak of our signal registers at 100dB, then we can consider the signal-to-noise ratio to be the difference between these two numbers. 100:35 = a signal-to-noise ratio of 65dB.

sine wave: The simplest waveform. The sine wave has the same shape as the mathematical sine function curve with a smooth and symmetrical crest and trough. The sound of a sine wave is most similar to the sound produced by a flute. Sine waves are used to calibrate electronic equipment, whereas white and pink noise are used to gather acoustical measurements.

skins: Slang term used to indicate the drum set and derived from the fact that early drums used animal skin (usually calf skin) for drum heads.

slapback: A single repeat of a signal with a delay time above 35ms.

slate: A verbal reference recorded (usually by the engineer) onto the master tape. This typically indicates song title, date, artist, etc. Often this verbal reference is mixed with a low-frequency sine wave (around 40Hz), which in fast forward and rewind, produces a higher tone used to locate the particular song or take.

SMPTE: The Society of Motion Picture and Television Engineers. This organization is responsible for many advancements in the film, audio and video industry, including the development of SMPTE time code. See **time code.**

snare drum: A drum with 20 to 30 wires across the bottom head that produce a buzz when the drum is struck. The snare drum is usually 5 to 8 inches deep and 13 to 15 inches in diameter. The snares are usually twisted metal strands. Some snares are made from organic material and are referred to as gut snares, which is short for cat gut. The snare drum's rhythmic function is typically constant and always very important to the rhythmic and emotional feel of the music. Most commercial musical styles contain a repetition of the snare drum hitting on beats two and four. Jazz uses the snare in the most random manner stylistically, although even in jazz, the snare adds dramatically to the rhythmic punch and dynamic excitement of the music.

solid-state amp: Uses transistors to boost a signal. Most studio power amplifiers used to power studio monitors are solid-state. When used within their normal operating range, solid-state amplifiers are typically more accurate, quieter and less distorted than an equivalent tube amplifier. When pushed past their normal operating range, solid-state amps become harsh and edgy. Solid-state amplification can be used to amplify a signal at any stage in the signal path, from the mic to the preamps to the final outputs of the console to the control room power amp. Some of the most highly regarded mics, preamplifiers and power amps use solid-state technology.

solo button: Lets you hear a track or instrument by itself. While a mix is up on the mixer, pushing the solo button on a channel eliminates all channels except the one soloed.

speaker wire: Wire designed for use between the power amp and the speakers. This has two identical wires. One goes to the red terminal, and the other goes to the black terminal. Always be sure the wire that's attached to the red terminal on the power amplifier is the same wire that's attached to the red terminal on the speaker and the wire that's attached to the black terminal on the power amplifier is attached to the black terminal on the speaker.

splash cymbal: A small cymbal used to accent punches and for special effects. Similar to a crash but smaller. Most splash cymbals are between 8 and 12 inches in diameter.

stereo: The two-speaker playback system in which tracks and/or channels can be positioned anywhere in the stereo panorama, from full left to full right.

sterile sound: A sound that's almost too clean, lacking warmth and smoothness. A very dry and close sound without the blending benefit of reverberation or natural ambience, often edgy in· the upper midrange (between 1.5 and 3kHz).

striping: Recording time code on one audio track of a multitrack recorder, video recorder or stereo recorder with a center track designed to record time code. Time code is usually recorded throughout the entire length of a tape before a time code related session begins. On a multitrack recorder, time code is almost always recorded (striped) on the track with the highest number (track 8 on an 8-track, track 24 on a 24-track, etc.).

studio: The separate room used for recording the vocalists or instrumentalists. The band plays in the studio, while the engineer and his or her equipment are in the control room.

studio monitors: Manufacturers refer to their speakers designed for studio use as studio monitors. In a large recording facility with a separate control room, isolation rooms and a large sound stage or studio, the speakers in the primary recording room (usually separate from the control room) are called the studio monitors.

sync pulse: This tempo-controlling system uses a specified number of electronic pulses per quarter note to drive the tempo of a sequencer. Most sync pulse is generated at 24 pulses per quarter note. Each pulse is identical. The only factor that establishes synchronization is how fast the pulses are being sent or received. This sync pulse can be recorded onto one audio track from the sync out jack of a sequencer. Later the output of the tape track can be plugged into the sync in jack of the sequencer. If the sequencer is set to listen to an external clock, every time 24 pulses go by, the sequencer begins the next quarter note. The faster the pulse the faster the tempo, or the slower the pulse the slower the tempo. Since each pulse is identical, there is no way for the sequencer to determine where it should be during a song in relation to the sync pulse. To be in sync with a previously recorded track, the tape must be rewound to the beginning of the song every time.

talkback: A one-way communications system that lets the engineer communicate with musicians or technical staff through the headphones or studio monitors.

tape hiss: Noise heard on playback of analog tape, especially when the musical signal isn't recorded hot enough on the tape.

test tones: Specific sine waves at various frequencies used for setting levels and calibrating electronic equipment. The most common tones produced are 100Hz, 1000Hz and 10kHz.

threshold: The control on a dynamic range processor (compressor, limiter, gate or expander) that determines when the voltage controlled amplifier starts to turn down or back up.

timbre: The tonal characteristic and textural color of a sound.

time code: The most common form of time code is SMPTE time code, which is used to synchronize audio, video and film. MTC is MIDI Time Code, which is the MIDI data equivalent to SMPTE time code. Time code is a binary, numerical code that is generated at a constant rate and can be recorded to tape. This code represents a continuously active 24-hour clock. Every point in time code is numerically unique and refers to its own specific time. Time code is indicated in hours, minutes, seconds, frames per second and sometimes sub-frames or time code bits. If a sequencer is set to begin playback at 1 hour, 20 minutes, 30 seconds and 15 frames (indicated by 01:20:30:15), the sequence will start as soon as the time code reader sees that time reference from the tape. Also, the sequencer can mathematically calculate the time reference of each beat of the song. No matter where you start the tape during a song, the sequencer will see the time code reference, calculate the measure and beat number of that time reference and begin playback in sync.

tip-ring-sleeve: The type of plug on stereo headphones. The tip is left, the ring is right and the sleeve is connected to the shield. This type of connector can be used for any application that requires three points. Balanced connections can be made with a tip-ring-sleeve connector.

tom: A drum that has no snares and is played with sticks. Toms usually have top and bottom heads, although the bottom heads can be removed for a certain type of sound. Most toms are between 10 and 18 inches in diameter and from 10 to 18 inches deep. Toms are usually mounted on stands or on a rack attached to the bass drum.

tracks: Horizontally distinguished zones on tape where audio signals are recorded. An 8-track multitrack has 8 divisions of the tape that run the length of the tape. Each of these divisions is called a track. Track also refers to a part of a MIDI sequence. Since MIDI recorders are modeled after the operational controls of analog tape recorders, MIDI sequencing terminology is identical in many ways to historic analog recording terminology. For the same reason, hard disk recorders also call the individual parts of a multitrack recording tracks.

transient: A fast attack, like that from a percussion instrument struck with a hard stick or mallet (cymbals, claves, tambourine, xylophone, etc.). Transients are an important concern in audio recording.

trim: Typically controls the amount of preamplification applied to the microphone signal at the input stage of the mixer. Trim is commonly used when referring to gain reduction.

tube amplifier: Uses a vacuum tube-based amplification process to boost a signal. Tube amplification is older technology than solid-state amplification and is typically noisier and less accurate. The advantage of a tube amplifier is apparent as the amp begins to distort. While solid-state distortion is harsh and objectionable, tube amp distortion is smooth and easy to listen to. Tube amplification can be used to amplify a signal at any stage in the signal path from the mic to the control room power amp. Some of the most highly regarded mics, preamplifiers and power amps use tube technology.

tubs: Slang for a drum set.

unbalanced line: A wiring scheme with one hot lead carrying the signal and a braided shield around the hot lead to diffuse extraneous signals. Unbalanced lines are subject to electrostatic noise and interference; therefore, cable length is practically restricted. Unbalanced lines are normally less than 25 feet in length.

unity gain: A status where a piece of equipment outputs the same signal strength that it receives at its input.

VCA: A voltage controlled amplifier. This amplifier turns a signal up or down depending on how much voltage it receives. Changing energy in a sound wave is what varies the voltage to these circuits.

volt: A unit used to describe the amount of electrical current pressure in a circuit.

VU meter: A signal source meter designed to read the average signal strength. A VU meter has a physical needle that moves across an arc to the right in response to signal increases and to the left in response to signal decreases. Because of the mass of the needle, VU meters are among the slowest types of commonly used metering systems.

wet: Totally effected. In the case of reverb, 100 percent wet is all reverberated sound with no dry sound.

XLR: A three-point connector like those used on most microphones. Balanced connections are typically made with XLR connectors or some other three-point connector.

Y cord: An adapting cable with three connectors joined in parallel. Can be used for splitting one output for send to two different inputs. Doesn't work optimally when attempting to send two different outputs to one input.

INDEX

Symbols

1/4" phone connectors, 9
+4dBm, 20
-10dBV, 20
4-track, 48, 122
4-track domain, 204
8-track, 122
10-band graphic, 51
10-band graphic EQ, 45
12-string, 137
16-track recording, 202
31-band graphic, 51
60-cycle hum, 13, 52

A

ac power cable, 13
acoustic guitar(s), 101, 134, 139, 142, 143
     dynamic processing and the, 139
     equalizing the, 142
     sounds, 138
acoustic piano, 101
acoustic room ambience, 101
acoustic room sound, 152
acoustical adjustments, 58
acoustical chambers, 95
acoustical environment, 93, 100, 153, 178
acoustical interaction of room ambience, 144
active direct boxes, 18
adjacent tracks, 39
adverse phase interactions, 178
AM radio, 25, 55
ambience, 130, 218
amplified electric, 127
amplifier
     characteristic sound of, 113
     headphone, 34
     miked, 37, 127
     solid-state, 128
     voltage controlled, 69
amps, guitar, 113
analog tape, 176
analytical listening, 7
attack time, 71, 74, 140, 215
attenuator, 2, 20, 22, 26, 58
     adjustment, 22
     line, 20
audible spectrum, 111
audio machine synchronizing, 195
auto correct, 199
automatic level control, 71, 213
aux(iliary) buses, 32, 33, 34, 67
auxiliary percussion, 199, 227
aux(iliary) sends, 58, 66
average level, 117, 178

B

baffle(s), 156, 184
balance, left/right, 57
balanced percussion, 229
bandwidth, 48
bass, 39, 46

bass drum, 104, 146, 166
bass drum, recording levels for the, 169
bass guitar, 46
bass roll-off switch, 136
bidirectional, 110
bleed onto the adjacent tracks, 226
blend the room sound with the dry sound, 230
bongos, 146, 182
bottom head, 175
bounce, 159
bouncing, 139
bouncing multiple instruments to one tape track, 39
braided shield, 9
brass, real, 101
breathing, 80
bridge, 137
brilliance, 47, 49
bus(es), 29
     aux(iliary), 32
     combining, 34
     effects, 29, 32
     fader, 20
     headphone, 34
     summing, 34
     track assignment, 34, 39
buzzy distortion, 121

C

cabasa, 182
cancel, 89
cardioid pickup pattern(s), 109, 132, 184
chamber reverb, 95, 125, 143
chambers, 93, 95
channel(s), 29, 58
     ins and outs, 58
     insert, 27, 66
chorus, 25, 65, 90, 91, 124, 144
     effects, 85
     mono, 92
claves, 149, 182
click sounds, 185
click track, 184
close proximity, 109
close-miking, 128, 136, 149, 167, 172, 175
     technique, 104, 159
     the amp, 130
close-sounding tracks, 130
combining bus, 34
combining close and distant mics, 130
combining direct and miked signals, 37
combining matrix, 34
commercial sound, 144
communications, 56
compact discs, 176
compressing on mixdown, 80
compressing the snare sound, 213
compression, 120, 122, 140
compressor, 65, 71, 76, 139, 213, 216
compressor/limiter, 69
condenser, 100, 128, 149, 182,

condenser mic(s), 101, 136, 138, 155, 173, 176
congas, 146, 182
connecting to the mixer, 14
connectors, 8
     1/4" phone, 9
     phone, 9
     RCA phono, 9
     XLR, 10
control room monitor selector, 54
cowbell, 146, 182
crash cymbals, 225
crosstalk, 207
cue sends, 32
cymbal microphones, 160
cymbals, 146, 149, 178, 182
     from a drum machine, 224
     live, 224
     real, 225

D

dampening material, 165
dB, 20
decay time(s), 98, 125
delay, 32, 93, 121
     amount, 122
     effects, 85
     length, 122
     modulated, 90
     repeating, 87
     slapback, 85
     times, 25, 92, 99
     vocal, 89
density, 99
     high, 99
     low, 99
depth and speed, 90
DI, 18
diffusion, 98
     high, 98
     low, 98
direct, advantages of running, 113
direct box(es), 18, 19, 22, 36, 116, 189
direct injection, 18
distortion, 4, 22, 39, 120, 122, 144, 199
double, 87
double coil pickups, 118
double, live, 122
double tracking, 143
doubling, 38, 65, 89
downward expander, 82
drop frame time code, 195
drum
     conditioning, 161
     fills, 199
     heads, 161
     microphones, 201
     mono, 189
     muffling the, 162
     preparation and tuning, 161
     setup, 201
     sound(s), 148, 161, 215

sticks, 165
tuning of the, 167
drum machine, 37, 185, 224
mix levels in the, 197
recording levels, 197
toms, 221
toms, tuning, 222
dry, 33
duct tape, 162
duplication, 60
dynamic processing and the acoustic guitar, 139
dynamic processors, 67, 82, 223
dynamic range, 69, 83, 139
dynamic range processors, 65, 69, 84

E

EBU, 195
echo(s), 65, 85
edge, 212
effects
bus, 29, 32
on the individual drums, 153
on the kick, 169
processors, 65, 85
return(s), 29, 67
reverberation, 92
sends, 32, 58, 173
stereo, 92
electric acoustic guitar, 134
electric acoustic guitar direct into a mixer, 134
electric guitar, 46, 134
amp, 138
recording an, 112
sounds, 119
speaker cabinets, 104
electrical power, 11
electronic calibration, 58
electronic doubling, 122
electronic metronome, 185
electronically out of phase, 23
electrostatic interference, 9
engineer, maintenance, 27
EQ, 20, 41, 58, 149
circuit, 27
fully parametric, 85
graphic, 51
parametric, 70, 88
section, 42
semiparametric, 49, 84
equalization, 43
equalization, purist's approach to, 127
equalized for mono, 126
equalizer(s), 42, 65, 84
equalizers, fixed-frequency, 50
equalizing
the acoustic guitar, 142
the guitar, 126
the kick, 206
the kick drum, 167
the toms, 176, 222
European standard time code, 195
exaggerate the attack, 213
exaggerated transients, 117
expander, 82, 120

F

faders, 32
far-field monitors, 8
feedback, 87, 91
filters, 53
fixed-frequency equalizers, 50
flange with delay, 143
flanger, 90, 124
flanging, 65
flat, 43, 47
frames, 195
frequency, 43
oscillator, 60
ranges, definition of, 47
response curve, 111
response of the human ear, 48

G

gain, 21
reduction, 76, 140
structure, 29, 38
gate, 82, 120, 181
gate the kick, 208
gated reverb, 65, 98, 159, 209
gated reverb sound, 174
gate/expander, 80
gating the snare, 213
generate time code, 194
glockenspiel, 182
gobos, 184
grind, 46
ground hum, 13, 51
ground lift switch, 19
ground pin, 13
grounding, 13
grounding problems, 13
guiro, 149, 182
guitar(s), 37, 87
acoustic, 101, 134, 139, 142, 143
equalizing the, 142
miking the, 135
purist's approach to the, 143
steel string, 136
amplified electric, 127
amps, 113
and bass blending together, 46
basic types of electric, 118
cable, 7
classical, 136
clean, 127
distorted, 116
electric, 46, 134
electric acoustic, 134
electric acoustic direct into a mixer, 134
equalizing the, 126
hollow-body electric jazz, 119
nylon string classical, 136
rhythm, 46
sound, direct, 37
strings, 139
guitarist, 112

H

hall(s), 93, 143
hall reverb, 65, 95, 124, 173

headphone(s), 10, 34, 56, 143, 185, 224
amplifier, 34
bus, 34
mix, 184
output level, 34
heart-shaped pickup pattern, 109
hertz, 43
hi-hat, 179
mic, 160
panning the, 180
high density, 99
high diffusion, 98
high input levels, 27
high-frequency clarity, 105
high impedance, 17
high-impedance instruments, 116
highpass filter, 52
highs, 42, 47
hollow-body electric jazz guitar, 119
hot lead, 9
hot levels, 221
hot wire, 9
human feel, 200
humbucking pickups, 118

I

impedance, 17
proper, 34
transformer, 18
in phase, 23
initial reflection(s), 87, 132
in-line consoles, 2
in-line module, 2
input(s)
faders, 29, 39
gain, 58
instrument, 20
level comparison, 26
meter, 33
preamp, 21, 102
stage, 17
instrument selection, 117, 139
interaction between microphones, 181
interference, 9
inverse reverb, 95
inverting phase, 92
isolating the drum tracks, 181

J

jazz guitar, 119

K

keyboards, 144
kick (drums), 146, 159, 166, 205, 206
equalizing the, 167
panning the, 210
recording levels for the, 169
with the front head off, 206

L

large recording room, 219
layering, 38
lead vocal track, 226
leakage, 173, 181
LED(s), 22, 76

left/right balance, 78
level(s),
    proper input, 27
    proper adjustment, 39
LFO, 89, 90
light-emitting diode, 22
light-gauge strings, 139
limiter, 77, 120
line, 39
    attenuator, 20
    in, 19
    level, 20, 102
    level strength, 20
    out, 19
line-matching transformer, 18
live cymbals, 224
live double, 122
live double track, 143
low density, 99
low diffusion, 98
low impedance, 17, 116, 189
low input levels, 27
lower midrange, 47
low-frequency roll-off, 101
lowpass filter, 52
lows, 42, 47, 207

M

maintenance engineer, 27
managing the signal path, 29
maracas, 182
marimba, 182
medium- and heavy-gauge strings, 139
meters, 23, 26
meters, VU, 23, 29, 58, 76, 182, 212
mic(rophone)(s), 39
    at the center of the speaker, 129
    at the outer edge of the speaker, 130
    choice for snare drum, 172
    combining close and distant, 130
    condenser, 101, 136, 138, 155, 173,
       176
    cymbal, 160
    drum, 201
    gain trim, 21
    hi-hat, 160
    interaction between, 181
    level, 20, 102
    manufacturers, 182
    moving-coil, 104, 128, 136, 149, 166
    overhead, 178
    placement, 138, 142, 166
    preamp, 20, 21
    recording a drum set with one, 149
    ribbon, 106, 136
    room, 132, 134
    talkback, 56
    techniques, 128, 134, 136, 144
    types, 101
mic/line inputs, 32
mic/line switch, 58
MIDI, 100, 189, 199
    sound module, 100
    Time Code, 195
mids, 47, 206
miked amplifier, 37, 127
miking
    the acoustic guitar, 135

the speaker cabinet, 147
    theories of drum, 169
milliwatts, 20
minus, 10, 20
mix, 46, 142, 179, 216
    final, 169
    headphone, 184
    level, 56
    levels in the drum machine, 197
    mono, 55
mixdown, 29, 43, 80, 83, 122, 169
    master output, 60
    recorder, 32, 54, 56
mixer(s), 20, 25, 29, 32, 34, 39, 54, 69, 112,
    120, 189
mixer, EQ circuitry, 41
mixing board, 2
modulated delay, 90
modulation, 87, 89
monaural sound, 154
monitor(s)
    section, 53
    sends, 32
    far-field, 8
    near-field reference, 7
monitoring, 7
mono, 25, 124, 125, 136, 178, 189
    chorus, 92
    drums, 189
moving-coil, 100, 107, 128
muffling the drum, 162
multi-effects, 29, 124
multi-effects process, 29
multi-effects processor, 32, 99
multiple effects, 124
multiple guitar parts, 125
multiple reverb, 217
multitrack, 29, 34, 132, 159
multitrack, digital, 39
mute(s), 29, 41, 58

N

narrow band, 51
narrow bandwidth, 85
near-field reference monitor, 7
new strings, 139
noise, getting rid of, 82
notch filter, 51, 85
nylon string classical guitar, 136

O

old strings, 139
omni configuration, 101
omnidirectional, 110, 210
operating principle of the condenser mic,
    101
operating principle of the moving-coil mic,
    105
operating principle of the ribbon mic, 108
optimum signal transfer, 36
oscillator, 56
out of phase, 23
outboard processor, 41
output buses, 34
overdrive, 120, 182
overdriven input, 22
overhead microphone(s), 178

overheads on a close-miked kit, 178
oversaturating, 213
oversaturation, 176, 226
overtones, 170

P

pad, 22
pan, 29, 37, 58, 122, 124, 134, 159, 179
    control, 37, 179
    pot, 37
panning, 57, 125
    the hi-hat, 180
    the kick, 210
    the snare, 221
    the toms, 223
panoramic potentiometer, 37
parametric EQ, 50, 66
passive direct boxes, 18
patch bay, 58, 69
patching in the drum machine, 189
peak LEDs, 23
peak meters, 23
perception of room size, 121
percussion, 101
    family, 146
    miscellaneous, 182, 226
    recording, 182
percussive sounds, 99
percussive transient, 207
personal 4-track multitrack, 48
personal 4-track recorder, 34
PFL, 41
phantom power, 19, 102
phantom power switch, 19
phase, 23, 26, 90
    inverting, 92
    problems, 26
    relationship, 89
    reversal, 25, 91
    shifter, 90
    shifting, 65, 124
    stereo, 92
phasing, 25
phone connectors, 9
pick(s), 139, 142
    de-emphasize the sound of the, 140
    sound, 139
    thick, 139
pickup(s)
    double coil, 118
    heart-shaped, 109
    humbucking, 118
    pattern, 109
    single coil, 118
    types, 118
ping-ponging, 39
plate reverb, 65, 95, 210
plates, 93, 95
plus four, 20
polar patterns, 109
post-EQ, 49
post-EQ/insert, 41
power amp, 4, 7
power surges, 12
powered outputs, 58
powering down, 13
powering up, 13
practical application for the combining bus, 35

practical applications for splitting a signal, 36
pre and post, 32
preamp, 2, 20, 26, 29, 58
    level controls, 20
    stage, 22
predelay, 98, 125
pre-EQ, 41
pre-EQ/insert, 41
pre-fader-listen, 41
presence, 47
print reverb, 173
processor(s)
    dynamic, 67, 82, 223
    dynamic range, 65, 69, 83, 139
    effects, 65, 85
    multi-effects, 29, 32, 99
    outboard, 41
    signal, 20, 58, 62
professional recordings, 26
programming drum parts, 199
programming, real-time, 199
protect speakers, 13
pumping, 80
punch-in, 22
purist, 43
purist's approach to equalization, 148
purist's approach to the acoustic guitar, 164

Q

Q, 48
quantize, 199
quantize strength, 200

R

range control, 82
ratio, 73, 76, 140, 213
ratio control, 82
raw kick sound, 167
RCA phono connectors, 9
read time code, 194
real brass, 101
real cymbals, 225
real strings, 101
real-time programming, 199
real-time recording, 200
record levels, 60
recorder, digital, 176, 222
recorder line ins and outs, 58
recording
    a drum set with one microphone, 149
    an electric guitar, 112
    hot to tape, 116
    level, 29
    level(s)
        for a bass drum, 169
        for kick drum, 169, 207
        for snare drum, 174, 212
        for toms, 221
    percussion, 182
    real-time, 220
reference tone, 57, 60
reflected sound, 93
reflections, 93
regenerating, 121
regeneration(s), 91, 93
release time, 71, 76, 140, 213

repeating delay, 87
retake, 22
return, 32
return channel, 87
reverb(s), 32, 33, 85, 124, 143, 144, 169, 173
    digital, 93
    gated, 65, 98, 159, 209
    hall, 65, 95, 124, 173
    inverse, 95
    multiple, 217
    on cymbals, 225
    on the gated snare, 181
    plate, 65, 95, 210
    reverse, 95
    room, 95
    sends, 58
reverberation, 98
    devices, 223
    effects, 92
    on the snare drum, 173, 216
    on the toms, 178, 223
    settings, 143
Rhodes-type keyboard, 90
rhythm guitar, 46
rhythmic feel, 184
ribbon, 128
ribbon mics, 106, 136
RMS, 4
room(s), 93
    ambience, 144
    mic, 132, 134
    size, 87

S

safety, 13
sampled guitar sounds, 144
sampling, 173, 176
screens, 184
semiparametric EQ, 49, 84
send, 32
separating and organizing tracks, 200
separation, 184
session procedures, 58
shaker(s), 146, 149, 182
shelving EQ, 53
signal path, 27, 41, 54, 216
signal path, managing the, 29
signal processor, 20
    basics, 62
    ins and outs, 58
signal strength, 34
signals, combining direct and miked, 37
signal-to-noise, 22
signal-to-noise ratio, 4, 197
simulated guitar parts, 144
simulated tube distortion, 121
single coil pickups, 118
single-note picking parts, 139
sizzle, 224
slapback, 65, 87
slapback delay, 85
slate, 56
slave to external sync, 197
SMPTE, 194, 205
snare (drum), 104, 146, 156, 159, 169, 211
    mechanism, 171
    mic, 173

panning the, 221
recording levels for the, 174, 212
reverberation on the, 173, 216
sound(s), 170, 174
tuning of the, 213
solid-state amp, 128
solo, 29
solo button(s), 41, 58
solutions to equalization problems, 142
sonic blend, 34
sound(s)
    acoustic guitar, 138
    commercial, 144
    direct guitar, 37
    electric guitar, 119
    gated reverb, 174
    hole, 137
    module(s), 58, 189, 224
    module levels, 199
    monaural, 154
    of the pick, 136
    perception, 93
    pick, 139
    reflected, 93
    snare, 170, 174
    source, 37
    stereo, 136
speaker cabinet, 127
speaker cabinet sound, 127
speaker wire, 297
spikes, 12
split mixer, 2
split one output, 36
split vs. in-line, 2
standard track assignment, 201
steel string acoustic guitar, 136, 137
stereo, 25, 124, 125, 144, 159, 189
    chorus, 92
    effects, 92
    image, 159, 223
    imaging, 57
    line output, 11
    master control, 56
    mic technique, 155
    pair, 159
    pattern, 178
    phase, 92
    sound, 136
    spectrum, 89
    to mono, 55
    X-Y, 155
string noise, 52
strings
    light-gauge, 139
    medium- and heavy-gauge, 139
    new, 139
    old, 139
    real, 101
striping, 196
studio monitors, 297
sub-bass, 47
sub-mix, 159
sub-mixing, 193
sum, 34, 89
summing
    bus, 34
    matrix, 34
    to mono, 89
surges, 12

switching matrix, 34
sync out, 196
sync pulse, 193, 196
synchronized to time code, 193
synchronizing, 193
synth, 37, 38
synthesized and sampled guitar sounds, 144

T

talkback, 56
talkback mic, 56
tambourine, 146, 149, 182, 226
tape, 39
tape noise, 127
tape recorder, 20
task-specific microphones, 149
television, 25, 55
tension, 175
test tones, 56
thick pick, 139
threshold, 71, 76, 83, 140, 215
timbales, 182
timbre, 43
time code, 193, 204
     drop frame, 195
     European standard, 195
     generate, 194
     synchronized to, 193
Time Code, 193, 194
toms, 104, 146, 159, 174, 221
     drum machine, 221
     equalizing the, 176, 222
     panning the, 223
     recording levels for, 221
     reverberation on the, 178
tone generator, 58
tones, 56
top head, 172, 175
track(s)
     assignment(s), 29, 34
     assignment bus, 34, 39
     assignment matrix, 34
     edge, 196
     evaluating for cleanliness, 41
     isolating the drum, 181
     lead vocal, 226
     live double, 143
     separating and organizing, 200
     vocal, 71, 87
tracking session, 41
transient(s), 23, 106, 111, 116, 173, 176,
     178, 182, 224
     exaggerated, 117
     peaks, 29
triangle, 146, 149, 182
trim, 21
true stereo sound, 134
tube amp, 128
tuning, 117, 139
     drum machine toms, 222
     the drum, 167
     the snare, 213

U

unidirectional mic, 109
unity points, 39
upper midrange, 47

upward expander, 82

V

VCA, 69, 70, 76
verbalization, 120
vocal, 87
     delay, 89
     mics, 101
     track, 71, 87
vocals, 76, 101
voltage controlled amplifier, 69
volts, 20
VU meter(s), 23, 29, 58, 76, 182, 212

W

weather stripping, 171, 175
wet, 34
wet/dry, 33
wire, proper, 7
wood-tipped sticks, 165
woodwinds, 101

X

XLR, 116
XLR connectors, 10
X-Y configuration, 155, 158, 178, 225
xylophone, 182

Y

Y cable, 34, 36

Acknowledgments

Front Cover Photo

The Sy Klopps Studio
San Francisco, California
Photographer: Michael Mendelson

Back Cover Photos

Left:
Coast Recorders
A full-service, 48-track music studio
665 Harrison Street
San Francisco, CA 94107
(415) 546-0200
Fax: (415) 546-9411
Photographer: John Cuniberti

Right:
Harvey Mandel's home studio
Pacifica, California
Harvey Mandel is powered by Parker Guitars, Crate Amps, Dean Markley
Strings, DiMarzio Pickups and Electric Snake Productions Inc.
Web Site: www.punmaster.com/mandel
E-mail: snake@punmast
Management: David Gross Entertainment; Fax: (415) 380-8198
Photographer: Michael Mendelson

Compact Disc Manufacturer

CRT Custom Products Inc.
7532 Hickory Hills Court
Whites Creek, TN 37189
(800) 453-2533
In Tennessee: (615) 876-5490
Fax: (615) 876-4260